School Improvement for Real

D0496316

As societies continue to set educational goals that are – on current perform-ance – beyond the capacity of the system to deliver, strategies for enhancing student learning through school and classroom intervention have become increasingly important.

Yet, as David Hopkins argues in this book, many of the educational initia-tives developed recently under the umbrella of school improvement are inadequate or unhelpful. Simply blaming teachers and delegating financial responsibility, he maintains, has little positive impact on classroom practice. Similarly, school heads who restrict their influence to bureaucratic inter-vention, ignoring the learning level, should not be surprised when student achievement scores fail to rise. This is the bleak context within which school improvement has to operate today. It is a situation predisposed towards short-term remedies for profound problems, in organisational settings not always conducive to enhancing student achievement and learning.

School Improvement for Real offers a genuine alternative: a strategy for educational change that focuses on student achievement by modifying classroom practice, and adapting the management arrangements within the school to support teaching and learning. This book outlines an approach to school improvement that has a medium-term, systemic orientation, provid-ing both principles and suggestions for better practice. It is only through viewing school improvement holistically and by adopting a strategic, inclusive response that the challenge of enhancing the level of student learning and achievement can be met. This specific approach is defined in practical detail by reference to both research and practice. This will be an extremely topical and much needed text for all those involved in educational leadership, from headteachers and principals to researchers in education and their tutors.

David Hopkins is Professor and Dean of Education at the University of Not-tingham, Chair of the Leicester City Partnership Board and a member of the Governing Council of the National College for School Leaderships. His pub-lications include *A Teacher's Guide to Classroom Research*, 3rd edition, and *Improving the Quality of Education for All*, and co-editing *The International Handbook of Educational Change*; and co-authoring *Models of Learning: Tools for Teaching*, 2nd edition.

Educational Change and Development
Series editors: Andy Hargreaves
Ontario Institute for Studies in Education, Canada
Ivor F. Goodson
Centre for Applied Research in Education, University of East Anglia, Norwich, UK, and Warner Graduate School, University of Rochester, New York, USA

School Improvement for Real

David Hopkins

London and New York

First published 2001
by RoutledgeFalmer
2 Park Square, Milton Park, Abingdon, Oxon, OX14 4RN

Transferred to Digital Printing 2005

Simultaneously published in the USA and Canada
by RoutledgeFalmer
270 Madison Ave, New York NY 10016

© 2001 David Hopkins

Typeset in Times by
The Running Head Limited, Cambridge

British Library Cataloguing in Publication Data
A catalogue record for this book is available from the British Library

Library of Congress Cataloging in Publication Data
A library record of this data has been requested

ISBN 0–415–23075–6 (hbk)
ISBN 0–415–23076–4 (pbk)

To Marloes

The crucial point is that the proposal is not to be regarded as an unqualified recommendation but rather as a provisional specification claiming no more than to be worth putting to the test of practice. Such proposals claim to be intelligent rather than correct.

Lawrence Stenhouse – *An Introduction to Curriculum Research and Development*

[The] differences between schools in outcome were systematically related to their characteristics as social institutions . . . All of these factors were open to modification by the staff, rather than fixed by external constraints . . . The implication is that the individual actions or measures may combine to create a particular ethos, or set of values, attitudes and behaviours which will become characteristic of the school as a whole.

Michael Rutter – *Fifteen Thousand Hours*

It goes without saying that this is a large project for one mind to try to put between two covers; I am painfully aware that I may not have succeeded, that I may have bitten off too much and may have tried to put it too sparely so that it could all fit in. As in most of my other work, I have reached far beyond my competence and have probably secured for good a reputation for flamboyant gestures. But the times still crowd me and give me no rest, and I see no way to avoid ambitious synthetic attempts; either we get some kind of grip on the accumulation of thought or we continue to wallow helplessly, to starve amidst plenty. So I gamble with science and write, but the game seems to me very serious and necessary.

Ernest Becker – *Escape from Evil*

Contents

A personal introduction

During my now almost 20-year involvement with the 'school improvement movement' I have struggled to find a role in helping schools become more effective places for both students and teachers to learn. As one who is committed to action, yet works in a university and consequently inhabits education's twilight zone, finding a role that embraces theory, research, policy and practice has not always been easy. The quest to establish a genuine voice for school improvement within a centralised policy context seems to me however to be a task that is as worthwhile as it is necessary.

The metaphor of the 'journey' is often used to describe the approach we take to school improvement. Some colleagues, particularly those in schools, find it a helpful image, capturing as it does the medium term, inclusive and at times uncertain character of educational change that has the enhancement of student learning and achievement at its core. As I have been attempting to translate the experience of working with students, schools, and school systems over the years into book form, I have realised that the approach to school improvement that we have developed is somewhat distinctive from much of normative practice. The image of the 'journey' represents an attempt to differentiate our emphasis on capacity building and teaching and learning, from the quick-fix solutions and short-term responses that characterise many current school improvement efforts.

So different and distinctive is this approach to much of what goes on nowadays under the label of school improvement, I felt it important in this book to articulate the values base of what we and others understand by 'real' or 'authentic' school improvement. As school improvement becomes an increasingly important feature on the educational landscape so the phrase itself assumes increasing plasticity. Given this I thought that it may be useful to review the theoretical, research and practical reasons as to why we do what we do when we work with teachers and their schools, and intervene in school systems. In the pages that follow I move beyond descriptions of conventional approaches to school improvement in order to examine the values underpinning this specific and principled approach to educational reform.

This is not however another exercise in critiquing and debunking the research and practice of others. There has been, in my opinion, too much of that particular form of intellectual narcissism of late. Rather it is a modest attempt to explore the foundations of a style of school improvement that is becoming increasingly influential. In demonstrating that there are good reasons for doing what we do, I hope that others will be encouraged to become more self-conscious about their school improvement efforts. For it is only through such a process of reflection that we can become more refined and increasingly systematic and strategic in terms of our practice.

This book has taken longer than I would have liked to prepare, and during this time I have been nagged by three thoughts that have imposed themselves on my thinking and practice. In many ways the substance of this book is an attempt to respond to these concerns. Taken together they give a flavour of the values and the sense of urgency that leads my colleagues and myself to work in the way that we do.

The first is the necessity for school improvement efforts to drive down to the 'learning level'. It has become increasingly apparent that unless school improvement strategies impact directly on learning and achievement then we are surely wasting our time. This concern is well caught in Michael Huberman's (1992a: 11) graphic warning that:

> By not addressing the impact on pupils, we will have indulged in some magical thinking as before: that adoption meant implementation . . . that implementation meant institutionalisation . . . that enhanced teacher capacity means enhanced pupil achievement or development . . . If changes in organisational and instructional practices are not followed down to the level of effects on pupils, we will have to admit more openly that we are essentially investing in staff development rather than in the improvement of pupils' abilities.

If I have learned nothing else over the past two decades it is that creating powerful and effective learning experiences for students is the heartland of school improvement. Yet even this is not enough. There has to be a will to learn on the part of the learner, and in my experience this is so often conditioned by the environment in which the student finds herself. My own experience of school improvement interventions in a wide range of settings, suggests that all too often there is a powerful and insidious collusion at work in many social, urban and educational settings that create an hegemony which fundamentally depresses learning – 'the kids around here just can't learn' or 'that is a nice caring school what a pity about the results!' The challenge therefore is to discover how an ethos of high expectations can be created in a context where many believe there is little cause for optimism.

The second nagging idea is something of a paradox. In recent years I have been privileged to share my ideas on school improvement with educational activists in many different and diverse parts of the world. I have worked in a number of the countries of the old USSR such as Kyrgytstan, Estonia and Latvia, in Eastern Europe, the Balkans, South Africa, Nepal, and Hong

Kong, as well as most European countries, North America and Australia. I have been enormously impressed by the commitment to education of those I have met, especially those in countries where resources are very limited and the geographical challenges are seemingly insurmountable. What else has struck me is that despite the dramatic differences in context, both the educational challenges facing school systems around the world and their solutions remain very much the same.

Raising levels of achievement, enhancing the learning repertoires of students and the creation of powerful learning experiences are educational challenges that are independent of GDP. So too is the need to prepare and sustain effective and innovative teachers, to establish the organisational conditions within the school that support ongoing as well as developmental activities, and to create administrative and support settings locally, regionally and nationally that sustain development and effectiveness at the various levels within the system. Despite the wide variation in setting the response is remarkably similar. Effective teaching and learning are not, it appears, culturally bounded, nor are the organisational settings within which they occur.

My final concern is that we will not accelerate student learning at the levels most governments and certainly educational activists such as myself desire, unless *we redesign the school around learning*. This apparently innocuous suggestion has profound and radical implications. Let me take a little time to unpack it.

In my other life I am a professional mountain guide. I was recently in Nepal leading a charity trek. During the trek I visited a number of schools most of which were many days' walk from the nearest road. What I saw in those schools – the commitment of the headteacher and staff and the pride in learning shown by the students humbled me. As I rested by the trail, or took some tea in a village, young children would often besiege me wanting to try out their English or show me their workbooks.

But I also took back with me from Nepal another rather more disconcerting thought. Despite the abject poverty, deprivation and primitive conditions of the schools that I visited, they were in terms of their architecture and organisation, allowing of course for the lack of glass in the windows and for the mud floors, uncannily reminiscent of the schools in which I spend much of my daily work life. It was not difficult to recognise a school in Nepal because it shared many of the essential features of any western school. The point is a simple but profound one. I should have been more surprised than I was. There should have been greater differences in the organisation of learning between schools in Nepal and England. Yet they remain strenuously similar.

As I was reflecting on this conundrum I recalled a conversation with Phil Runkel in the summer of 1979 about the degree of continuity in the organisation of schooling. He was complaining that despite there being schools where something recognisably different or radical was going on, he could not think of a single school where things were so different that he was confused about which room to search for to find the headteacher or principal, to whom to speak to about what, and what questions to ask to understand what the school was doing. In an aside he reflected poignantly that before he ended his professional career he wished to see a school that plunged him into that kind of confusion. Despite having that conversation over 20 years ago I also yearn for such dissonance. Surely if we are serious about learning we should be continually redesigning the school environment to keep it aligned with our learning goals.

These are some of the thoughts that have been exercising me while I have been writing this book. I have been doing this at a time of great educational change, but also at a time when such centrally imposed changes are having some difficulty in reaching down to the 'learning level'. As one who for many years has been espousing the virtues of a particular approach to school improvement I feel that it is now an appropriate time to provide a more complete statement about the role of school improvement in educational reform and the values underpinning it.

In preparing the book I faced a number of problems. The first is that in doing so I would have to draw on my previous writings and so face a potential problem of repetition. Second, as an active 'school improver' myself, I would inevitably focus on the approaches we use and have developed over the years, thus facing a perception of being too partisan. Third, I have had a range of audiences in mind – teachers, headteachers or principals, those in the support system and academics. But even making such a list raises for me a particular problem. Try as I may I only seem able to write for one audience. My natural voice seems to be pitched at the informed practitioner or the researcher/scholar with a penchant for action, in a phrase – the committed individual.

In writing the book I have accepted that I will never completely resolve all of these concerns, but I have continually attempted to address them throughout the writing and re-writing process. I hope that I have at least been partially successful, and on those occasions when I have failed that my various audiences will be sufficiently generous to understand the reasons why.

Although in this introduction I have tended to refer to 'my' journey of school improvement it has in reality been a communal experience. It is this that explains the rather self-conscious use of the personal and collective pronouns in this introduction. The approach to school improvement described in this book has been both a collaborative responsibility and shared achievement of those of us who have worked together over the years, hence the use of 'we' and 'our' in these introductory pages. Having said that, this book represents an individual interpretation of the implications of that work.

I have also been unusually personal in this introduction. In part this is a reflection of my writing style, but I have purposely written in a discursive and self-conscious fashion. This is because the author of any book that purports to be about values has a clear responsibility to be explicit about the value position he or she holds. Having done that in this introduction I will return in the main body of the book to a less personalised and more analytic writing style; I will however fail to completely eschew the use of the personal pronoun!

It is in the nature of all good adventures that the support and collaboration of many others have buttressed the uncertainty of outcome. In this regard I have been more than unusually fortunate. A large number of scholars and school improvement practitioners have shared generously with me their time, good nature, intelligence, insight and critical acumen over the years. They are too many to mention here, but whatever is of worth on the following pages is most probably due to them.

I do need however to acknowledge individually those colleagues and friends with whom I have written about school improvement over the past ten years or so. I am extremely fortunate to have colleagues who have challenged me and from whom I have learned so much. The intensity of the experience and discourse that eventually led to the printed word has been so great that at times it has been difficult to separate out whose ideas and words belong to whom. I have tried hard however to respect and acknowledge the privilege and responsibility of co-authorship on the pages which follow. In this regard I am especially grateful to Mel Ainscow, John Beresford, Robert Bollen, Emily Calhoun, Michael Fullan, John Gray, David H. Hargreaves, Alma Harris, David Jackson, Bruce Joyce, Ben Levin, Barbara MacGilchrist, Dave Reynolds, Jean Rudduck, Marv Wideen and Mel West. To some of these colleagues, especially Mel Ainscow, Alma Harris, David Jackson, Bruce Joyce, Ben Levin, Dave Reynolds and Mel West I owe an especial debt of gratitude for they have allowed me to include in this book extracts of writing that we have previously published elsewhere. David Jackson in particular has been characteristically generous in permitting me to incorporate some of his material and many of his ideas on leadership in chapter 7. I am afraid that the acknowledgements I make to his work do little justice to the practice and writing of one who is no doubt the leading 'instructional leader' of his generation. In addition, the case studies in the book have been based on material originally prepared by Emily Calhoun, David Jackson, Bruce Joyce, Marcia Puckey, Collette Singleton, Brenda Thomas, Ruth Watts and Judith Wordsworth. Special thanks are due to Avril Rathbone who not only assisted with the typing, but also played a pivotal role in preparing the manuscript for production.

I owe a particular debt of gratitude to Andy Hargreaves, David Jackson and Dave Reynolds who took the time to read the second draft of the manuscript in detail, and made careful and radical suggestions for restructuring and rewriting. Although this has meant that I have had to spend a summer vacation writing instead of climbing, their comments have encouraged me to produce a tighter, more focussed and I hope in the end a more useful book. One is indeed fortunate to have colleagues such as these. For much of the time that I was working on the manuscript I was living in the Chamonix valley, at the foot of Mont Blanc. The majesty of the environment encouraged and sustained me, and when even that was insufficient motivation Sylvie and Pete Allison provided other forms of sustenance on and off the hill. My thanks to them too.

Any sustained piece of writing is an exercise in biography. It would be foolish to claim otherwise. In an obvious way this book reflects the experiences and insights I have gained since my last writing on this topic. Hopefully these experiences and insights will have added value to what was previously written. But the biographical element goes deeper. As a mountaineer I have become used to fear, strenuous effort, disciplined activity, unforeseen dangers, and seeing things through to the end – all common features of contemporary school improvement! I am also a product of my time and my parents' time. The fact that my father, as the only surviving child from seven confinements, was raised in a mining village in South Wales where education was seen as the only means of 'escaping the pit', may have something to do with the commitment to learning and achievement which pervades these pages.

The immediate past has had a similar influence. During the preceding twelve years I have become the proud father of Jeroen, Jessica and Dylan. Their mother tells me that my writing and practice have become much more learning and classroom focussed since they have become part of our lives. Whatever the truth in that, it is certainly the case that as they have developed their own individual learning histories they have consistently challenged my own ideas on education and forced me to rethink and rewrite. In a profound way, I am continually trying to adjust my educational thinking to keep pace with their development.

This book is dedicated to my wife Marloes Hopkins de Groot. We have been together now for sixteen years. When we first met I promised her that I had 'just one more book to write'. Given that some 30 books later 'the book' is still not written testifies to the support that she has given me during our time together. This book however, on 'school improvement for real', may be getting me a little closer. Over the years she has shared with me, usually at our dinner table, the genesis of this and much else of my writing with grace, fortitude, and a critically incisive intelligence. Her being with me on the journey – that has made all the difference.

David Hopkins
Argentière – Mont Blanc
Summer 2000

Acknowledgements

The author and publishers are grateful to the following for giving permission for the sole or joint authored work to be used in this book:

Professor Mel Ainscow, University of Manchester
Dr Emily Calhoun, The Phoenix Alliance
Professor Mats Ekholm, Skolverket, Sweden
Professor Michael Fullan, University of Toronto
Professor John Gray, Homerton College, University of Cambridge
Dr Alma Harris, School of Education, University of Nottingham
David Jackson, National College for School Leadership
Dr Bruce Joyce, Booksend Laboratories
Professor Ben Levin, Deputy Minister for Education and Training, Manitoba
Mrs Marcia Puckey, Hempshill Hall School, Nottingham
Professor David Reynolds, School of Education, University of Exeter
Professor Pam Sammons, Institute of Education, University of London
Mrs Colette Singleton, Bigwood School, Nottingham
Dr Sam Stringfield, Johns Hopkins University
Mrs Ruth Watts, Swanwick Hall School, Derbyshire
Professor Mel West, University of Manchester
Judith Wordsworth, 'Success For All' Foundation, UK

The author and publishers are also grateful for permission to reproduce the following tables and figures in this book:

Table 3.1 – Professor Michael Fullan
Table 3.2 – Professor Pam Sammons
Table 3.4 – Professor Charles Teddlie and Professor Sam Stringfield
Table 5.1 – Dr Bruce Joyce
Figure 3.1 – Professor Mats Ekholm
Figure 5.2 – Dr Bruce Joyce
Figure 7.2 – David Jackson
Figure 7.3 – David Jackson

Figures

Tables

1 Educational reform and school improvement

Those of us who spend much of our professional lives labouring in that part of the educational vineyard known as 'school improvement' have recently been celebrating. For decades now we have been the poor relations of the field, tolerated, talked to at parties, but not really regarded as being a main player. But as western societies have in recent years grappled with the challenges of economic growth and social dislocation, our particular contribution to educational change has increasingly been recognised as important and helpful. As societies continue to set educational goals that are, on current performance, beyond the capacity of the system to deliver, those whose work focusses on strategies for enhancing student learning through school and classroom intervention are taken more seriously.

Many of the educational initiatives that have been recently spawned under the school improvement umbrella are unfortunately, however, simply tinkering at the edges. Governments whose policies emphasise accountability and managerial change fail to realise that if teachers knew how to teach more effectively they would themselves have done so decades ago. Blaming teachers and delegating financial responsibility have little positive impact on classroom practice. Similarly, school headteachers or principals who restrict their influence to bureaucratic intervention and ignore the 'learning level' should not be surprised when student achievement scores fail to rise. Even those consultants and others who do offer training on 'thinking skills' and 'learning styles' are missing the point when they fail to recognise that many of their prescriptions have a short shelf life. Even when there is a subsequent attempt at implementation following a 'one-off' workshop, 'tissue rejection' is usually the result.

At the same time that pressure on schools and school systems has increased, so too has the context of schooling changed dramatically. In most western educational systems there has been a move from a somewhat paternalistic approach to education to a situation where schools are not only encouraged, but are increasingly required, to take responsibility for their own development. The emphasis on self-improvement has increased in the past decade as a consequence of the trend in most western countries of decentralising the responsibility for the implementation of educational reform. Alongside this increase in political pressure for institutional renewal, there has been a steady realisation that traditional strategies for educational change are not working. In recent years it has become starkly apparent that as strategies for educational reform, neither centralisation nor decentralisation work and that a better way must be found.

This is the rather bleak context within which school improvement has to operate at the turn of the century. It is a situation that is predisposed towards short-term remedies for profound problems, in organisational settings not always conducive to enhancing levels of student achievement and learning. The emergence of school improvement from the shadows is therefore a mixed blessing. As with any new idea, much is expected of it, particularly from those desperately seeking for simple and rapid solutions to complex challenges. School improvement's time in the sun will be short lived unless it can persuade its new found friends that it is not a 'quick fix' response to educational change.

The purpose of this book is to outline an approach to school improvement that has a medium-term and systemic orientation, and to describe the principles on which it is based. It is only through viewing school improvement holistically and by adopting a strategic and inclusive response that the challenge of enhancing the level of student learning and achievement will be met. This specific approach to school improvement – termed here as 'real' or 'authentic' school improvement – is defined in some detail in this and subsequent chapters. Initially it is best regarded as a strategy for educational change that focusses on student achievement by modifying classroom practice and adapting the management arrangements within the school to support teaching and learning.

In this first chapter the various challenges to this strategy for school improvement inherent in the current context are described, and the response that constitutes the argument of the book, that to be successful one has to develop an authentic and principled approach, is outlined. In particular in this chapter:

- the current international educational policy context is outlined
- some limits to these reform strategies are suggested
- the case of educational reform in developing countries is briefly considered
- some contrasting definitions of school improvement are reviewed
- an overview of the book as a whole is provided.

The international policy context

The last ten or fifteen years of this century have been a time of great challenge as well as considerable excitement for educational systems around the world. Governments everywhere have been embarking on substantial programmes of reform in an attempt to develop more effective school systems and raise levels of student learning and achievement. Schools in many countries have been subject to a barrage of legislation and policy that has meant changes in curriculum, assessment, governance and financing. England has perhaps had more of this than most countries, but the phenomenon of large-scale reform by central governments is world wide (Levin, 1998).

A general strategy has been to centralise educational policy while at the same time placing the responsibility for implementation on the school. This tension has made the task of implementing change both complex and challenging. The balancing of centrally directed change and locally developed improvement has proved most difficult to achieve in practice. To the cynic this looks as if governments have created a situation where they can have their cake and eat it too! If policies fail to meet aspirations, the fault can then be attributed not to the policy maker, but to the schools, teachers and local authorities that have failed to put them into practice.

Within this larger scheme, reforms have tended to focus on:

- *Curriculum:* governments have instituted more restrictive curriculum requirements including increased emphasis on science, technology, and so-called basic skills such as literacy. Traditional subject divisions have been reinforced in many cases.
- *Accountability:* governments have increased testing of students and have made the results public, and in some cases put in place extensive external inspection of schools.
- *Governance:* while governments have centralised curriculum and assessment, they have also decentralised many decisions from intermediate bodies such as school districts or local authorities to individual schools, and have given parents an increased role in school governance, all of which has put new pressures on professional staff.
- *Market forces:* governments have tried to introduce market elements to schooling through increasing the opportunity – or requirement – for parents to choose schools (or, in some cases, for schools to choose parents and students).
- *Status of teachers:* in a number of countries the status of teachers and their organisations has been attacked directly through unilateral changes by governments to the status of unions or to collective bargaining arrangements.

(Hopkins and Levin, 2000: 18–19)

It is almost inconceivable that countries and educational systems with very different political cultures and stages of economic development should all be pursuing what is to all appearances a very similar policy agenda. Some commentators have reacted positively to such a policy consensus and have posited an international process of 'mutual learning', where educational systems having carefully analysed the challenges facing themselves and through learning from each other's experiences have adopted a similar range of policy options. I am not so sanguine. It is more the case of what Halpin and Troyna

(1995) have called 'policy borrowing' for largely symbolic purposes. 'Faddism' – the adoption of any current vogue, irrespective of its 'fit' to a particular problem or challenge, just to be seen to be doing something – is a well documented response to the pressure for external change at the school level (Slavin, 1989). 'Policy borrowing' seems to me to be the same phenomenon raised to an international or systems level.

In summary and in reflecting on the international 'policy epidemic' of the past decade or so one is struck by the radical shifts in policy on the one hand, and by the continuity of experience in schools on the other. The old adage of the 'more things change the more they stay the same' comes to mind. The conundrum here is not only how policy can affect practice, but also how schools can pursue an improvement agenda within a centralised change context. The thesis of this book is that those reform strategies that do positively impact on student learning and achievement, and the organisational culture of the school, are based on principles derived from the theory, research and practice related to effective school development. In beginning to build this argument and develop the theme, some of the reasons why it is difficult for centralised reform to impact positively on the daily life of schools are explored in the following section.

The limits of current reform strategies

It is an irony of quite breathtaking proportions that the dramatic increase in educational reform efforts in most western countries over the past decade is having insufficient impact on levels of student achievement. Admittedly there are pockets of success, such as the claims made for the English National Literacy Strategy by Barber and Sebba (1999). A recent analysis of trends in examination results in English secondary schools however, suggests only a modest year-on-year increase even in those schools that are 'improving rapidly' (Gray *et al.*, 1999). On the other hand the failure of recent reforms to accelerate student achievement in line with policy objectives has been widely documented (e.g., Sebring *et al.*, 1996; Rinehart and Lindle, 1997; Hopkins and Levin, 2000).

A clear indication of the pathology of central policy change was given a few years ago by Milbrey McLaughlin (1990) in her reanalysis of the extensive Rand Change Agent study originally conducted in the United States during the 1970s. In the paper McLaughlin (1990: 12) puts it this way:

> A general finding of the Change Agent study that has become almost a truism is that it is exceedingly difficult for policy to change practice, especially across levels of government. Contrary to the one-to-one relationship assumed to exist between policy and practice, the Change Agent study demonstrated that the nature, amount, and pace of change at the local level was a product of local factors that were largely beyond the control of higher-level policy makers.

McLaughlin (1990: 12) comes to the salutary conclusion that 'policy cannot mandate what matters'. Here are three reasons why educational reforms do not in general have the desired impact.

First, many reforms focus on the wrong variables. There is now an increasingly strong research base that suggests that initiatives such as local management of schools, external inspection, organisation development, or teacher appraisal only indirectly affect student performance. These 'distal variables' as Margaret Wang and her colleagues (1993) point out are too far removed from the daily learning experiences of most students. Those variables that do impact positively on student learning are, to use their term, 'proximal'. According to their meta-analysis of variables that do correlate with higher levels of student achievement the three key proximal variables are psychological, instructional and home environment. The clear implications for policy are that any strategy to promote student learning needs to give attention to engaging students and parents as active participants, and expanding the teaching and learning repertoires of teachers and students respectively. Second, although the focus on teaching and learning is necessary, it is also an insufficient condition for school improvement. Richard Elmore, a leading American commentator on school reform explains it this way (Elmore, 1995: 366):

> Principles of [best] practice [related to teaching and learning] . . . have difficulty taking root in schools for essentially two reasons: (a) they require content knowledge and pedagogical skill that few teachers presently have, and (b) they challenge certain basic patterns in the organisation of schooling. Neither problem can be solved independently of the other, nor is teaching practice likely to change in the absence of solutions that operate simultaneously on both fronts.

What Elmore is arguing for is an approach to educational change that at the same time focusses on the organisational conditions of the school as well as the way teaching and learning is organised. The more the organisation of the school remains the same the less likely it is for there to be changes in classroom practice that directly and positively impact on student learning. The importance of the dynamic between changes in classroom practice and the concomitant modification to school organisational arrangements is a major theme in this book.

Third, most reforms do not adopt a systemic perspective. The need for 'systemic reform' has been one of the rallying calls of recent policy initiatives. Yet much of what currently goes on under the label 'systemic' is neither systemic, nor does it have much impact on student performance. It is helpful to think about this problem along two dimensions – that policies need to be both 'system wide' and 'system deep'. 'System wide' applies to the coherence and contingency across a policy spectrum, whereas 'system deep' refers to clarity and coherence at both the top and the bottom of the system – at the level of policy and in the minds of the majority of teachers.

'System wide' applies to the overall coherence of the policy framework. There needs to be 'joined up thinking' between policies, and they need to be informed by the same values base. A negative example is found in the ideology of the New Labour government in Britain. In an article in the recent *Political Quarterly*, Michael Freeden (1999: 50) argues that 'the ideology of new labour can only be understood as an internal arena of competition, indeterminacy and uncertainty over the key meanings of the political values and concepts with which it engages'. This, Freeden argues, leads to core concepts being prone to multiple meanings, and 'in a number of areas incompatible meanings of the core and adjacent concepts . . . still exist side by side' (Freeden, 1999: 50). Although New Labour's educational policies reflect only a mild form of this pathology they are still illustrative of this general trend.

The move towards 'restructuring' in the US provides another negative example, this time of 'system deep'. As Elmore (1995: 357) again comments:

> This current incapacity of policymakers to connect broad-scale policy fixes with the details of teaching and learning in schools is part of a long historical tradition in the United States. David Tyack (1991) has characterised the current interest in school restructuring as a contemporary instance of a long-standing process he calls 'tinkering towards utopia', in which competing political interests use the policy process to express their views about how schools should operate. These views often have less to do with the details of teaching practice and school organisation than with making schools responsive to particular political interests. Attention to teaching and learning in education reform is episodic . . . So the gap between best practice and ordinary practice, and the lack of closure between policy and practice, is a recurring problem that reveals a deep incapacity of schools to engage in cumulative learning over time directed at tangible results for students.

David Cohen (1995: 16) has similarly argued that systemic reform (the current buzz phrase in the lexicon of American educational reform):

> seems to assume that instruction is a homogenous and unified system that can be driven by a small set of policy instruments – i.e., standards and assessments. But I have argued that instruction includes several related 'systems' – teachers' knowledge, their professional values and commitments, and the social resources of practice. One difficulty for systemic reform has been that these elements of instructional practice are distinctively weak in the United States, and a second has been that the instruments of policy that governments deployed since 1985 were not well designed to repair these weaknesses in practice. A third has been that the three elements of instruction seem to be weakly interdependent. Hence, making change in teachers' knowledge and skill, for example,

would not necessarily lead to change in teachers' values and professional commitments . . . The apparent logic of systemic reform is that instruction is a homogenous and unified system that can be driven by a small set of policy instruments, but these considerations suggest that changing one element of practice may not produce significant change in other elements.

When government policy does not impact directly on student outcomes it is by and large because it lacks an implementation or more broadly a school improvement perspective. It matters little how 'good' the policy may be – unless it is implemented, there will be little impact on outcomes. The logic of this position is that if governmental policy wishes to impact upon schools, teachers and students it needs to be informed by what is known about how schools improve. This discussion of current policy initiatives in 'developed' educational systems, suggests that although they may contain some of the key ingredients for a successful contemporary approach to school improvement, they are unlikely to deliver the promised higher levels of achievement. In general the approach being advocated is insufficiently strategic and ignores what is known about integrative and successful school improvement efforts.

It is for reasons such as this that one cannot be over optimistic about whether current reform initiatives will lead to dramatically enhanced levels of student learning and achievement. It also explains why the approach to school improvement adopted in this book is directed at simultaneous change at both classroom and school levels within a principled strategic and systemic policy context. The argument being built in this chapter is that because policy prescriptions do not by and large impact on practice, new ways of formulating education change need to be developed. Some of the reasons why centralised policy initiatives are unlikely to achieve the goal of raising levels of student achievement have been identified. The discussion has in the main reflected the experience in 'western' educational systems. Before proposing an approach to school improvement which meets the authentic challenge of educational change, it is worth briefly examining whether this analysis of educational reform is similar to those challenges found in the world's developing educational systems.

Educational reform in developing countries

As the previous two sections reflected in the main experience in so called 'western' countries, it may be instructive to explore the reform context in developing countries also. This discussion although inevitably brief and partial will additionally presage a number of the themes more fully discussed later in the book.

The distinction between 'developing' and 'western' educational systems is well caught by Harber and Davies in their *School Management and Effectiveness in Developing Countries* (1997: 4):

Our use of the term 'developing countries' mostly refers to those countries which have undergone and continue to experience economic and
political problems at the 'stringency' end of the continuum. Similarly,
when we use the term 'western', we are using this as a shorthand for
literature and thinking which has emerged from industrialised areas such
as the USA, the UK and Northern Europe as well as Australasia. It
refers to an economic and ideological reality rather than a geographical
one.

One of the few authoritative and wide-ranging studies of educational change
in developing countries is that reported by Per Dalin and his colleagues in
How Schools Improve (Dalin, 1994). This book reports on World Bank sponsored research that was carried out from 1987 to 1992 in 31 primary schools
in Colombia, Ethiopia and Bangladesh. Dalin notes that prior to the *How
Schools Improve* study:

many people assumed that there were certain 'obvious truths' about
reform:

- reforms should be incremental and gradual rather than wide-ranging
- tight inspection and control are essential for success
- the issue is designing a reform and its materials so well that it can be
  implemented faithfully and well with minimal training and assistance, in other words teachers are 'consumers' of new reform ideas
- success depends mainly on the quality of the reform ideas
- schools in general are resistant to reforms
- either 'top-down' or 'bottom-up' strategies work – depending on the
  educational context referred to.

(Dalin, 1994: xvii)

As Dalin notes, all these 'obvious truths' have been shown to be false, both
in the *How Schools Improve* study as it relates to developing countries, and in
other recent large-scale studies of educational reform in industrialised countries. The HSI study findings on effective reform strategies can be summarised in the following ways (adapted from Dalin, 1994: 251–2):

- *Educational reform is a local process* Schools determine the degree of
  success of any national policy; they can block implementation, enfeeble
  it or bring it to effective life. For schools to improve, they need to play an
  active and creative role in both policy formulation and implementation.
- *Central support is vital* The issue for the central ministry is how to support local schools in their efforts to implement national policy. The placing of responsibility for implementation at the level of the individual
  school presupposes a strong support structure from the system at large,

one that must be built around the real and diverse needs of schools in development. The implication for the central level is the establishing of an infrastructure for implementation that recognises that a multi-agency approach is needed to effectively support the local level.

- *Effective system linkages are essential* The strategy in complex systems is to identify effective linkages and networks, non-bureaucratic in nature, between the national, district and local levels. For communication within the system to be effective, it needs to be both 'wide' and 'deep'. A clear administrative role that combines pressure and support and secures the delivery of needed resources without inhibiting local empowerment is also required.
- *The reform process is a learning process* The process is evolutionary and developmental in nature. It cannot be blueprinted ahead of time. The key to success is to get good data from all parts of the system on a continuous basis, studied and worked on at the school/district level, and subsequently at the central level. This implies a competent supervision and monitoring system.
- *Think systemic and big* A vision of reform that affects school life substantially will have more effect than a cautious, incremental approach. Any major reforms in complex systems need to build structures and capabilities at all levels. Ad hoc solutions will not work in the long run, only institution building based on sustained commitment works.
- *Focus on classroom practice* The clue is to focus on the dynamics of teaching and learning within the classroom and the individual school, since this dynamic to a large extent determines implementation success. It is essential that the supporting materials are of good quality, and that they integrate both content and instructional strategy, whether nationally developed and locally adapted, or locally built from the start.
- *See teachers as learners* Good materials and facilities are a necessary but insufficient condition. Teacher mastery is crucial for impact on students, and that can best be developed through a systematic local learning process that encourages reflection through in-service training, supervision and coaching in a collegial atmosphere.
- *Commitment is essential at all levels* Commitment is crucial at the central level for sustained effort and the maintenance of needed support structures. It is also essential at the district and school level, however, it cannot be transmitted directly to schools. Commitment at the school level results from empowered successful action, personal mastery that starts with good assistance and develops from practice. In effect, local empowerment builds emotional as well as administrative and problem-solving capacity.
- *Both local and central initiatives work* An innovative idea that starts locally, nationally or with external donors can succeed, if programmes meet the criteria of national commitment, local capacity building and linkage, in a configuration that makes sense for the particular country.

- *Parent and community participation contribute to success* Parent and community participation lead to commitment and contribute to outcomes. In
  particular, they are essential for the development and maintenance of
  primary schools in rural areas. Effective participation includes a real role
  for parents in decision-making.

These findings echo what was found in earlier studies of educational change
in developing countries (see for example Verspoor, 1989). They are also reflected in other major studies of national reform efforts in the industrialised
countries (Dalin, 1973; Berman and McLaughlin, 1977; Crandall, 1982), and
in in-depth studies of smaller-scale innovations (Huberman and Miles, 1984;
Louis and Miles, 1990). It is on the basis of this evidence that Dalin (1994:
253) concludes that these ten lessons are 'generic and quite fundamental'. As
I intimated in the Introduction, these conclusions by and large reflect my own
experience and interpretation of the evidence.
    Further support for this position is found in the work of Pam Christie and
her studies of school improvement in South Africa. In her paper 'Schools as
(dis) organisations' Christie describes 'the breakdown of the culture of learning and teaching' in many South African schools in terms of organisational
breakdown. She writes:

> Instead of being able to focus on their substantive task of learning and
> teaching, schools have become caught up in forms of conflict, aggression
> and uncertainty that cannot be contained within a weak organisational
> structure. Principals, teachers and students have lost focus and have
> directed their energies towards the malfunctioning of the institution, at
> the expense of substantive learning and teaching. The breakdown in
> schools is in part at least a breakdown of rhythmical, disciplined learning
> and teaching – the ostensible, conscious goal of the work group.
>
> (Christie, 1998: 293)

Christie (1998: 293) concludes:

> The accompanying emotions of apathy, depression, anxiety, disempower-
> ment and projection are intimately related to this organisational break-
> down. And all of this makes up the complex texture, social discourse
> and informal logic of everyday life in these schools, i.e., the culture of
> learning and teaching.

So although the broad generic strategies may be similar, as ever it is the
context that defines the difference. It also defines the parameters of the response. Based on her analysis of 'Schools as (dis) organisations' in South
Africa, Christie (1998: 294–6) identifies five guiding principles for intervention within that context, particularly from external agencies committed to an
ethic of collaboration:

- As a first step, government education departments need to recognise the complex group and organisational dynamics crippling the work of these schools, as a basis for working with them.
- Second, in line with this, departments need to view as their major task the regeneration of these schools as functioning organisations.
- A third principle for intervening in these schools is that the importance of the substantive task of learning and teaching needs to be bolstered, so that schools are encouraged to engage with 'real work' rather than 'psycho-politics'.
- Fourth, organisational failure needs to be recognised and remedied in terms of school management and leadership.
- Fifth, our research suggests that it is important to build a sense of agency and responsibility at the school level. While there are important steps for departments to take, it is crucial for interventions to work from the basis that schools themselves need to take at least partial ownership of problems and work towards their resolution.

Although the context of schools in South Africa, as Christie so graphically describes, is far more extreme than those in most western countries, the underlying issues are unfortunately all too familiar. The breakdown in the 'culture of learning and teaching' is the result of organisational dysfunction exacerbated in the South African context by the policies and practices of apartheid. It is however a mistake to respond simply at the organisational level, as Christie notes – 'the substantive task of teaching and learning (also) needs to be bolstered'. This 'breakdown' is however not too dissimilar to the situation in some inner-city secondary schools in many western countries, and the response here also needs to be at both the organisational and classroom levels.

This brief excursion into the problems of educational reform in developing countries serves to reinforce the view that although the challenges for school improvement are at one level generic, the solutions need to be context specific. This is a continuing theme in this book. So too is the unwavering commitment to school improvement as a strategy for educational change that focusses on both the quality of teaching and learning *and* the organisational conditions that support it. A more complete definition of an approach to school improvement that is built on such principles and values is found in the following section.

Towards a definition of school improvement

There are a number of ways in which the phrase 'school improvement' is used. The most common sense meaning relates to general efforts to make schools better places for pupils and students to learn in. This is a sensible interpretation of the phrase and its most general usage. Such a definition however covers a range of activities ranging from the 'quick-fix' approaches alluded to earlier to the more principled strategy described below. Even among the most sophisticated of commentators, there are significant differences of opinion.

John Gray (Gray *et al.*, 1999) for example, describes an improving school, 'as one which secures year-on-year improvement in the outcomes of successive cohorts of similar pupils . . . In other words it increases its effectiveness over time.' By way of contrast Peter Mortimore has recently described school improvement as, 'the process of "improving" the way a school organises, promotes and supports learning . . . It includes changing aims, expectations, organisations (sometimes people), ways of learning, methods of teaching and organisational culture.' Although not inimical, these definitions offer diverse perspectives. To Gray, student outcomes are pre-eminent, to Mortimore, it is the process that is vital. Taken at face value it is as if the Gray definition regards as unproblematic or irrelevant the means of improvement, whereas the Mortimore definition could be regarded as valuing process and school culture over student learning. It is unproductive to push the contrast further, as it could parody the positions of these commentators who have elsewhere enriched the literature with more detailed and catholic definitions (see for example Gray *et al.*, 1996; Mortimore, 1998). The discussion does serve to illustrate the point that as conceptual pluralism spreads, so clarity of definition becomes increasingly necessary.

Roland Barth (1990) has also identified two contrasting approaches to school improvement that rest on sets of very different assumptions. In *Improving Schools From Within* he described the dominant approach as being predicated on a set of assumptions that has led to an approach to school reform that is based on a proliferation of 'lists'. There are lists of the characteristics of the 'effective' school, teacher, and pupil, lists of minimum competencies, lists of regulations, performance indicators and so on. Barth claims that what is dangerous and self-defeating about this view of the world is the mindset that informs it. Inherent in the approach is a set of assumptions about people, how they feel, how they should behave, and about how organisations work (see Hopkins *et al.*, 1994: chapter 1).

Barth then argues for basing school reform on the skills, aspirations and energy of those closest to the school: teachers, senior management, governors and parents. He asserts that a 'community of learners' approach to school improvement derives from a radically different set of assumptions than those of the list makers. These assumptions are:

- Schools have the capacity to improve themselves, if the *conditions* are right. A major responsibility of those outside the school is to help provide these conditions for those inside.
- When the need and purpose is there, when the conditions are right, adults and students alike learn and each energises and contributes to the learning of the other.
- What needs to be improved about schools is their *culture*, the quality of interpersonal relationships, and the nature and quality of learning experiences.

- School improvement is an effort to determine and provide, from without and within, conditions under which the adults and youngsters who inhabit schools will promote and sustain learning among them.

(Barth, 1990: 45 *my italics*)

The definition of school improvement adopted in this book has some similarities with the positions of Gray, Mortimore and Barth. School improvement was described earlier as a distinct approach to educational change that aims to enhance student outcomes *as well as* strengthening the school's capacity for managing change. It is concerned with raising student achievement through focussing on the teaching–learning process and the conditions that support it. Although this definition will be elaborated below and in further chapters, it is in this specific sense that the phrase 'school improvement' will be used throughout the rest of the book. At times the phrase will be qualified by the adjective 'real' or 'authentic' in order to differentiate the approach taken here to the ubiquitous 'quick fix' alternative.

Overview of the book

It has been argued in this opening chapter that school improvement is an appropriate response to the current pressures for educational reform. Although well intentioned, many policies are unable to directly address and influence the learning level. The approach to school improvement described in this book provides a way of linking policy and practice, that results in more effective schools, effective teachers and most importantly effective learning on the part of students.

In the following chapter, 'The foundations of authentic school improvement', the principles of school improvement are elaborated, and located within the intellectual tradition established by Kurt Lewin. Lewin's development of action research and his pioneering studies of the dialectic between group dynamics and individual growth provide some of the key ideas upon which authentic school improvement is based. The theoretical basis for action research is referred to in the light of Jurgen Habermas' observation that action research is an appropriate methodology for critical theory. Following this, school improvement's evolution from the research and practice of organisation development, and emergence from a range of contemporary influences are described.

School improvement's development as an identifiable strategy and approach has been heavily influenced by the recent history of research in the areas of educational change and school effectiveness. Consequently, in chapter 3 the importance of Michael Fullan's implementation perspective to contemporary school improvement efforts is emphasised. The research tradition of school effectiveness is complementary to that of school improvement and of late the two traditions have learned much from each other. As a result, the best of current practice reflects a transcendence or merging of the two paradigms. Unfortunately this has not always been the case and at times the proponents of each approach have sometimes appeared to be in tension. The intellectual and strategic debt owed by authentic school improvement to school effectiveness is acknowledged and some of the characteristics of the new merged paradigm are described.

On the basis of the accounts and analysis of the three previous chapters, in chapter 4 the territory of 'School improvement in an era of change' is outlined. Its development from the OECD's International School Improvement Project (ISIP), and its relationship with school effectiveness are reviewed, and a range of contemporary approaches, including the 'Improving the Quality of Education for All' (IQEA) school improvement network and the 'Success For All' (SFA) literacy programme developed by Bob Slavin and Nancy Madden, are critiqued. The issue of the various sources of school improvement is addressed, and the chapter concludes with a comprehensive model for school improvement that focusses both on the learning needs of students and on establishing the appropriate organisational conditions within the school.

Chapter 5, 'Powerful learning and powerful teaching', is crucial to the development of the central argument of the book. Without a focus on teaching and learning school improvement efforts are doomed to 'tinkering'. Teaching and learning is the heartland of authentic school improvement yet curiously a secure language for describing the technical aspects of teaching and learning is not well established in most educational systems. In this chapter an argument is made for the centrality of teaching and learning to the school improvement process and a comprehensive framework for establishing a principled and practical approach to student learning and achievement is advanced. In particular the work of Bruce Joyce and his approach to 'Models of teaching' is emphasised.

As has already been argued in this chapter, without establishing the appropriate organisational conditions within the school, improvement efforts cannot be sustained. In chapter 6, 'Creating the conditions for school improvement', an analysis is made of those school and classroom level conditions necessary to support enhanced levels of teacher development and student learning. This chapter draws on the approach to school improvement developed by the IQEA network that established a theoretical and practical framework for this aspect of the improvement process.

It is now a truism that effective leadership is a cornerstone for successful schooling. In chapter 7 contemporary concepts of school leadership are discussed, and an argument is made in terms of school improvement for the importance of 'instructional leadership'. The roles of leaders throughout the school are considered, especially the importance of school improvement groups. The role of staff development in supporting teaching and learning provides an additional focus for this chapter. The various elements of an effective staff development infrastructure are described, as well as its relationship with the school culture.

In chapter 8 examples of effective school leadership and cultural change are provided through accounts of successful school improvement efforts. These vignettes lay the basis for an analysis of successful patterns of development, together with a discussion of the importance of the learning focus and the process of cultural change.

One of the crucial problems in most national educational change strategies is the implicit assumption that 'one size fits all'. This assumption is self-evidently incorrect. The basis of a differential approach to school improvement requires an understanding of the concept of 'capacity', the various growth states of schools and the innovations and interventions best suited to schools at the different stages of their development. In chapter 9 these issues are addressed together with a review of the effect sizes and the suitability of a range of school and classroom interventions for school improvement purposes.

One of the main points made in this initial chapter is that central educational policy fails to impact on practice to the extent that it ignores a school improvement perspective. Many of these themes are pulled together in chapter 10 in order to provide some policy directions to support the approach to school improvement taken in the book. No school is an island and an implicit theme throughout is that school improvement works best within a supportive local and national environment. In this chapter the implications for policy from the research on school improvement are outlined, the contribution made by the LEA or school district and the role of networks are described, and a policy framework for national authorities is proposed.

Commentary

A clear statement has been made in the introduction and this chapter about the crucial values underpinning a systemic approach to school reform that focusses on the learning and achievement of students. As is seen in more detail in the following chapter, a key set of principles underpin 'real' school improvement. It is an approach that is emancipatory and empowering, and that disciplines both one's educational goals and ways of working. By adopting this perspective, schools and those who live out their daily lives within them, are no longer the 'victims' of change, but become managers of the change process. By using the opportunity of external change as a stimulus, and by taking advantage of external support and the evidence of good practice and research, these educators subject the specificities of reform to their own professional scrutiny and judgement in the pursuit of enhanced learning for their students. What this looks like in practice, and how it can be achieved, is the focus of what follows.

2 The foundations of authentic school improvement

A central theme of this book is that school improvement should be a principled approach to educational change, based on values that have theoretical coherence and practical implications. Unfortunately there is often an 'actual – ideal' conflation in the rhetoric surrounding school improvement. Although one may argue for a principled and strategic approach, the reality is often a quick fix and pragmatic response to the challenge of educational reform. Sadly, the drive for short-term gain in the current 'epidemic' of reform initiatives has replaced principle with expediency, and consequently failed to achieve long-term impact.

We now know enough about the theory and practice of educational change to successfully improve schools. Those engaged in such school improvement efforts do not just intervene in schools to carry through a particular change strategy; they are actively implementing improvement strategies that help both students and teachers to enhance their learning and achievements. They are also collaboratively researching the process in order to create new knowledge about schools, the change process, and their own practice. More importantly they are increasing the capacity of the school, the headteachers, teachers and students, to manage their own improvement process.

These approaches to school improvement are being called here 'authentic school improvement'. They stand in contrast to 'target setting' and 'high stakes accountability' reform strategies, and short-term quick fix approaches, all of which are informed by different expectations, values and *modus operandi*. Reviews of successful school improvement efforts around the world suggest that they are based on a number of key principles (e.g., Hargreaves *et al.*, 1998). Taken together, these principles provide the framework for the approach to authentic school improvement taken in this book. They reflect the values described in the Introduction and chapter 1, and characterise the majority of successful school improvement programmes.

In general 'authentic' school improvement programmes are:

- *Achievement focussed* – they focus on enhancing student learning and achievement, in a broader sense than mere examination results or test scores.

- *Empowering in aspiration* – they intend to provide those involved in the change process with the skills of learning and 'change agentry' that will raise levels of expectation and confidence throughout the educational community.
- *Research based and theory rich* – they base their strategies on programmes and programme elements that have an established track record of effectiveness, that research their own effectiveness and connect to and build on other bodies of knowledge and disciplines.
- *Context specific* – they pay attention to the unique features of the school situation and build strategies on the basis of an analysis of that particular context.
- *Capacity building in nature* – they aim to build the organisational conditions that support continuous improvement.
- *Enquiry driven* – they appreciate that reflection-in-action is an integral and self-sustaining process.
- *Implementation oriented* – they take a direct focus on the quality of classroom practice and student learning.
- *Interventionist and strategic* – they are purposely designed to improve the current situation in the school or system and take a medium-term view of the management of change, and plan and prioritise developments accordingly.
- *Externally supported* – they build agencies around the school that provide focussed support, and create and facilitate networks that disseminate and sustain 'good practice'.
- *Systemic* – they accept the reality of a centralised policy context, but also realise the need to adapt external change for internal purpose, and to exploit the creativity and synergies existing within the system.

Although the principles are based on an analysis across many programmes, obviously not all programmes will share these characteristics. Even the most successful school improvement efforts will not necessarily embody all of the principles, and there will be inevitable variation within the principles as well. That the principles share a high degree of intellectual coherence is not serendipitous. The principles, although empirically based, reflect an 'ideal type' of school improvement profile.

Table 2.1 represents a first attempt to define the influences on authentic school improvement. Although illustrative rather than exhaustive, the table identifies some of the wide range of influences that have helped determine this particular approach to school improvement. The figure also serves to chart the intellectual history of 'authentic' school improvement as it is described in this and following chapters. These principles therefore fulfil a number of important functions. They:

- define a particular approach to school improvement
- can be used to organise the theoretical, research and practical implications that define school improvement as a field of enquiry

Table 2.1 The principles of authentic school improvement

The principles of authentic school improvement	Examples of theoretical, research, policy or practical influences on school improvement
Achievement focussed	The moral and social justice responsibility to enhance student learning, and the unrelenting focus on the quality of teaching and learning.
Empowering in aspiration	The moral imperative of emancipation, of increasing individual responsibility, the enhancement of skills and confidence in the tradition of Dewey, Freire and Stenhouse.
Research based and theory rich	The use of teaching and learning and organisational development strategies with robust empirical support for the developing of a variety of curriculum and teaching programmes or models; and the location of the approach within a philosophical tradition e.g., Critical Theory.
Context specific	The influence of the contemporary school effectiveness research that points to the importance of context specificity and the fallacy of the 'one size fits all' change strategy.
Capacity building in nature	The necessity to ensure sustainability, the nurturing of professional learning communities, and the establishing of local infrastructures and networks.
Enquiry driven	The uses of data to energise, inform and direct action. The influence of the 'reflective practitioner' ethic and a commitment to dissemination and utilisation.
Implementation oriented	The research on the management of change, in particular the importance of individual meaning, the consistency of classroom effects and the creation of a commitment to active implementation.
Interventionist and strategic	The influence of 'Lewinian' Action Research and Organisation Development principles and strategies, and the contemporary emphasis on development planning.
Externally supported	The centralisation/decentralisation polarity of most National educational policies places increasing emphasis on networking and external support agencies to facilitate implementation.
Systemic	This relates not just to the need to accept political realities, but also to ensure policy coherence horizontally and vertically, and the use of pressure and support to exploit the creativity and synergies within the system.

- provide a set of criteria that can be used to differentiate broad approaches to school improvement
- can also be used more specifically to help analyse and define individual school improvement efforts or programmes
- contain a series of implications for policy that could enable them to more directly influence the achievement and learning of all students.

The purpose of this chapter therefore is to discuss some of those ideas that have influenced authentic school improvement, and to provide a brief history of its evolution as a distinctive strategy for educational change. This review is undertaken by:

- exploring the values base of authentic school improvement by situating it within Habermas' 'tri-paradigmatic framework of human interests'
- referring to the work of Kurt Lewin and his articulation of action research and notion of group dynamics
- describing how the 'organisation development movement' laid the operational basis for an authentic school improvement strategy
- explaining how school self-evaluation and how contemporary school development approaches contributed to the evolution of authentic school improvement.

The school improvement values base

Paulo Freire once commented that 'methodological confusion can always be traced to ideological error'. Unless we are clear about and have a consensus over the values underpinning any particular strategy then it will founder. Where the values implicit in a school improvement strategy are not consistent or conflict with those held by the school or system, not only will confusion flourish and unexpected outcomes materialise, but a situation requiring intervention and support may also be made worse. In the absence of a consistent and articulate values base, the direct impact of a particular strategy will be inhibited or distorted.

It is now well established that different perspectives can be taken towards school improvement and indeed towards education and educational research more generally. Carr and Kemmis (1986), Aoki (1979) and Habermas (1972) among others have identified two dominant and contrasting trends in social and educational research and innovation – positivism and the interpretative perspective. Carr and Kemmis (1986: 103) summarise the contrast like this:

> What emerges from the discussion of positivism is the naive way in which it takes the 'objective' character of reality for granted and then interprets that reality as something governed by inescapable laws. In consequence, it tends to confirm a spurious scientific respectability on prevailing 'commonsense' and offers no way of effecting practical change, other

than through technical control. A major corrective to positivism provided by the interpretive approach is the recognition that the commonsense view of reality, far from being an 'objective' given, itself constitutes the major problem for theorizing and research. From the interpretive perspective, social reality is not something that exists and can be known independently of the knower. Rather, it is a subjective reality constructed and sustained through the meanings and actions of individuals.

In the field of educational change strategies that fit the positivist and interpretative paradigms, respectively, can be characterised as *adoptive* and *adaptive* models of change (Hopkins, 1984).

The *adoptive* approach tends to disregard variables within the individual school environment. This approach is preoccupied with a top-down approach to change: it assumes that change is linear, initiated by an authority figure, and is motivated by external pressure. The best known version of this approach is probably the Research, Development and Dissemination (RD&D) model of educational change. This top-down, or centre–periphery model of change was developed to assist the implementation of centralised curriculum innovations in the mid-1960s and later (Guba and Clark, 1965).

Adaptive models of educational change are more sensitive to the context of the individual school and local situation. They appreciate the environment in which they intervene, and are concerned to develop a capacity for change within the school rather than to adopt a specific approach per se. Strategies for school development planning as a means of managing and adapting centralised change exemplify this approach (Hargreaves and Hopkins, 1991).

Neither of these broad approaches provides an entirely satisfactory basis for authentic school improvement. Yet advocates of both the positive and the interpretative perspective assume 'that the two positions they represent more or less exhaust the range of possible options available for educational research to adopt' (Carr and Kemmis, 1986: 105). Yet as Carr and Kemmis (1986: 129–30) continue, there are major objections to both approaches:

> the positivist idea that knowledge has a purely instrumental value in solving educational problems and the consequent tendency to see all educational issues as technical in character needs to be firmly resisted . . . However, the recognition that educational theory must be grounded in the interpretations of teachers, is not in itself sufficient. For while it may be true that consciousness 'defines reality', it is equally true that reality may systematically distort consciousness. Indeed, one of the major weaknesses of the interpretive model is its failure to realize how the self-understandings of individuals may be shaped by illusory beliefs which sustain irrational and contradictory forms of social life.

A third approach, that of 'critical theory' addresses both of these weaknesses. This approach originated with the 'Frankfurt School' of philosophy – a community of scholars based in that German city, many of whom then immi-grated to the United States during the Second World War. The overriding concern of the Frankfurt School was 'to articulate a view of theory that has the central task of emancipating people from the positivist "domination of thought" through their own understandings and actions' (Carr and Kemmis, 1986: 130).

Audi (1995: 278–9) argues that:

> Critical theory is primarily a way of doing philosophy, integrating the normative aspects of philosophical reflection with the explanatory achieve-ments of the social sciences. The ultimate goal of its programme is to link theory and practice, to provide insight, and to empower subjects to change their oppressive circumstances and achieve human emancipation, a rational society that satisfies human needs and powers.

In his study of critical theory and its educational implications, Gibson (1986: 5–6) describes its central characteristic like this:

> Critical theory acknowledges the sense of frustration and powerlessness that many feel as they see their personal destinies out of their control, and in the hands of (often unknown) others . . . Critical theory attempts to reveal those factors that prevent groups and individuals taking control of, or even influencing, those decisions that crucially affect their lives . . . In the exploration of the nature and limits of power, authority and freedom, critical theory claims to afford insight into how greater degrees of auto-nomy could be available.

Making available 'greater degrees of autonomy' marks out critical theory's true distinctiveness: its claim to be emancipatory. Not only does it provide enlightenment (deeper awareness of your true interests); more than that (indeed, because of that), it can set you free. Unlike 'scientific' theory, it claims to provide guidance as to what to do. This concept of emancipation – enabling people to exert more influence and direction over their own lives – is central to critical theory and to authentic school improvement.

In *Knowledge and Human Interests* Habermas (1972), one of the leading members of the Frankfurt School, describes the three ways in which humans know and construe the world. These, he terms, 'technical', 'practical' and 'emancipatory'. For Habermas, knowledge is the outcome of human activity that is motivated by natural needs and interests. These interests guide and shape the way knowledge is constituted in different human activities. The technical orientation relates to positivism, the practical orientation to the interpretative paradigm, and the emancipatory one to critical theory. Aoki (1979: 10–14) has applied these orientations to education in terms of curric-ulum enquiry research.

Aoki terms positivism or the technical orientation as the *empirical analytic*. This he claims, has been until recently the dominant perspective in most educational research communities, particularly those in North America. The 'scientific' enterprise, as most educators know it, has been embedded in this orientation and has carried with it the weight of tradition and prestige. Research in education has often been defined in terms of this orientation, and rigour in this paradigm implies complex research designs and sophisticated statistical analyses.

As Aoki (1979: 10) notes, researchers within this orientation assume a detached stance towards their world, which they attempt to subdue through intellect and will. Intellectual control of this world is approached indirectly, mediated by conceptual constructs, and knowledge about the world is gained through guided observation and carefully designed and controlled manipulation. The scientific experiment is the exemplary paradigm.

Table 2.2a summarises the *empirical analytic* orientation.

The *situational interpretative paradigm*, on the other hand, involves individuals in meaning-giving activities as they construct their personal world. The structure of these meanings is their present reality. As Aoki (1979: 11) explains, in a social situation where things, people and events move together, there are many ways in which actions and events are given meaning. People continuously interpret the events they experience, and these interpretations differ from person to person. People give personal meanings to each situation experienced, and they interpret the same event in different ways.

The activity of concern for those in the interpretative framework is *communication*. The key research interests of situational interpretative researchers are insights into human experiences as they are lived. They therefore direct their efforts towards clarifying, authenticating and bringing to full human awareness the meaning structures within the social, cultural process. They seek forms of knowledge far different from those generated by cause and effect. Their focus is on the way in which individuals cognitively appropriate their social world.

Table 2.2b summarises the *situational interpretative* orientation.

The third form of research is within the *orientation* represented by *critical theory*. Whereas in the empirical-analytic research mode the root activity is manipulative work, and in the interpretative one it is communication, the critical focus is on *reflection*. Reflection uncovers and makes explicit tacit and hidden assumptions and intentions at hand. Critical researchers question descriptive accounts, and search for tacitly held intentions and assumptions, through a process of critical reflection.

As Aoki (1979: 13) notes, in critical enquiry the researcher becomes part of the object of enquiry. Here, researchers become involved with their subjects, they enter into their world and engage them in mutually reflective activity. The researchers question their subjects and themselves, they both become participants in an open dialogue. This process of reflection is also oriented towards implications for action, guided by the newly gained consciousness and critical knowing. Critical theory is interested in bringing about a reorientation through transformation of the assumptions and intentions upon

Table 2.2a A summary of empirical-analytic (technical) orientation

---

Root activity: intellectual and technical work (relates us to our natural world)

Interest: in intellectual and technical control of world; interest also in efficiency, certainty and predictability

Knowledge form: nomological knowledge (facts, generalisations, cause and effect laws, and theories)

Understanding is in terms of facts

Knowing: empirical knowing

Explaining: giving causal, functional or hypothetico-deductive reasons

Person/world relationship: 'we act upon our world'

Reality is out there

Life in this world can be explained with certainty and predictability

School improvement focus is often short term, using bureaucratic policy options and narrow outcome measures

---

Source: adapted from Aoki, 1979: 8–9

Table 2.2b A summary of situational interpretative orientation

---

Root activity: communication (relates us to our social world)

Interest: in experientially meaningful, authentic intersubjective understanding (in terms of meanings to actors)

Knowledge form: situational knowledge (knowing of structure of interpretative meanings)

Understanding is in terms of meanings people give to situations

Knowing: giving meaning

Explaining: striking a resonant chord by clarifying motives, common meanings and authentic experiences

Person/world relationship: 'we are in our social world'

Reality is inter-subjectively constituted

Life is a mystery

School improvement focus is often on process and culture and on creating a harmonious school environment

---

Source: adapted from Aoki, 1979, 8–9

Table 2.2c A summary of critical orientation

Root activity: reflection (relates us to ourselves and our social world)

Interest: in improving human condition by rendering transparent tacit assumptions and hidden assumptions and by initiating a process of transformation designed to liberate

Knowledge form: normative knowledge; knowledge of thought and action to improve human/social condition

Understanding is in terms of reflection

Knowing: critical knowing that combines reflection and action

Explaining: tracing to underlying unreflected aspects to call for action

Person/world relationship: 'we reflect upon and transform our world'

Reality is in praxis (thought and action)

Life can be improved

School improvement focus is authentic, with an emphasis on student learning, intervention and empowerment

---

Source: adapted from Aoki, 1979: 8–9

which thought and action rest. Critical theory seeks to liberate individuals from hidden assumptions and techniques, and promote a theory of the individual and society that is grounded in the moral attitude of liberation.

Table 2.2c summarises the *critical* orientation.

In moving beyond the polarity implied by the positivistic–interpretative distinction, Habermas' 'tri-paradigmatic' framework provides a way of categorising the range of strategies for educational change and school improvement. The emphasis within *positivism* or the *empirical analytic orientation* of values such as control, efficiency, and cause and effect most often results in school improvement strategies that are bureaucratic, 'quick fix' and based on a narrow range of outcomes. The *interpretative orientation* prizes giving meaning and portraying subjectivity and emphasise school improvement strategies that focus on process over product and the creation of an harmonious and supportive culture. The *critical orientation* however is different from both, committed as it is to reflection and understanding, to a belief that the world can be improved. School improvement strategies within this orientation are *authentic* and emphasise student learning as well as achievement, intervention and capacity building.

To summarise briefly – most successful forms of school improvement are characterised by a relatively consistent set of values, and these were presented earlier as a set of principles. This approach to school improvement is being called 'authentic' in order to distinguish it from other forms with different values, strategies and expectations. Habermas' 'tri-paradigmatic' framework was used to explore the value base of authentic school improvement, which is most closely associated with the critical theory paradigm. The implication being that if critical theory is emancipatory then by the same token school improvement is too. Yet even powerful ideas have little power to affect everyday life unless they assume an action orientation. The key question must be what are the strategic implications of critical theory and what does that mean for authentic school improvement? The genesis of a response is found in the assertion of Robert Young (1989) that to Habermas the only emancipatory form of research was action research. A discussion of the evolution of action research as a methodology for both critical theory and authentic school improvement provides the focus for the discussion in the following section.

The legacy of Kurt Lewin: action research

The origins of action research are generally attributed to Kurt Lewin, who in the immediate post-war period proposed it as a methodology for intervening in and researching the major social problems of the day (Adelman, 1993). Rapoport (1970), neatly summarised its twin purpose when he wrote that action research: 'aims to contribute both to the practical concerns of people in an immediate problematic situation and to the goals of social science by joint collaboration within a mutually acceptable ethical framework'.

Kemmis (1983), expanded on this definition as follows:

> Action research is a form of self-reflective enquiry undertaken by participants in social (including educational) situations in order to improve the rationality and justice of a) their own social or educational practices, b) their understanding of these practices, and c) the situations in which the practices are carried out. It is most rationally empowering when undertaken by participants collaboratively, though it is often undertaken by individuals, and sometimes in co-operation with 'outsiders.' In education, action research has been employed in school-based curriculum development, professional development, school improvement programs, and systems planning and policy development.

Lewin himself maintained that through action research advances in theory and needed social changes might simultaneously be achieved. Action research, according to Lewin (quoted in Kemmis, 1982: 13), 'consisted in analysis, fact-finding, conceptualisation, planning execution, more fact-finding or evaluation; and then a repetition of this whole circle of activities; indeed a spiral of such circles'.

As Carr and Kemmis (1986: 164–5) note, Lewin presaged three important characteristics of modern action research: its participatory character, its democratic impulse, and its simultaneous contribution to social science and social change. He identified the two essential aims of all action research: to improve and to involve. Action research aims at improvement in three areas: first, the improvement of a *practice*, second, the improvement of the *understanding* of the practice by its practitioners; and third, the improvement of the *situation* in which the practice takes place. The aim of *involvement* stands shoulder to shoulder with the aim of *improvement*.

Lewin's ideas on action research were almost immediately applied to education, as well as social science more generally. The work of Stephen Corey (1953) at Teacher's College, Columbia University, in particular his book *Action Research to Improve School Practice*, spread the word about action research into 'main stream' American education. Somewhat later but equally influentially, Lawrence Stenhouse and his colleagues in England, used action research principles to inform their approach to curriculum development and the concept of the 'teacher as researcher' (see Stenhouse, 1975). Lewin's ideas have therefore been highly influential. It is not just action research that serves the authentic purpose of school improvement, but also his research into group dynamics.

The legacy of Kurt Lewin: group dynamics

Given his commitment to action research it should be unsurprising that Lewin's other major contribution to thought and action focussed on the dynamic between the individual and their social organisation. As Lewin (1943) himself wrote:

> Although the scientific investigations of group work are but a few years old, I don't hesitate to predict that group work – that is, the handling of human beings not as isolated individuals, but in the social setting of groups – will soon be one of the most important theoretical and practical fields . . . There is no hope for creating a better world without a deeper scientific insight into the function of leadership and culture, and of other essentials of group life.

This prediction was widely welcomed. It was based in part on the pioneering research that Lewin undertook with Lippett and White in the late 1930s (Lewin *et al.*, 1939). In their definitive study they studied the influences on groups and their members of different leadership patterns. Groups of 10- and 11-year-old children met regularly for several weeks under the leadership of an adult who behaved in one of three ways: democratically, autocratically, or in a laissez-faire manner. The effects of these leadership styles on the behaviour of group members were large and dramatic. Severe forms of scapegoating, for example, occurred in the autocratic groups and at the end of the experiment the children in some of those groups destroyed the things they had constructed. This study made it clear that important social issues could be produced in the laboratory and studied experimentally (reported in Johnson and Johnson, 1994: 31). Lewin's advocacy of the study of group dynamics, was notable not just for his early championing of the use of experimental methodology and development of theory, but also for his insistence that theory and research be relevant to social practice.

Again as the Johnson brothers note (1994: 33) much of Lewin's research highlighted the importance of active participation in groups in order to learn new skills, develop new attitudes, and obtain new knowledge about groups. His research demonstrated that learning is achieved most productively in groups whose members can interact and then reflect on their mutual experiences. In this way members are able to spark one another's creativity in deriving conclusions about group dynamics. From Lewin, therefore, came the characteristic emphasis on studying one's own experiences in order to learn about group dynamics and on behaving democratically in structuring learning situations. The emphasis was however not entirely on the individual *qua* the group. It was also, as is seen in the following section, on the nature of the organisation as a social institution, and how that could be the focus of change and development in order to promote the healthy growth of its members.

Organisation development

One can trace the emergence of organisation development (OD) back to the social psychological writings and practice of Kurt Lewin (1947) with his emphasis on the influence of the organisation on the behaviour of its members, and the popularisation of 'action research' as *the* research methodology for social action and emancipation. From the early experimentation with group dynamics, through the emergence of T-groups, McGregor's work with Union Carbide in 1957, and the ESSO experiment in the late 1950s, OD began to develop a distinctive character, with an attendant technology and philosophy (Hopkins, 1982).

In the 1960s it was Matthew Miles (1967) whose seminal paper on 'organisational health' advocated the adaptation of OD techniques to schools. Miles was one of the first commentators to understand the dynamic between the organisational condition of schools and the quality of education they provide. This insight lays the foundation for much contemporary work in the area of educational change, school effectiveness and school improvement. In the paper Miles (1975: 231) describes organisational health as:

> a set of fairly durable second-order system properties, which tend to transcend short-run effectiveness. A healthy organisation in this sense not only survives in its environment, but also continues to cope adequately over the long haul, and continuously develops and extends its surviving and coping abilities.

Miles describes ten dimensions of organisational health. His first three dimensions are relatively 'tasky' and deal with goals, the transmission of information, and the way in which decisions are made. His second group of three dimensions relate to the internal state of the organisation and with maintenance needs: more specifically the effective use of resources, cohesiveness and morale. His final set of dimensions are concerned with the organisation's ability to deal with growth and change – notions of innovativeness, autonomy, adaptation vis-à-vis the environment, and problem solving.

When Miles subsequently analysed schools as organisations against these criteria he diagnosed them as being seriously ill! His analysis presaged subsequent descriptions of the pathology of schools as organisations such as Weick's (1976) characterisation of them as 'loosely coupled' systems, and comments such as schools 'are a collection of individual entrepreneurs surrounded by a common parking lot', or a 'group of classrooms held together by a common heating and cooling system'. This also explains the twin emphasis in authentic school improvement strategies on the organisational conditions of schooling as well as the teaching and learning process.

Miles then described a series of strategies designed to induce a greater degree of organisational health such as team training, survey feedback, role workshops, target setting, diagnosis and problem solving, and organisational experiment. Some of these strategies may have an anachronistic ring to them by today's standards, but there are a number of common themes flowing through all of them that have a more contemporary flavour. These are for example, self-study or review, the promotion of networking, increased communication, culture as a focus for change, the use of temporary systems, and the importance of external support.

Of the various OD strategies described in the research literature, survey or data feedback was 'the only treatment associated with substantial improvement' (Bowers, 1973: 21). As Bowers (1973: 45) notes, 'where the survey feedback is employed with skill and experience, it becomes a sophisticated tool for using the data as a springboard to development'. When used in the educational context, most OD advocates suggested the use of a survey feedback (SF), problem solving (PS) and collective decision-making (CD) design. This approach aids goal clarification by giving information on what the staff of a school perceives as goals. Its design improves information flow and communication, encourages adaptation, and creates a climate for consensual decision making. Finally, the follow-through phase presents a model for problem solving that can be internalised and used as a resource in the future. The links between survey feedback as an OD methodology and the evolving educational strategy of school self-evaluation are clear to see.

The publication of *OD in Schools* (Schmuck and Miles, 1971) was the first mature expression of the impact of OD in education. In a later 'State of the Art' paper, Fullan *et al.* (1980) concluded that OD in schools had 'diffused to a larger extent than we and others had realised'. An example of a well-developed approach to institutional self-renewal based on OD techniques is found in the *Handbook of Organisational Development in Schools* (Schmuck and Runkel, 1985). This work also served to provide insights into what constitutes the school's capacity for problem solving. According to Schmuck (1984: 29) it is reflected in a series of meta-skills – systematic diagnosis, searching for information and resources, mobilising collaborative action, 'synergy', and the staff's ability to evaluate how effectively the previous meta-skills were implemented.

Three conclusions can also be drawn from this brief analysis. First, OD approaches emphasise the importance of the organisational health determinant of effectiveness. Second and consequently, a major emphasis in many school improvement interventions is based on an approach that attempts to 'humanise' the organisational context within which teachers and students live. Third, and possibly under-emphasised at the time, was the empirical support given to the effectiveness of strategies, such as survey feedback, that diagnosed the internal conditions of the organisation as a precursor to development. It is on such approaches to OD in schools that much of the process emphasis in authentic school improvement interventions was initially based.

The emergence of authentic school improvement

Running parallel to the specific application and development of OD techniques was the beginning of widespread research into, and understanding of, the change process and the school as an organisation. The OECD/CERI project 'Case Studies of Educational Innovation' (Dalin, 1973), and the Rand Corporation 'Change Agent' study (Berman and McLaughlin, 1977), for example, highlighted the limitations of externally imposed changes, the importance of focussing on the school as the unit of change, and the need to take the change process seriously. Similarly, the research on schools as organisations, of which Sarason's (1982) *The Culture of the School and the Problem of Change* is an outstanding example, demonstrated the importance of linking curriculum innovation to organisational change.

There was a marked change in the character of school renewal efforts in the late 1970s and early 1980s. Three influences accounted for this change in emphasis (Hopkins, 1994):

- First was an increase in demands for school accountability. In the United Kingdom, for example, the reaction to the pressure for accountability took the form of a variety of local education authority (LEA) schemes for school self-evaluation.
- Second was the increased emphasis in the early 1980s on school leader development. School self-evaluation was at that time regarded as one of the few strategies available to school leaders for introducing innovation and 'renewing' the organisation of the school. The school leader training scheme in Sweden was a prime example of such developments (Bjornemalm and Ahlstrom, 1987).
- Third was the international trend towards whole scale national educational reform that began in the 1980s. School self-evaluation or school based review (SBR) was seen by many as a strategy for implementing external change. The 'Renewed Primary School' (RPS) project in Belgium

for example, devised an 'entry' procedure based on the principles of SBR (Depoortere *et al.*, 1987).

Cutting across these influences was the common denominator of school self-evaluation. At this time it was viewed as one of the few improvement strategies that could not only strengthen the capacity of the school to develop or renew itself, but also provide evidence for accountability purposes and a structure for managing the change process. The OECD International School Improvement Project (ISIP), in particular, took a leading role in conceptualising and disseminating examples of various schemes for school based review (see chapter 4 and Bollen and Hopkins, 1987; Hopkins, 1987b, 1988).

The following three brief examples represent the 'state of the art' of school self-evaluation and school improvement at this stage of development. These approaches although building on the technology of OD aligned themselves more self-consciously to the organisation and culture of the school. All were widely used in their country of origin, and two of them in many other countries of the world.

The Schools Council Guidelines for Internal Review and Development (GRIDS) project was designed to help teachers review and develop the curriculum and organisation of their school, and two practical handbooks, one primary, one secondary were produced for the purpose. In its second stage GRIDS was modified in order to: recognise the need to be externally accountable, widen the roles of those who contribute to a review, assist with the identification of in-service needs, and the management of change. New materials were also developed to assist teachers in establishing criteria for effectiveness and in using GRIDS in secondary schools at the department level (Abbott *et al.*, 1988).

The Institutional Development Programme (IDP) originated within IMTEC (International Movement Towards Educational Change), the Norwegian Educational Foundation, as a result of international collaboration that began in Scandinavia in 1974. The IDP was based on a survey feedback design with the emphasis being placed on a standardised questionnaire, consultant support and a systematic feedback-development process (Dalin and Rust, 1983). The IDP is based on an explicit conceptual framework about the nature of schools, and the feedback on the administration of the GIL (Guide to Institutional Learning) questionnaire. The IMTEC concept of consultancy includes an emphasis on skill training for participants and developing ownership at the school level. All this activity is based on the realisation that although the IDP process is generalisable, the actual reality of change varies from school to school (Dalin and Rolff, 1993).

The *Systematic Analysis for School Improvement* (SAS) project was based at the Department of Education of the University of Utrecht. The SAS is essentially a diagnostic instrument for linking of staff development and school improvement to the school's organisation. The SAS is dependent on computer analysis and external support for data feedback, interpretation and further action. In the Netherlands, educational policy is developed through the piloting of innovative projects and experimental schemes. Schools receive additional resources and external assistance for collaborating in such projects. An SAS review was used to assist schools in identifying priorities and design action plans as a basis for participation in a specific innovation project. As the Dutch support structure has a national network, which allows all schools access to the SAS database, this allows schools to compare themselves with national norms (Voogt, 1988).

During the early 1980s school-based review or evaluation, despite confusion over purpose, established itself as a major strategy for managing the change process and institutional renewal. The empirical support for its success as a school improvement strategy, however, is at best ambivalent (Clift *et al.*, 1987). For most schools it proved easier to identify priorities for future development than to implement selected targets within a specific time frame. Because of this, and a failure to implement the total process, for example training for feedback and follow up, school self-evaluation had, despite its popularity, a limited impact on the daily life of schools.

By the mid-1980s the amount of change expected of schools was increasing dramatically. This increase in expectations was also accompanied by fundamental changes in the way schools were managed and governed. Although this went by different names in different countries – self-managing schools, site-based management, development planning, local management of schools, restructuring – the key idea of giving schools more responsibility for their own management remained similar. The common aspiration of these initiatives was the 'renewed' or 'self managing' school. Although self-evaluation was still seen as a major strategy for achieving this goal, it was now regarded not as simply the initial stage in a cycle, but was spread throughout the process as an integral part of a systemic change strategy. These efforts were more broadly based than the original schemes for school self-evaluation, and, as seen in the following examples assumed a different character in different countries.

The concept of the *self-managing school* was developed in Tasmania and Victoria, Australia, in the mid-1980s. Since then, it has been adapted and emulated in many other school systems, most notably in Edmonton, Alberta. This approach was developed initially as a response to the devolution of financial resources to the school level, which by itself is no guarantee of school improvement. The aspirations of this approach can only be achieved if financial plans reflect educational plans, and if resources are allocated to support the priorities that a school has set itself. The approach, described by its originators Caldwell and Spinks (1988) as 'Collaborative School Management', aspired to integrate goal setting, policy making, budgeting, implementation and evaluation within a context of decision making that involved the school's staff, students, community and governing body.

The DES project on school development plans (SDPs) in England and Wales, was also an attempt to develop a strategy that would, among other things, help governors, headteachers and staff change the culture of their school. Development planning provides an illustration of an authentic school improvement strategy, combining as it does curriculum innovation with modifications to the school's management arrangements. It is also a strategy that became widespread in British schools in the 1990s as teachers and school leaders struggled to take control of the process of change (*vide* Hargreaves *et al.*, 1989; Hargreaves and Hopkins, 1991).

In a similar way, 'restructuring' efforts in the United States of America were attempting a more fundamental approach to educational reform by transforming the organisation of the school in the quest for enhanced student achievement. The restructuring phenomenon is generally traced to the release in 1986 of two influential reform reports *Tomorrow's Teachers* by the Holmes Group and *Teachers for the 21st Century* by the Carnegie Forum. It was also seen by some as a means of implementing the findings of, or the legacy from, the school effectiveness research (Murphy, 1992b).

Elmore (1990) suggested that there are three commonly agreed aspects to restructuring:

- changing the way teaching and learning occurs in schools
- changing the organisation and internal features of schools – the so called 'workplace conditions'
- changing the distribution of power between the school and its clients.

Unless these three conditions or changes occur simultaneously, so Elmore argues, there is little likelihood of marked improvements in student outcomes or the achievement of the core goals of the school. Restructuring, like many other authentic school improvement initiatives, will remain at the level of rhetoric unless its 'deep structure' or key principles are implemented.

This brief review of the evolution of authentic school improvement has emphasised its origins in survey feedback strategies for organisation development. It soon became evident that self-evaluation is necessary but not sufficient as the initial step in a cycle, and should re-occur, often in different forms, throughout the process. The experience with centralised change from the mid-1980s onwards, also illustrated that simply devolving budgets, broadening the governance of schools or engaging in planning is no guarantee of authentic school improvement. To be successful, models for school management and development need to achieve fundamental and lasting organisational change. This is the legacy of Lewin's influence. As he pointed out half a century ago, strategies are needed that not only involve cycles of research and action, but also directly address the organisational culture of the school.

Commentary

This chapter has focussed on the origins and foundations of authentic school improvement. The purpose has been to demonstrate that this approach to school improvement has solid foundations grounded in half a century of theory, research and development.

School improvement as a field of study has evolved subtly but decisively over the past 50 years. This evolution has passed through five phases. The first was the contribution of Lewin, his formulation of action research and the application of his ideas on group dynamics to organisation development. Second was the influence of organisational development strategies on education in the 1960s and 1970s. The third was the use of strategies for school self-evaluation, as a response to the increasing demand for school accountability in the late 1970s and early 1980s. Fourth, was the emphasis on school-based development, and the management at the school level of complex changes and multiple innovations. The fifth phase of 'authentic school improvement', has only recently been entered. As will be seen in subsequent chapters it is characterised by attempts to enhance student achievement through the use of specific instructional strategies that also have an impact on the organisation and culture of the school.

The purpose of beginning the chapter with a discussion of values and principles is to emphasise that one's view of schooling must be related both to epistemology and action. By claiming that authentic school improvement follows in the tradition of critical theory is to claim that it is emancipatory in purpose, theory and action. This is a claim that is sustained on the pages that follow.

3 A perspective on educational change and school effectiveness

In the earlier discussion of the 'epidemic' of educational change, it became clear that against a background of continuing change, expectations for student achievement seem to rise beyond the capacity of the system to deliver. It has also been argued that authentic school improvement as a strategy for educational change holds some potential for closing this gap. Any prospect for raising standards of learning and achievement however, must be regarded as extremely fragile unless school improvement strategies are designed to accommodate the complexity of educational change. Two perspectives on this complexity that have a major influence on the design of authentic school improvement strategies are considered in this chapter.

The first is that change, if it is to mean anything at all, has to have an impact at the classroom level – on the hearts and minds of teachers and students. Without this appreciation there is the danger, to use Charters and Jones' (1973) felicitous phrase, of 'appraising non-events'. Educational change is not simply about policies, although they do provide a framework for action, but about the *implementation* of policies – how they are interpreted by and impact on students, teachers and schools. If the study of change is to be taken seriously, then it must be realised that its success is ultimately an individual achievement. In order to have a positive impact on teachers and the progress of students, authentic school improvement strategies need to adopt an implementation perspective.

The second insight is that irrespective of the amount of change expected of schools by society, some schools are more able than others to respond to this challenge. Over the past 20 years the research evidence on the characteristics of those schools that create more effective learning environments for their students has been steadily accumulating. Authentic school improvement strategies need therefore to help schools become more effective learning environments *at the same time* as they are implementing reform policies.

The literature and experience of planned educational change has a relatively long and distinguished history (Fullan, 1991; Hargreaves *et al.*, 1998), and the research on school effectiveness has now reached a state of maturity (Mortimore, 1998; Teddlie and Reynolds, 2000). The field of school improvement as a whole, however, lags behind both of these areas of research and practice, and has much to learn from them. In this chapter the contribution that the recent history of educational change and school effectiveness makes to the emerging conceptualisation of authentic school improvement is reviewed.

A perspective on educational change

The amount of change expected of schools has increased exponentially over the past fifteen years. Yet even this situation is beginning to change. Change is now endemic, it is becoming all pervasive, and unfortunately traditional responses are no longer coping with the situation. What is required are radically different ways of looking at, responding to, and managing change. Fullan (1992) has phrased the problem in a particularly helpful way:

> Many of us who have pursued the theory and practice of planned change over the past 25 years have now decided to take a different tack. This change in strategy is based on the conclusion that educational reform not only does not work as the theories say it should, but more fundamentally that it can never work that way. Educational reform is complex, non-linear, frequently arbitrary, and always highly political. It is rife with unpredictable shifts and fragmented initiatives. I am afraid that this is the nature of the beast in complex socio-political societies.

The phrase *systemic change* is often used to describe the current situation, where change proliferates, is unpredictable, and is all-pervasive. It is a situation that requires a radical response. The basic problem is that our maps of change are faulty (Fullan and Miles, 1992: 745). It is difficult to get to one's destination, if the directions you are following are incorrect. It is these faulty assumptions that leave one helpless, de-skilled and frustrated at the inability to come to terms with a changing world. A 'paradigm shift' is required, to use Kuhn's phrase, in the approach to change. New mind sets and lines of action are required, as Fullan notes, to enable survival, and to have a chance of progressing under these complex, less than helpful conditions. Such shifts in understanding and beliefs are difficult to achieve, but without them we will continue to wallow helplessly in the face of the inevitable.

The purpose of this section of the chapter is to provide a perspective on the implications of educational change for authentic school improvement. The treatment will inevitably be brief, and more detailed discussions are found elsewhere (see for example: Fullan, 1991; Hopkins *et al.*, 1994: chapter 3; Hargreaves *et al.*, 1998; Joyce *et al.*, 1999). In the spirit of understanding and managing the change process, the section below:

- reviews briefly the history of educational change
- explores the meaning of educational change

- analyses the three stages of the change process
- comments on the difficulty of managing multiple changes in times of change.

The recent history of educational change

It is surprising to realise, as Fullan (1991: 5) has pointed out, how short is the history of serious investigation into the change process in schools. He noted four major phases in the study of planned educational change over the past 40 years or so. In *School Improvement in an Era of Change*, we described the four phases as lasting for approximately a decade and being characterised by a particular set of external circumstances and change strategies (for more detail see Hopkins *et al.*, 1994: 22–4).

The first, which dates from the mid-1960s, was the emphasis on the *adoption of curriculum materials*. Educational change strategies were conceived within a top-down or 'centre–periphery' model. On both sides of the Atlantic the curriculum reform movement was intended to have major impact on student achievement through the production and dissemination of exemplary curriculum materials. Although the materials were often of high quality, in the main they failed to have an impact of teaching. Although this analysis applies more to North America than to the UK, the materials emanating from the Schools Council in the late 1960s (see Stenhouse, 1980, for a comprehensive account of these projects) cannot escape censure. Also few of these projects paid anything more than lip service to the essential connection between teaching strategy and curriculum development (Hopkins, 1987a).

The second phase, covering most of the 1970s, was essentially one *understanding the process of implementation*. An adaptive style of educational change strategies was assumed during this period, as it became increasingly apparent that top-down models of change did not work. It was now acknowledged that implementation does not occur spontaneously as a result of legislative fiat, and that teachers require in-service training to acquire new knowledge and skills. It became clear that implementation is an extremely complex and lengthy process that requires a sensitive combination of strategic planning, individual learning and commitment to succeed. The contribution of Michael Fullan during this phase, in particular his *Meaning of Educational Change* (1982) was pivotal.

The third phase, roughly from the late 1970s to the late 1980s was one of *school development*. The dominant change strategies, such as self-evaluation, were essentially school-based. It was during this time that the first studies of school effectiveness were published (Rutter *et al.*, 1979; Reynolds, 1985), and that a consensus was established over the characteristics of effective schools (Purkey and Smith, 1983; Wilson and Corcoran, 1988). It was also during this period that some major large-scale studies of school improvement projects were conducted such as the DESSI and the ISIP (Crandall *et al.*, 1982, 1986; Hargreaves, 1984; Huberman and Miles, 1984; van Velzen *et al.*, 1985; Hopkins, 1987b; Rosenholtz, 1989; Louis and Miles, 1990.

The fourth phase, *systemic reform*, has lasted throughout the 1990s. This approach to change has combined centralisation and decentralisation strategies. During this period there has been a struggle to relate strategies and research knowledge to the realities of schools in pragmatic, systematic and sensitive ways. There has been a move away from studying change as a phenomenon towards actually participating in the process of school development. The best of the current work on educational change is now coming from those who in the authentic spirit of action research are studying change as they are engaged in bringing it about (Dalin, 1994; Barber, 1996; Slavin, 1996; Stringfield *et al.*, 1996; Hargreaves *et al.*, 1998; Mortimore, 1998; Fullan, 1999; Gray *et al.*, 1999; Joyce *et al.*, 1999).

This historical review of studies of innovation and planned change is one way of organising the literature. Per Dalin has recently commented somewhat wryly that during these four phases the change community began by trying to fix things, then people, then cultures, and more recently systems! However elegant the formulation, such analyses tell us little about what educational change actually is; this is the task of the following section.

The meaning of educational change

Those innovations or adaptations of practice that intervene in, or modify, the learning process achieve the greatest impact on student progress. Changes in curriculum, teaching methods, grouping practices, and assessment procedures have the greatest potential to enhance the performance of students, and so should provide the key focus for school improvement efforts.

Unfortunately the implementation of those changes that positively affect the learning of students is very difficult to achieve. This is because the focus of policy implementation is usually on some aspect of curriculum and the production of guidelines or materials. Yet educational changes that directly impact on the learning of students usually involve teachers in not only adopting new or additional teaching materials, but also (Fullan, 1991) in:

- acquiring new *knowledge*
- adopting new *behaviours* (e.g., modifying teaching styles)
- and, sometimes, in modifying their *beliefs or values*.

If classroom practice is to be affected, however, then teachers' behaviours and practices as well as their beliefs and understandings need to be addressed. As Fullan (1991: 32) reminds us, real change, 'whether desired or not, represents a serious personal and collective experience characterised by ambivalence and uncertainty' for the individual involved. There are a number

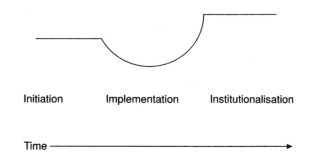

Initiation   Implementation   Institutionalisation

Time ───►

Figure 3.1 Fullan's concept of the 'implementation dip'

of implications for authentic school improvement that stem from this (Fullan, 1985: 396):

- change takes place over time
- change initially involves anxiety and uncertainty
- technical and psychological support is crucial
- the learning of new skills is incremental and developmental
- organisational conditions within and in relation to the school make it more or less likely that the school improvement will occur
- successful change involves pressure and support within a collaborative setting.

It is exactly because change is a process whereby individuals need to 'alter their ways of thinking and doing' that most changes fail to progress beyond early implementation. It is this phenomenon that Fullan (1991) has graphically referred to as 'the implementation dip'. The 'implementation dip' incorporates that constellation of factors that creates the sense of anxiety and those feelings of incompetence so often associated with re-learning and meaningful change. This is the phase of dissonance, of 'internal turbulence', that is as predictable as it is at the same time uncomfortable. Many research studies have found however that without a period of destabilisation, successful, long lasting change is unlikely to occur (Huberman and Miles, 1984).

The implications for authentic school improvement are that conditions need to be created within the school to ensure that individuals are supported through these inevitable but difficult and challenging times. The school's internal conditions should be organised around the realisation that change is a process whereby individuals alter their ways of thinking and doing. What these conditions are and how they can be established in schools provides the focus for chapter 6.

The three stages of the change process

Besides understanding the change process, educators also need to become more skilled in its use. As Miles (1986) and Fullan (1991) have demonstrated, the change process consists of a series of three overlapping phases: initiation, implementation, and institutionalisation (see Figure 3.2). Although these phases often co-exist in practice, there are some advantages in describing them separately as we did in *School Improvement in an Era of Change* (for more detail see Hopkins *et al.*, 1994: 36–8). It is particularly important to understand what happens during each phase and what behaviours within each phase make for success.

The *initiation* phase is about deciding to embark on innovation, and of developing commitment towards the process. The key activities in the initiation phase are the decision to start, and a review of the school's current state as regards the particular change. Matthew Miles (1986) made an analysis of the various stages of school improvement. This is a list of factors that Miles believes make for successful initiation:

- the innovation should be tied to a *local agenda* and high profile *local need*
- a clear, *well-structured* approach to change
- an active *advocate* or champion who understands the innovation and supports it
- *active initiation* to start the innovation (top-down is OK under certain conditions)
- good *quality* innovation.

Implementation is the phase of the process that has received the most attention. It is the phase of attempted use of the innovation. The key activities occurring during implementation are the carrying out of action plans, the developing and sustaining of commitment, the checking of progress and overcoming problems. The key factors making for success at this stage, according to Miles (1986), are:

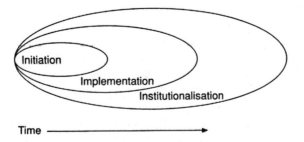

Figure 3.2 The three overlapping phases of the change process (Miles *et al.*, 1987)

- clear responsibility for *orchestration/co-ordination* (head, co-ordinator, external consultant)
- *shared control over implementation* (top-down is not OK); good cross-hierarchical work and relations; empowerment of both individuals and the school
- mix of *pressure,* insistence on *'doing it right',* and *support*
- adequate and *sustained staff development* and *in-service training*
- *rewards for teachers* early in the process (empowerment, collegiality, meeting needs, classroom help, load reduction, supply cover, expenses, resources).

Institutionalisation is the phase when innovation and change stop being re-garded as something new and become part of the school's usual way of doing things. The move from implementation to institutionalisation often involves the transformation of a pilot project, to a school-wide initiative, often with-out the advantage of the previously available funding. Key activities at this stage according to Miles (1986) are:

- an emphasis on 'embedding' the change within the school's structures, its organisation and resources
- the elimination of *competing* or contradictory *practices*
- strong and purposeful *links to other change efforts,* the curriculum and classroom teaching
- *widespread use* in the school and local area
- an adequate *bank of local facilitators,* (e.g., advisory teachers) for skills training.

Many change efforts fail to progress beyond early implementation because those involved do not realise that each of these phases have different charac-teristics and require different strategies for success to be achieved.

On the difficulty of managing multiple changes in times of flux

Differentiating between the three phases of initiation, implementation and institutionalisation is very helpful, as is the articulation of the appropriate activities at each stage. Nowadays however one is rarely involved with just one innovation. A school can be going through a number of change cycles at any one time. This places great stress on the organisational capacity of the school and the confidence and maturity of those leading the change process. How to build this capacity and confidence is the key challenge for authentic school improvement efforts.

In the early phases of a school improvement effort, the process of initia-tion, implementation and institutionalisation will be going on on at least two levels. The first is at the classroom level – putting into practice a change in curriculum and instruction. At the level of the school, the cycle of initiation, implementation and institutionalisation is concerned with capacity building – the process of learning how to change. In particular the way in which in-service activities, planning, and enquiry are organised in order to support authentic school improvement.

Once a school has developed the 'capacity to change' then successive cycles of innovation become much easier. In the early stages of a school improvement effort where the schools' organisation is not well attuned to change, more effort needs to be given initially to building capacity and possibility limiting the amount of classroom change (see chapter 8). Once the capacity is in place then managing multiple cycles of innovation become both possible and desirable.

A second issue raised by the initiation, implementation and institutionalisation analysis, are the skills required of change agents. Besides the specific activities required during each of the phases, there are also a series of 'cross cutting' or generic skill clusters that characterise the behaviours of effective change agents. There are a number of reviews of change agent skills: for example, from the organisation development literature (Schmuck and Runkel, 1985); from accounts of school improvement (Hopkins *et al.*, 1996: chapter 7); and the research on change agents themselves (Miles *et al.*, 1988). A review of this research and experience suggests the following abilities to be the most important:

- to generate trust
- to understand and diagnose the state of the school's organisation
- to plan into the medium term and to see the bigger picture
- to work productively in groups
- to access the required technical resources and advice be it research, good practice, or specifications of teaching and learning
- to give people the confidence to continue.

There is however another key skill needed for managing the contemporary process of change. It is the ability to deal with complexity. Traditional mindsets based on rational approaches to school improvement will not work in the current climate, and if employed will probably make matters worse. It is not that educational change is irrational, but as Patterson *et al.* (1986) noted, it is often non-rational and does not respect normative logical conventions.

Michael Fullan has over the years been at the cutting edge of thinking about educational change. His most recent work, in particular the *Change Forces Trilogy*, has reflected on the dialectic between rationality and chaos. The tension between top-down versus bottom-up change in a situation where change is multi-dimensional and pervasive, was a major theme in the first volume, *Change Forces*. In this book, Fullan identified 'eight basic lessons of the new paradigm of change' (Fullan, 1993: 21–2). These lessons provide an appropriate summary of this review of educational change for the purposes of authentic school improvement. They resonate with what has already been

Table 3.1 Fullan's eight basic lessons of the new paradigm of change

Lesson 1	You can't mandate what matters. (The more complex the change the less you can force it.)
Lesson 2	Change is a journey not a blueprint. (Change is non-linear, loaded with uncertainty and excitement and sometimes perverse.)
Lesson 3	Problems are our friends. (Problems are inevitable and you can't learn without them.)
Lesson 4	Vision and strategic planning come later. (Premature visions and planning blind.)
Lesson 5	Individualism and collectivism must have equal power. (There are no one-sided solutions to isolation and group-think.)
Lesson 6	Neither centralisation nor decentralisation works. (Both top-down and bottom-up strategies are necessary.)
Lesson 7	Connection with the wider environment is critical for success. (The best organisations learn externally as well as internally.)
Lesson 8	Every person is a change agent. (Change is too important to leave to the experts, personal mind set and mastery is the ultimate protection.)

Source: Fullan, 1993: 21–2

written; and examples of how they work in practice are seen on the pages that follow. As Fullan warns, however, each lesson is something of a paradox (which should be no surprise), and they should be regarded as a complete set, each benefiting from the wisdom of the other seven (see Table 3.1).

The research on school effectiveness

Over the past 20 years or so, a vast amount of evidence to support the commonsense notion that individual schools can make a difference to student progress has been accumulated. The school effectiveness research, besides articulating the characteristics of effective schools, has demonstrated unequivocally that given the right conditions *all* students can learn. The research knowledge about the characteristics of those schools and classrooms 'whose pupils progress further than might be expected from considerations of intake' (Mortimore, 1991: 216) is among the most robust there is in the quest for educational reform. Once again the treatment of the research literature on school effects will inevitably be brief. The intention is to outline the main contours of the knowledge base in order to provide a link with authentic school improvement. The interested reader is referred to recent reviews of the school effectiveness research and to our own original overview on which some of the following is based (Scheerens, 1992; Mortimore, 1998; Teddlie and Reynolds, 2000; Hopkins *et al.*, 1994 chapter 4). This survey of the school effectiveness research:

- briefly reviews the origins of this research tradition
- outlines the school effectiveness characteristics

- estimates the amount of the 'school effect'
- describes the legacy of school effectiveness
- begins to establish a framework for considering school improvement strategies.

The origins of the school effectiveness research

Up until quite recently the ability of schools to make a difference to student learning was widely doubted. Even as late as the 1960s and 1970s, well known studies and 'blue riband' reports, many of which influenced national policy, looked to factors other than the school as predictors of a student's academic performance. The family, in particular, was regarded as being far more important. The Coleman *et al.* (1966) study in the United States of America, and the Plowden (Central Advisory Council for Education (England) 1967) report in Britain were highly influential both publicly and politically, and both strongly maintained that the home influence outweighed that of the school. Other more controversial views were also advanced. Jensen (1969) reasserted the claim that hereditary influences were pre-eminent, while Bowles and Gintis (1976) in their critique of *Schooling in Capitalist America*, claimed that educational inequalities are rooted in the basic subcultures and social biases of our economy. The one thing that these widely divergent views had in common was that they all vastly underestimated the influence of the school on pupil progress.

By the late 1970s however the prevailing view began to change in the face of an emerging consensus that *schools do make a difference*. In the United States of America this was largely due to the advocacy of Ron Edmonds. His commitment to reducing racial inequality in inner city American schools and his original 'five factor theory' is well known. Edmonds' (1979) description of the effective school correlates is as follows:

1   emphasis on student acquisition of basic skills
2   high expectations for students
3   strong administrative leadership
4   frequent monitoring of student progress
5   orderly climate conducive to learning.

One of the earliest studies conducted in the United Kingdom was by Michael Rutter and his colleagues (1979) who compared the 'effectiveness' of ten secondary schools in South London on a range of student outcome measures. The 'effective schools' described in their book *Fifteen Thousand Hours*, were characterised by factors 'as varied as the degree of academic emphasis, teacher actions in lessons, the availability of incentives and rewards, good conditions for pupils, and the extent to which children are able to take responsibility' (Rutter *et al.*, 1979: 178). It was this constellation of factors that Rutter and his colleagues later referred to as the school's 'ethos'. They further claimed (Rutter *et al.*, 1979: 179) that the:

> cumulative effect of these various social factors was considerably greater than the effect of any of the individual factors on their own. The implication is that the individual actions or measures may combine to create a particular ethos, or set of values, attitudes and behaviours which will become characteristic of the school as a whole.

By the beginning of the 1980s, at a time when the cold winds of accountability were beginning to blow through most 'western' educational systems, there came striking evidence that at last schools had something to be held accountable for. The effective schools research makes it very clear that there are significant differences between schools on a variety of student outcomes, after full account has been taken of the pupil's prior learning history and family background at the time she enters the school. In terms of the contemporary debate over league tables, this is the 'value added' to a pupil over and above what ability and socio-economic status would naturally bring her. This is not to say that an individual's learning history and family background is not important: but it is to say that schools contribute differentially to pupil achievement. The school a child goes to *does* matter.

The school effectiveness characteristics

The features of effective schools as outlined by Edmonds and Rutter have already been noted. By and large, subsequent research supported these findings. There is broad agreement that the following eight criteria are representative of the organisational factors that characterise effective schools (e.g., Purkey and Smith, 1983):

1   curriculum-focussed school leadership
2   supportive climate within the school
3   emphasis on curriculum and teaching
4   clear goals and high expectations for students
5   a system for monitoring performance and achievement
6   on-going staff development and in-service training
7   parental involvement and support
8   LEA and external support.

These factors do not, however, address the dynamics of schools as organisations. There appear to be four additional factors that infuse some meaning and life into the process of improvement within the school. These so-called *process factors* provide the means of achieving the organisational factors;

they lubricate the system and 'fuel the dynamics of interaction' (Fullan, 1985: 400). They have been described as follows (Fullan, 1985: 400):

1 A feel for the process of leadership; this is difficult to characterise because the complexity of factors involved tends to deny rational planning. A useful analogy would be that organisations are to be sailed rather than driven.
2 A guiding value system; this refers to a consensus on high expectations, explicit goals, clear rules, a genuine caring about individuals, etc.
3 Intense interaction and communication; this refers to simultaneous support and pressure at both horizontal and vertical levels within the school.
4 Collaborative planning and implementation; this needs to occur both within the school and externally, particularly in the local education authority.

A further summary of the school effects research is summarised in Table 3.2 (Sammons *et al.*, 1995).

Table 3.2 Eleven factors for effective schools

1 Shared leadership	Firm and purposeful
	A participative approach
	The leading professional
2 Shared vision and goals	Unity of purpose
	Consistency of practice
	Collegiality and collaboration
3 A learning environment	An orderly atmosphere
	An attractive working environment
4 Concentration on teaching and learning	Maximisation of learning time
	Academic emphasis
	Focus on achievement
5 High expectations	High expectations all round
	Communicating expectations
	Providing intellectual challenge
6 Positive reinforcement	Clear and fair discipline
	Feedback
7 Monitoring progress	Monitoring pupil performance
	Evaluating school performance
8 Pupil rights and responsibilities	Raising pupil self-esteem
	Positions of responsibility
	Control of work
9 Purposeful teaching	Efficient organisation
	Clarity of purpose
	Structured lessons
	Adaptive practice
10 A learning organisation	School-based staff development
11 Home–school partnership	Parental involvement

Source: Sammons *et al.*, 1995

How much difference does a school make?

This discussion of school effectiveness characteristics leads to the obvious question: how great is the school effect? Not surprisingly, the various research studies differ, but as we noted a few years ago, more recent studies support earlier claims of greater effects than originally thought, although individual learning histories and home and socio-economic factors still predominate (Hopkins *et al.*, 1994: 45).

Reynolds (1992: 3), on the basis of John Gray's (1981) early work, suggests that as a rule of thumb 'the competitive edge' possessed by the most effective fifth of state secondary schools, as compared with the least effective fifth, was equivalent to one and a half of the old 'O' level public examinations per child. More recent research suggests that the difference in 'value added' to student performance by the most and least effective schools is equivalent to 7 GCSE passes at Grade C as compared to Grade E. A more international way of explaining the difference between the 'top' 10 per cent and 'bottom' 10 per cent of schools is equal to the difference between the mean 20 years ago and the mean today. In other words the best schools give their students some twenty years of educational improvement. That order of magnitude, and greater, is commonly found in a number of studies (e.g., Reynolds *et al.*, 1987; Nuttall *et al.*, 1989; Smith and Tomlinson, 1989; Gray *et al.*, 1990; Cuttance, 1992).

Scheerens (1992) in his authoritative study of the school effects research noted that his attempt to synthesise the various research studies was 'a sobering experience'. This was due to the variation in the way the research has been reported, and he like others sought different ways of estimating the school effect. He used the concept of 'effect size' (which is the effect of the school in terms of percentages of standard deviation, see chapter 5 for a further explanation) to estimate the quantum of the school effect. Using the 0.67 standard deviation result from the Purkey and Smith (1983) study he concluded that this was an effect of average size (Scheerens, 1992: 71). Yet this average effect still equates to an entire year's difference in the experience of a student in one of the most effective schools (top 20 per cent) as compared with students who are unfortunate enough to go to one of the least effective schools (bottom 20 per cent).

There are many other striking results from individual studies that confirm the relative importance of the school effect. Mortimore and his colleagues (1988) for example, used a longitudinal study to express the magnitude of the school effect in junior schools as compared with home influence over a three-year period. They concluded that over this time period the school was roughly four times more important in accounting for pupil progress in reading than were background factors, and ten times more important in accounting for progress in mathematics (Mortimore *et al.*, 1988: 186, 188).

The issue of the magnitude of effect is dealt with at length in the extremely comprehensive *International Handbook of School Effectiveness Research*

(Teddlie and Reynolds, 2000, chapter 3). By and large their extensive description of school effects research tends to confirm the research just cited. Interestingly, they also comment on their frustration at attempting to summarise the results concerning the magnitude of school effects. This frustration relates both to the variation in the way in which the research is reported as well as the complexity of the issues raised.

This complexity relates to a range of important issues in the contemporary school effectiveness debate. Four in particular are relevant to this discussion:

- The first stems from the difficulty in comparing results across different contexts. Indeed 'context specificity' is now a key issue in school effectiveness research (see Teddlie and Reynolds, 2000, chapter 5).
- Second is the issue of the constitution of the school effect. How much is due to the ethos of the school, and how much to the teacher? Again a definitive response is illusive, due to the difficulty of obtaining an authoritative meta-analysis across different contexts. Another rule of thumb would spread the effect fairly evenly across school and classroom, depending of course upon context. Most commentators agree that at least the effect is shared, but some commentators claim a higher classroom effect (Creemers, 1994).
- Third, in the same way as the amount of effect is open to debate, so too is the consistency of the effect. Early studies suggested stability in outcomes over a period of years, but the recent studies are more ambivalent. Nuttall and his colleagues (1989) in the ILEA study noted marked differences in school performance during the period 1985–7 and a lack of stability over the three-year period. They therefore advised caution when interpreting the results of any study that relied solely on one year's data or one cohort of students. Similarly, in our recent study of 'improving schools' we found little evidence that schools sustained improvement year-on-year over the five years of the research, although most schools were consistent in terms of trend in performance (Gray *et al.*, 1999).
- Fourth is the differential impact of school effectiveness on sub-groups. Nuttall and his colleagues (1989), in their research on the effectiveness of ILEA schools, for example, showed large differences for different types of pupil in the relative effectiveness of schools in London. The ILEA research suggests that the difference in experience between able and less able pupils vary markedly between schools. The performance of schools also varied in the ways they impacted upon boys and girls, and in their effects upon students from different ethnic groups. Some schools narrowed the gap between these different groups over time and other schools widened them in both instances. Not only have the differential effects they noted been substantiated by other studies, but also the differential effectiveness of departments or curriculum areas has also been established (Harris *et al.*, 1995).

The legacy of the school effectiveness research

It may appear from this review of the school effectiveness research that the quest for the Holy Grail of authentic educational reform is already at an end, that the knowledge generated by those working within the effective schools tradition provides the answer to the challenge of raising student achievement. Unfortunately, this is not the case. There are a number of problems related to the way in which the school effectiveness research is conducted that inhibits both its validity, and the practical applications of the research (e.g., Elliott, 1996; Thrupp, 1999; West and Hopkins, 2001).

These problems aside, the contribution of the effective school research to authentic school improvement is indeed highly significant. Murphy (1992a, b) has re-formulated the debate in a very helpful way. He argues that the school effects correlates are simply the means to an end – student learning. From that perspective it is not the correlates themselves that are important, but rather the principles that support them. Indeed the correlates may look very different in the future; they certainly change in differing contexts at present, although the concept of effectiveness remains the same. It was this line of argument that encouraged Murphy to look at the 'real legacy of the effective school movement'. He identified four aspects to the legacy (Murphy, 1992a: 94–6):

- *The educability of learners* At the heart of the effective schools movement is an attack on the prevailing notion of the distribution of achievement according to a normal curve. There is a clear demonstration that all students can learn.
- *A focus on outcomes* For a variety of reasons educators tend to avoid serious inspection of the educational process. Effective school advocates argue persuasively that rigorous assessments of schooling are needed and that one can judge the quality of education only by examining student outcomes, especially indices of learning. Equally important, they define success not in absolute terms, but as the value added to what students brought to the educational process.
- *Taking responsibility for students* The third major contribution of the effective schools movement is its attack on the practice of blaming the victim for the shortcomings of the school itself. The movement has been insistent that the school community takes a fair share of the responsibility for what happens to the youth in its care.
- *Attention to consistency throughout the school community* One of the most powerful and enduring lessons from all the research on effective schools is that the better schools are more tightly linked – structurally, symbolically and culturally – than the less effective ones. They operate more as an organic whole and less as a loose collection of disparate sub-systems. An overarching sense of consistency and co-ordination is a key element that cuts across the effectiveness correlates and permeates our better schools.

This analysis represents a major contribution both to the effective schools literature as well as a challenge to school improvement. The legacy of the effective schools movement as outlined by Murphy leads away from the effective schools research per se into the territory of authentic school improvement.

Towards a framework for considering school improvement strategies

At the start of the next chapter the argument is made for an integration of school effectiveness research and school improvement practice. Before that it is instructive to briefly review two research studies that combine these two perspectives.

In her book *Teacher's Workplace*, Rosenholtz (1989) argues that the social organisation of the school directly affects the commitment of teachers and the achievement of students. She writes evocatively of the 'learning enriched school', where the excitement and motivation of learning is a full part of the daily lives of both students and teachers. Rosenholtz distinguishes between two stereotypical schools – the 'moving' school and the 'stuck' school. She found perhaps unsurprisingly, that the 'moving' schools produced higher outcomes for students than those pupils in the so-called 'stuck' schools. Table 3.3 shows a set of characteristics of 'stuck' and 'moving' schools that is based on Rosenholtz's work.

The second example formed part of Stringfield and Teddlie's (1988, 1991), longitudinal study of School Effectiveness in Louisiana. As part of this work they identified sixteen secondary schools that were either highly effective or ineffective over a period of time, that is the students in these schools continued to perform either significantly above or below expectation based on previous learning history and family background. They report the characteristics of these contrasting school types at three levels: school and principal, classroom, and student. These 'data categories', which are summarised in Table 3.4, provide very helpful insights into successful and unsuccessful schools (adapted from Hopkins *et al.*, 1994: 65). In the figure, some of the categories have an asterisk; these factors apply especially to the four schools in the sample that the observers felt were deliberately attempting to 'improve' themselves. This study is an excellent example of research that is concerned not

Table 3.3 The characteristics of 'stuck' and 'moving' schools

'Stuck'	*'Moving'*
Low consensus	High consensus
Teacher uncertainty	Teacher certainty
Low commitment	High commitment
Isolation	Cohesiveness
Individualised	Collaborative
Learning impoverished	Learning enriched

Table 3.4 Factors observed to differentiate effective and ineffective schools

School level	Stable high achieving school	Stable low achieving school
Student	High to moderate time on task*	Low or uneven time on task; students 'escape' from class and reduce academic time
	School makes academic sense to students	School is intellectual anarchy
Classroom	Planned academic push*	Classes progress at leisurely pace
	Teachers articulate academic plans	Minimal to no planning – 'following the curriculum'; 'going through the motions'
	High to moderate interactive teaching – 'get the show on the road', and so on*	Low or uneven interactive teaching rates
	Teachers seek new teaching techniques	Teachers teach in isolation
	Varied curriculum	Many 'ditto sheets' and workbooks
School and principal	Friendly, serious academic atmosphere* – 'we're here to teach, students are here to learn'	Occasionally friendly, never academically focussed – 'if kids had a better attitude, we could teach better'
	Respect for academic time* Accurate schedules	Lack of academic focus Timetables overestimate instructional time – 'extended break' etc.
	Special needs classes well co-ordinated	Resources (especially for special needs pupils) working at cross-purposes
	Principals know curricula and instructional details, often mention specifics	Principals rarely discuss academic specifics
	Principals seek and integrate new intellectual experiences for schools	Principals define their work bureaucratically
	Principals actively recruit new teachers*	Principals passively accept new teachers
	Focussed, often school-wide staff development	Diffuse staff development
	Principals move ineffective teachers out*	Principals rarely observe classes – 'all our teachers are good'
	Student-focussed, academically-oriented library*	Rarely used or non-academic library
	Prominently posted academic 'honour roll'*	No school academic rewards

Source: Adapted from Stringfield and Teddlie, 1991: 362

only with creating effective schools and classrooms, but also with school improvement.

These analyses provide us with heuristic and engaging descriptions of highly effective and ineffective schools. But neither of the studies directly addresses the question of how schools become more or less effective. What is of central importance for authentic school improvement approaches is how do ineffective schools assume the characteristics of highly effective schools and so produce higher levels of achievement for their students? The signal contribution of the school effectiveness research has been to identify and describe the characteristics of those schools. It is the responsibility of authentic school improvement to devise the strategies that can help the ineffective schools become less so, and the effective schools more so.

Commentary

During the current period of educational reform, it is becoming increasingly apparent that change and improvement are not necessarily synonymous. Although it is true that external pressure is often the cause, or at least the impetus, for most educational change, this is not to imply that such changes are always desirable. Indeed some externally imposed change should be resisted, or at least adapted to meet the school's own purpose. The single most important criterion for the introduction of any change into a school or educational system should be its potential for enhancing the learning of students. In this chapter the two research literatures most relevant to authentic school improvement have been reviewed, and their perspective on this dilemma solicited.

The importance of implementation and the management of systemic change have dominated the research on educational change in recent years. Perhaps the best way of coping with these demands is to make change everyone's business. As Fullan and Miles (1992: 745) comment, 'no change would be more fundamental than a dramatic expansion of the capacity of individuals and organisations to understand and deal with change'. Everyone within a school needs to become in some sense a change agent, someone who is skilful and knowledgeable about the business of change. Educators should be as skilful in managing the change process as they are in curriculum and instruction.

One of the most optimistic and well supported conclusions from the school effects research, was that of Rutter's when he commented that, 'the differences between schools in outcome were systematically related to their characteristics as social institutions', and that 'all of these factors were open to modification by the staff, rather than fixed by external constraints' (Rutter *et al.*, 1979: 178). The social organisation of the school and the consistent commitment of staff to a core set of educational principles provide the foundations for the value the school adds to a student's learning, progress and achievement.

Both of these insights have profound implications for approaches to authentic school improvement. It is only in the synergy of the knowledge from these disciplines that a coherent response to the contemporary world of rapid, centrally determined, and externally enforced educational change can be developed. Some glimpses of that future are found in the following chapter.

4 School improvement in an era of change

During its relatively short history, school improvement as an approach to educational change has passed through 'three ages'. Although the intellectual background to school improvement can be traced back to the work of Kurt Lewin in the immediate post war period, it was only in the late 1970s and early 1980s that it took shape as a practical approach to educational change. Many of the 'first age of school improvement' initiatives were 'free floating'. There was a focus on individual strategies such as organisational change, school self-evaluation, the role of leadership, and of external support. These initiatives were loosely connected to student learning, were too fragmented in conception and application, and therefore struggled to impact upon classroom practice. As a consequence, these 'first age' initiatives did not match the criteria previously outlined for authentic school improvement.

Many of the elements for a 'second age' of school improvement, more in line with the 'authentic principles' were however in place by the early 1990s. The catalyst for a qualitative move forward came from the beginnings of a merger of the two traditions of school effectiveness research and school improvement practice. By this time the two traditions were in a position to give tools to practitioners that were directly applicable and useful in the new policy context. So for example 'value added' measures of school performance provided schools with a methodology for gauging their effectiveness and in so doing sharpened the focus of reform efforts on student learning. Similarly the school improvement tradition was at last providing schools with guidelines and strategies for implementation that were sufficiently powerful to take educational change into the classroom. Approaches to staff development based on partnership teaching (Joyce and Showers, 1995), designs for development planning that focussed on learning and that linked together organisational and classroom change within a medium-term time frame (Hopkins and MacGilchrist, 1998), are but two examples. In addition, the educational reform initiatives of the early to mid-1990s that reflected a more centralised attempt to reform schooling and impact on learning were beginning to bite.

Despite this, the full legacy of the interaction between school effectiveness and improvement has not been fully exploited. Improvement on a national scale is very patchy. There is a lack of a strategic dimension to most national reforms and a consequent failure to significantly accelerate the learning of pupils. Success at the local level is often the result of either a strong and opportunistic leader or a happy series of serendipities. It is clear that neither the first nor second ages of school improvement have made sufficient impact on the 'learning level'. Educational systems need not only to consolidate what has been learned from the second age of school improvement, but also to move onto a third that fully embodies the principles of authentic school improvement.

Many of the features of the 'first age' of school improvement have already been outlined. In this chapter what is known about the 'second age' will be consolidated, and some indication given of what the 'third age of school improvement' based on the authentic principles will consist. The contours of the 'third age' of authentic school improvement will become clearer as the discussion in subsequent chapters unfolds. In this chapter:

- the contribution of the OECD International School Improvement Project is described
- the integration of school effectiveness and school improvement traditions reviewed
- the school improvement response to educational change is assessed
- the 'Success For All' and 'Improving the Quality of Education for All' programmes are described as examples of authentic school improvement initiatives
- a framework for authentic successful school improvement is proposed.

The OECD International School Improvement Project

A major impetus to the development of school improvement as a strategic response to the challenge of educational change was given by the OECD through its Centre for Educational research and development (CERI), which between 1982 and 1986 sponsored an International School Improvement Project (ISIP). ISIP built on previous OECD/CERI initiatives such as *The Creativity of the School* (Nisbet, 1973) and the INSET (Hopkins, 1986) projects. Although school self-evaluation was regarded as an important strategy for school improvement, the ISIP took a more holistic and systemic view of educational change. At a time when the educational system as a whole faced not only retrenchment but also pressure for change, a project that focussed on school improvement – at change at the meso level, at strategies for strengthening the school's capacity for problem solving, at making the school more reflexive to change, as well as enhancing the teaching–learning process – was seen as both important and necessary. More detail of the knowledge that emanated from ISIP is found elsewhere (van Velzen *et al.*, 1985; Hopkins, 1987b, 1990),

ISIP proposed a very different way of thinking about change than the ubiquitous 'top-down' approach. When the school is regarded as the 'centre' of change, then strategies for change need to take this new perspective into account. School improvement for example, was defined in the ISIP as (van Velzen *et al.*, 1985: 48): 'A systematic, sustained effort aimed at change in learning conditions and other related internal conditions in one or more schools, with the ultimate aim of accomplishing educational goals more effectively'.

School improvement as an approach to educational change, according to ISIP, therefore rested on a number of assumptions (Hopkins *et al.*, 1994: 69):

- *The school as the centre of change* This means that external reforms need to be sensitive to the situation in individual schools, rather than assuming that all schools are the same. It also implies that school improvement efforts need to adopt a 'classroom-exceeding' perspective, without ignoring the classroom.
- *A systematic approach to change* School improvement is a carefully planned and managed process that takes place over a period of several years.
- *A key focus for change is the 'internal conditions' of schools* These include not only the teaching–learning activities used in the school, but also the schools' procedures, role allocation, and resource use that support the teaching–learning process.
- *Accomplishing educational goals more effectively* Educational goals reflect the particular mission of a school, and represent what the school itself regards as desirable. This suggests a broader definition of outcome than student scores on achievement tests, even though for some schools these may be pre-eminent. Schools also serve the more general developmental needs of students, the professional development of teachers and the needs of its community.
- *A multi-level perspective* Although the school is the centre of change it does not act alone. The school is embedded in an educational system that has to work collaboratively or symbiotically if the highest degrees of quality are to be achieved. This means that the roles of teachers, heads, governors, parents, support people (advisers, higher education, consultants etc.), and local authorities should be defined, harnessed and committed to the process of school improvement.
- *Integrative implementation strategies* This implies a linkage between 'top-down' and 'bottom-up'; remembering of course that both approaches can apply at a number of different levels in the system. Ideally 'top-down' provides policy aims, an overall strategy, and operational plans; a 'bottom-up' response involving, diagnosis, priority goal setting, and implementation complement this. The former provides the framework, resources, and a menu of alternatives; the latter, energy and school based implementation.
- *The drive towards institutionalisation* Change is only successful when it has become part of the natural behaviour of teachers in the school. Implementation by itself is not enough.

It was this philosophy and approach that underpinned the International School Improvement Project and laid the basis for further thinking and action. The ISIP also occurred at a fruitful time for the evolution of school improvement more generally. During this period some large-scale studies of school improvement projects were also conducted. The 'Study of Dissemination Efforts Supporting School Improvement' (see the ten volume report, *People, Policies and Practices: Examining the Chain of School Improvement* by David Crandall *et al.*, 1982) was particularly important. This mammoth study was responsible for the fine-grained analysis of *Innovation Up Close* (Huberman and Miles, 1984), and an analysis of policy implications (Crandall *et al.*, 1986). Much was consequently learned about the dynamics of the change process during this period.

School effectiveness and school improvement: towards integration

Recent years have seen a growing enthusiasm for combining the perspectives, approaches and findings of school effectiveness and school improvement in various ways. There is clear intellectual value in ensuring that the school improvement 'vehicle' and the school effectiveness 'knowledge base' are combined to enlarge our understanding both of the operation of school regimes and the possibility of their change. The centrality of school effectiveness and school improvement within the contemporary policy discourse and the needs of the educational system for relevant knowledge, have also ensured that any artificial, historical blocks upon the quality of our knowledge are rapidly disappearing as both knowledge bases are utilised by practitioners.

It is only comparatively recently, however, that school improvement programmes in their basic conceptualisation and design have reflected the influences of these multiple constituencies and bodies of knowledge. In the past major differences between the paradigms or belief systems of the 'school improvers' and of the school 'effectiveness research community' inhibited synergy. The detail of this is explored elsewhere (Reynolds, 1993; Reynolds *et al.*, 1993; Gray *et al.*, 1996; Reynolds *et al.*, 1996; Teddlie and Reynolds, 2000; Hopkins and Reynolds, 2001) but, briefly, school improvement historically celebrated:

- a 'bottom-up' orientation in which improvement was owned by the individual school and its staff
- a qualitative orientation to research methodology
- a concern with changing organisational processes rather than the outcomes of the school
- a concern to treat educational outcomes as not 'given' but problematic
- a concern to see schools as dynamic institutions requiring extended study more than 'snapshot' cross sectional studies.

These core assumptions clashed with those of school effectiveness, generating an absence until recently of any confluence of perspectives and programmes in the two fields. Effectiveness research by contrast evidenced historically:

- a pragmatic response to policy initiatives
- a commitment to quantitative methods
- a concern with the formal organisation of schools rather than with their more informal processes
- a focus upon outcomes which were accepted as being a 'good' that was not to be questioned
- a focus upon description of schools as static, steady-state organisations generated by brief research study.

After the clearly fragmented intellectual communities of the 1980s what is now emerging is a group of individuals who might be called pragmatists, rather than being either the 'scientists' of the school effectiveness paradigm, or the 'humanists' of the school improvement community. This new group avoids being either one thing or the other by combining elements of both traditions into a new paradigm, in which mixed methods rather than either quantitative or qualitative ones are utilised for description and explanation, and in which the improvement of schools is to be through 'pulling levers' selected from both former traditions. (See for example Gray *et al.*, 1999.)

School improvement and the response to external change

If the nature of school improvement itself has been evolving over the past twenty years, so has the context of schooling changed since the OECD ISIP project first articulated school improvement as a strategy for educational change. Contemporary school improvement is now characterised by increasing complexity. On the one hand, school improvement approaches are becoming more sophisticated as they move through the three ages described in this chapter. On the other hand, the pressure for externally imposed change is also increasing. The title of this chapter was deliberately chosen to emphasise the need for school improvement strategies to evolve and become more authentic, in order to meet the challenge of external change. At the start of a new century it is not sufficient for school improvement to develop on its own terms, it also needs to be responsive to the changing demands of the external educational environment.

Strategies for authentic school improvement are needed because externally imposed changes are not capable of directly enhancing the learning and achievement of students. In many jurisdictions, claims that centralised policy will lead to standards inevitably and inexorably rising have now been exposed as rhetoric. It is now very clear that accountability measures such as inspection, or guidelines for national curricula, and schemes for national assessment have difficulty in impacting directly on practice. If, as McLaughlin argues (1990), policy does not mandate what matters and local implementation determines outcomes, then some form of linkage to mediate between policy and outcome is required. One solution that is proposed in the final chapter is to develop policies within an authentic school improvement framework; the other is for schools and those agencies close to the school to develop their own response.

These responses are neither ideal nor uniform. Research and experience illustrate a range of approaches that vary in their ability to address the challenge of external change. In trying to make sense of the range of response it is helpful to analyse them across two dimensions. The first dimension contrasts the response as either 'curricular' or 'organic'. A curricular response is self-explanatory, as it is a direct response to the curricular focus of many current policies. An organic response focusses on building a capacity within the school in order to manage change. The other dimension contrasts the response as either 'comprehensive' or 'diffuse'. In response to a particular curriculum oriented policy a school may adopt an already well developed, and tried and tested programme. This would be a comprehensive response. It is more usual however for the school to rely more on its own resources, and to do more of what it has already done successfully. This could be termed a 'diffuse' response.

Some examples of this range of possibilities are given in Table 4.1. This way of analysing school improvement captures not only the variety of responses that schools typically adopt in responding to external change, but it also provides a way of organising and differentiating between a number of school improvement programmes and the associated literature.

A *diffuse–curricular response* to external change is the most common. Schools react as best they can, but often in an ad hoc and unco-ordinated way. Detailed examples of this response are found in the case studies reported in our book *Improving Schools* (Gray *et al.*, 1999). The objective for the research was to explore how secondary schools become more effective over time. We found that different schools at differing levels of effectiveness and with different improvement trajectories exhibited contrasting 'routes to improvement' (see chapter 9).

All of the schools in the study, however, irrespective of being 'slow' or 'rapid' improvers, exhibited a diffuse–curricular response to external change.

Table 4.1 Examples of school improvement responses to external change

	Curricular	Organic
Diffuse	'The common curriculum of school improvement'	'The "doors" to school improvement'
Comprehensive	'Success For All'	'Improving the quality of education for all'

This tactical response was a direct reaction to the externally imposed target setting agenda, in particular the pressure to raise examination results at age sixteen. These tactics included: monitoring performance, introducing extra classes for certain groups of students, implementing 'codes of conduct', giving students greater responsibility, changing examination boards, and so on. They comprise what we termed the 'common curriculum' of school improvement (Gray *et al.*, 1999).

This combination of tactics are powerful enough to raise the performance of low or slowly achieving schools up towards average levels of performance but no further. Although very popular such *diffuse–curricular responses* are by no means a panacea. There appears to be a ceiling on the amount of improvement such an approach can deliver. At best it can bring a school from a moderately low level up to an average level of performance. Also, it appears that the effect is short-lived, it usually plateaus or decreases after two years. Such a tactical response may be popular and in many cases necessary, but it is by no means a sufficient condition for authentic school improvement.

The *diffuse–organic response* is highly visible in Bruce Joyce's review of the 'doors' to school improvement. These are a series of individual approaches, which he describes as being 'doors' that can open or unlock the process of school improvement. Joyce concludes that each approach emphasises different aspects of school culture at the outset – in other words, they provide a range of ways of 'getting into' school improvement. Each door opens a passageway into the culture of the school. His review reveals five major emphases (Joyce, 1991: 59):

1   *Collegiality:* the developing of collaborative and professional relations within a school staff and between their surrounding communities.
2   *Research:* where a school staff studies research findings about, for example, effective school and teaching practices, or the process of change.
3   *Action research:* where teachers collect and analyse information and data about their classrooms and schools, and their students' progress.
4   *Curriculum initiatives:* the introduction of changes within subject areas or, as in the case of the computer, across curriculum areas.
5   *Teaching strategies:* when teachers discuss, observe and acquire a range of teaching skills and strategies.

Joyce argues that all these emphases can eventually change the culture of the school substantially. He maintains that single approaches are unlikely to be as powerful an agent for school improvement as a synthesis. The implicit assumption made by Joyce is that behind the door are a series of interconnecting pathways that lead inexorably to school improvement. In reality this is rarely the case. Most school improvement strategies tend to focus on individual changes, and individual teachers and classrooms, rather than how these changes can fit in with and adapt the organisation and ethos of the school. Because of their singular nature, they fail to a greater or lesser degree to affect the culture of the school. As a consequence when the door is opened it only leads into a cul-de-sac. This partially accounts for the uneven effect of most of our educational reforms.

The broad conclusion from the analysis so far is that the diffuse responses to external change are inadequate. They do not match the criteria for authentic school improvement. If the problems of educational change are to be over-come some way needs to be found of integrating organisational and curric-ulum change within a coherent strategy. To continue with Joyce's metaphor, the doors to school improvement need to be opened simultaneously or con-secutively and the pathways behind them linked together. This would argue for the adoption of more comprehensive and well-specified approaches to school improvement.

The *comprehensive–curricular response* has a relatively long history, at least in terms of educational change. The 1960s have been described on both sides of the Atlantic as the 'decade of curriculum reform'. Although at that time many well-specified curricula were developed, few were sufficiently compre-hensive enough to integrate both curriculum content and instructional stra-tegies (Hopkins, 1987a). It is the integration of content and pedagogy that characterises programmes that are associated with high levels of student achievement (Slavin and Fashola, 1998). Stringfield and his colleagues (Stringfield *et al.*, 1996, 1998), in their recent review of effective school im-provement approaches, emphasise the need for carefully selected instruc-tional strategies embedded within curriculum programmes that are designed to meet the particular learning needs of students. Unfortunately, within the field of school improvement at present, it is clear that few such strategies exist. An exception to this is the 'Success For All' literacy programme that uses research-based approaches to curriculum, instruction, assessment and classroom management, with one-to-one tutoring being provided for those students falling behind in their reading (Slavin *et al.*, 1996).

Examples of the *comprehensive–organic response* are found in the various school improvement networks that are based on a particular philosophy or set of principles. They are a sort of school improvement 'club' where the rules of admission define a generalised approach to development work in schools. The Comer School Development Programme (Comer, 1992); the Coalition of Essential Schools based at Brown University which has evolved on the basis of the ideas of Theodore Sizer (1989); the League of Professional Schools at the University of Georgia led by Carl Glickman (1993); and the Learning Consortium in Toronto, including the 'Halton Project' (Fullan *et al.*, 1990; Stoll and Fink, 1996), are all fine examples of this approach to school im-provement. One of the weaknesses in such programmes is that the emphasis on principles, capacity building, and whole school processes is often at the expense of innovation at the classroom level. Without expanding the teach-er's repertoire of instructional strategies, it is unlikely that such programmes will have any significant impact on student achievement. The 'Improving the Quality of Education for All' (IQEA) project, however, provides one example of a comprehensive–organic approach that attempts to link whole school development to enhanced classroom practice (Hopkins *et al.*, 1994, 1996).

In terms of their contribution to enhancing the achievement of students, and to realising the aspirations of national educational policies, it is the comprehensive approaches to school improvement that are the most effective. Despite the difference in focus and emphasis between comprehensive 'curricular' and 'organic' programmes, in practice they share many of the features of authentic school improvement. The two comprehensive programmes with which I am the most familiar are 'Success For All' and the 'Improving the Quality of Education for All' projects. They are both examples of authentic school improvement programmes. As they will be used as exemplars throughout the rest of the book, they are described below in a little more detail.

'Success For All'

'Success For All' (SFA) is a comprehensive programme for restructuring primary schools where students are 'at risk' of not developing functional literacy by the end of their elementary education. SFA is based on two essential principles: prevention and immediate, intensive intervention. Learning problems are prevented by providing children with the best available classroom programmes and by engaging parents in support of their children's school success. When learning problems do appear, corrective interventions must be immediate, intensive, and minimally disruptive to students' progress in the regular programme. The components of 'Success For All' are briefly described below, although more detailed descriptions exist (Slavin *et al.*, 1994, 1996).

- *Reading programme* During a regular 90-minute reading period students who are performing at similar reading levels are grouped into the same class irrespective of age. The programme emphasises the development of basic language skills and sound and letter recognition skills in reception, with sound blending and phonics starting in Year 1. The initial reading programme uses a series of 'shared stories' that have a phonetically controlled and key word sight vocabulary. The programme utilises oral reading to pupil partners as well as the teacher, instruction in story structure and specific comprehension skills, and the integration of reading and writing. This is the 'Reading roots' component of the programme that would usually occur during Year 1. Subsequently, in the 'Reading wings' programme that usually starts in Year 2, students use a form of Co-operative Integrated Reading and Composition (CIRC) with novels. CIRC uses co-operative learning activities built around story structure, prediction, summarisation, vocabulary building, decoding practice, writing and direct instruction in reading comprehension skills.
- *Reading tutors* One of the most important elements of 'Success For All' is the use of one-to-one tutoring to support students' success in reading. Tutors work directly with individual students who are having difficulty

keeping up with their reading groups. The students are taken from their 'home-room classes' by tutors for intensive 20-minute sessions during times other than reading or maths periods. In general, tutors support students' success in the regular reading curriculum, rather than teaching different objectives. Year 1 students receive priority for tutoring, on the assumption that the primary function of the tutors is to help all students be successful in reading the first time, before they become reluctant readers. In the Nottingham SFA pilot, the Boots Company provided some 200 tutors to support this aspect of the programme.

- *Eight-week assessments* Every eight weeks, reading teachers assess students' progress through the programme. The results of these assessments are used to determine any necessary regrouping, who is to receive tutoring, to suggest adaptations in students' programmes, and to identify students who need other types of assistance, such as family interventions or vision/hearing screenings.

- *Pre-school and reception* The pre-school and reception programmes provide a balanced and developmentally appropriate learning experience for young children. The curriculum emphasises the development and use of language and provides a mix of academic readiness and music, art and movement activities. Readiness activities include the use of integrated thematic units, Peabody Language Development kits, and a programme called Story Telling and Retelling ('STaR') in which students retell stories told by teachers.

- *Programme facilitator* A half-time programme facilitator works at each school to oversee (with the head) the operation, training and implementation of 'Success For All'. The facilitator helps plan the 'Success For All' programme, assists the head with scheduling, and visits classes and tutoring sessions frequently to help teachers and tutors with individual problems. The programme facilitator may work with individual children in order to find successful strategies for teaching them and then return them to the tutors or teachers.

- *Teachers and in-service training* Teachers and tutors receive detailed teachers' manuals, supplemented by two days of in-service training at the beginning of the school year and several in-service training sessions throughout the year on such topics as classroom management, instructional pace, and the implementation of the curriculum.

Research conducted by Slavin and his colleagues suggests that the SFA programme has consistent and powerful impacts on children's reading performance (Slavin *et al.*, 1994, 1996; Slavin, 1996; Slavin and Madden, 1999). In summary, by the end of first grade students on average are reading at a level three months higher than students in matched control groups. By fifth grade they are reading a full year higher, and this difference is maintained into secondary school. The research on 'Success For All' finds particularly large impacts for children who are most at risk. A national dissemination programme in the US provides extensive training and support to a network of more than one thousand 'Success For All' schools in most states. Studies in Australia, Israel and Canada have shown that adaptations of 'Success For All' can be successful outside of their US context.

Our own research has demonstrated that SFA has the potential to be successful in England too (Hopkins *et al.*, 1999). The main conclusions from the initial pilot in the 'Meadows' family of schools in Nottingham, suggest that as a result of initial involvement in the SFA programme:

- Students appear to have made as much progress in one term in reading as they would normally have been expected to make in one year.
- Students' motivation, behaviour, attitude to and skill in learning have also increased.
- Teachers claim to have learned a great deal from SFA, particularly about the effective teaching of reading, co-operative teaching strategies and their own professional development.

In addition:

- SFA has forged community links and enhanced parental participation.
- An excellent 'fit' between 'Success For All' and the National Literacy Strategy was identified.

SFA has clearly demonstrated that in whatever context it is capable of raising literacy levels in areas of high underachievement and relative deprivation. In addition, the research and dissemination of 'Success For All' and other research-based strategies create dynamic opportunities for fundamental and lasting change in education. 'Success For All' is one of several comprehensive, school-wide models for school improvement that point towards a time when heads, principals and other educators will be able to make informed, thoughtful choices from among many alternative curriculum and instructional programmes, confident that each, if well implemented, will significantly enhance student achievement. As such, SFA reflects the principles of authentic school improvement (for an illustration see Table 4.2).

'Improving the Quality of Education for All'

The 'Improving the Quality of Education for All' (IQEA) project has over the past ten years collaborated with hundreds of schools in England and elsewhere in developing a model of school improvement and a programme of support. The IQEA programme aims to enhance student outcomes through focussing on the teaching–learning process as well as strengthening the school's capacity for managing change (Hopkins *et al.*, 1996). IQEA is also a research-based programme and reflects many of the principles of authentic school improvement (for an illustration see Table 4.3).

Table 4.2 'Success For All' as an authentic school improvement programme

The principles of authentic school improvement	Example of theoretical, research or practical influence
Achievement focussed	The social justice responsibility to ensure that all students can read.
Empowering in aspiration	The moral imperative of the principles of prevention and immediate, intensive intervention.
Research based and theory rich	Grounded in research on co-operative learning, reading and early childhood intervention, and the location of the approach within a general socio-psychological framework.
Context specific	The programme is only proposed in situations where it is appropriate – in schools facing the greatest challenges and where students are most at risk.
Capacity building in nature	The use of a whole school approach, high quality materials, staff development and external support to ensure sustainability.
Enquiry driven	The use of implementation checks and research data to energise, inform and direct action.
Implementation oriented	The importance of the consistency of classroom effects and use of facilitator.
Interventionist and strategic	The influence of 'Lewinian' approaches, and based on a medium term, holistic, and comprehensive approach to educational change.
Externally supported	Extensive and intensive support provided by the 'Success For All' Foundation, and local networks of SFA schools.
Systemic	Fits into and influences Federal policy and funding programmes, encourages a whole school and whole school district approach.

At the outset of IQEA a set of principles were articulated that provided a philosophical and practical starting point. These principles represent the expectations of the way project schools pursue school improvement, and serve as an *aide-mémoire* to all those involved. The operation of these principles creates synergism – together they are greater than the sum of their parts. The five principles of IQEA are:

- School improvement is a process that focusses on enhancing the quality of students' learning.
- The vision of the school should be one that embraces all members of the school community as both learners and contributors.

Table 4.3 'Improving the Quality of Education for All' as an authentic school improvement programme

The principles of authentic school improvement	Example of theoretical, research or practical influence
Achievement focussed	Moral commitment to student learning Influence of the school effectiveness research
Empowering in aspiration	The focus on enhancement of skills, confidence and learning capability Community involvement and responsibility
Research based and theory rich	Models of teaching and learning Organisational development strategies General influence of socio-psychological and critical theory
Context specific	Emphasis on adapting external change for internal purpose Works within school's own development plan Programme designed on basis of school-based data collection
Capacity building in nature	Peer coaching and staff development Cross-hierarchical working groups
Enquiry driven	Teacher as researcher Action research
Implementation oriented	Importance of individual meaning Consistency of classroom effects
Interventionist and strategic	'Lewinian' action research Development and maintenance distinction Survey data feedback and organisation development
Externally supported	Consultancy support from University Facilitation of networking Links with LEAs
Systemic	Influence of National Reform agenda Appreciation of local micro-politics Searches to increase policy coherence

- The school will see in external pressures for change important opportunities to secure its internal priorities.
- The school will seek to develop structures and create conditions that encourage collaboration and lead to the empowerment of individuals and groups.
- The school will seek to promote the view that monitoring and evaluation quality is a responsibility which all members of staff share.

This approach to school improvement is underpinned by a contract between the partners in the project – the school and its teachers, and in some cases, the

LEA or sponsoring agency, and the IQEA team. The contract defines the parameters of the project, and the obligations those involved owe to each other. It is intended to clarify expectations and to ensure the conditions necessary for success. In particular the contract emphasises that all staff be consulted, that school co-ordinators are appointed, that a 'critical mass' of teachers are actively involved in development work, and that sufficient time is made available for appropriate classroom and staff development activities. The IQEA team co-ordinates the support arrangements, provides training for the school co-ordinators and representatives, makes regular school visits, contributes to staff training, provides staff development materials, and monitors the implementation of each school's project. Handbooks and videos are produced to support staff development work, that includes training exercises and support materials (Ainscow *et al.*, 1994; Hopkins *et al.*, 1997; Beresford, 1998; Harris, 1999; Hopkins and Harris, 2000; Hopkins, 2001).

The following propositions provide an initial understanding of the IQEA approach to school improvement.

Proposition 1: school improvement will not occur unless clear decisions are made about development and maintenance

Given concerns about overload, decisions have to be made about what changes need to be implemented and how they are to be selected. This question reflects what is perhaps the most crucial challenge facing schools today – how to effectively balance change and stability. The distinction between a school's development and maintenance activities assists in decision-making (Hargreaves and Hopkins, 1991). *Maintenance* refers to the school carrying out its day-to-day activities, the fulfilling of its statutory obligations, and to supporting teaching and learning, all to the best of its ability. *Development* on the other hand refers to that amount of resource, time and energy the school reserves from the total it has available, for carrying forward those aims, aspirations and activities that 'add value' to what it already does. The distinction between development and maintenance allows the school to make more coherent decisions about the focus of its developmental energy, irrespective to some extent of the external reform agenda.

Proposition 2: successful school improvement involves adapting external change for internal purposes

Development planning was originally designed as a strategy to help schools manage change; as such it is commonly regarded as an important preliminary to school improvement. Working through the planning cycle is likely to involve the school in generating a number of 'priorities' for action – often too many to work on. This means that decisions about 'priorities' must be made – moving from the separate, perhaps even conflicting priorities of individuals or groups, to a systematically compiled set of priorities that represent the overall needs of a whole school community. It is through such an understanding of how to approach planning that schools begin to see the potential in adapting external change to internal purpose.

Proposition 3: without a clear focus on the internal conditions of the school, improvement efforts will quickly become marginalised

The IQEA experience suggests that school improvement works best when a clear and practical focus for development is linked to simultaneous work on the internal conditions within the school. Conditions are the internal features of the school, the 'arrangements' that enable it to get work done. Without an equal focus on conditions, even development priorities that directly affect classroom practice quickly become marginalised. As seen in chapter 6, within the IQEA project there are a number of 'conditions' within the school with its capacity for sustained development. Taken together these conditions result in the creation of opportunities for teachers to feel more powerful and confident about their work (Hopkins and West, 1994).

Proposition 4: school improvement will remain a marginal activity unless it impacts across all the levels of the school

Educational change will not be successful unless it impacts across all levels of the organisation. Within IQEA the focus is on three levels in particular. The senior team level is responsible for overall management and the establishment of policies, particularly with respect to how resources and strategies for staff development can be mobilised in support of school improvement efforts. The department or working group level comprises those established groups within the school responsible for curriculum, teaching and learning. Finally, at the individual teacher level the focus is on developing classroom practice through professional growth. These levels are integrated by the school improvement co-ordinates or cadre group (see chapter 7).

Proposition 5: data about the school's performance creates the energy for development

The need to ground policy decisions in data about how the school is functioning is paramount. Too often elaborate policy-making processes are established to validate the directions and priorities that school managers favour, rather than identify what is actually appropriate for the particular school. Although there is a feedback role for data gathering, the focus needs to remain on the collection of evidence of impact, not merely of implementation. Unless this distinction is kept in mind, school leaders could convince themselves that they were improving the school while in reality they were merely changing its policies. Involving teachers in this process provides them with a stimulus to make the changes work for the benefit of students.

Proposition 6: successful school improvement efforts engender a language about teaching and change

There is mounting evidence that the content of a lesson notwithstanding, the use of appropriate teaching strategies can significantly increase student achievement. A major goal for school improvement, therefore, is to help teachers become professionally flexible so that they can select, from a repertoire of possibilities, the teaching approach most suited to their particular content area, and the age, interests and aptitudes of their students. One of the characteristics of successful schools is that teachers talk about teaching. In IQEA schools this involves:

- teachers discussing with each other the nature of teaching strategies
- establishing specifications or guidelines for the chosen teaching strategies
- agreeing on standards used to assess student progress as a result
- mutual observation and partnership teaching in the classroom.

The IQEA approach to school improvement is not simply about the implementation of centralised reforms in a more effective way, the emphasis is on how schools can use the impetus of external reform to 'improve' or 'develop' themselves. Sometimes, what a school chooses to do in terms of school improvement will be consistent with the national reform agenda, at other times it will not. Whatever the case, the decision to engage in school improvement, at least in IQEA schools, is based on an aspiration to create cultures that enable teachers to effectively pursue what is the best for the young people in that school. When this occurs school staff not only begin to meet the real challenge of educational reform, but they also create classrooms and schools where both students and their teachers learn.

A framework for authentic school improvement

The framework for authentic school improvement found in Figure 4.1 builds on the argument of this chapter by focussing explicitly on the learning experiences, achievement and progress of pupils. In the centre of the series of concentric rings is powerful learning – the achievement and progress of students. The next ring is comprised of the essential ingredients of powerful teaching – the 'holy trinity' of teaching strategy, curriculum content and the learning needs of students. Powerful learning and powerful teaching are found in powerful schools – those schools that have organisational conditions supportive of high levels of teaching and learning. Some of the key elements of these conditions are found in the next ring – collaborative planning that focusses on student outcomes, staff development that is committed to the improvement of classroom practice, enquiry that fuels the process and the involvement of students in their own learning and the school community in education. This activity usually takes place within the context of a national

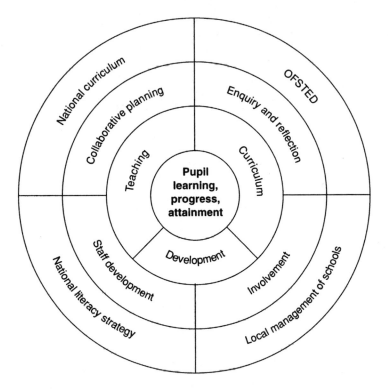

Figure 4.1 The circles of school improvement (The Centre for Teacher and School
  Development, the University of Nottingham)

reform agenda, as depicted by the outer ring. This is represented in the diagram by reference to the English context, e.g., the National Curriculum,
OFSTED inspections, Local Management of Schools (LMS), and National
Literacy Strategy (NLS). This aspect of the framework can easily be adapted
to other policy contexts. When all the rings are pulling in the same direction,
then the aspirations of authentic school improvement have much more chance
of success. All need to exist in a reciprocal relationship if student achievement
is to be enhanced.

Commentary

Authentic school improvement strategies focus both on how to accelerate the
progress and enhance the achievement of students, as well as establishing
effective management practices within the school. This is the key characteristic
of third age approaches to school improvement and explains why previous
strategies that tended to focus on either one or the other failed to enhance
pupil progress and achievement. In this chapter the main characteristics of the

second age of school improvement have been illustrated. In the subsequent discussions of the more comprehensive and well-specified approaches some indication has been given of what 'third age' or authentic school improvement strategies look like.

The 'new paradigm' represents a new way of thinking whose full ramifications have yet to be felt (see also chapter 7 in Teddlie and Reynolds, 2000, and Hopkins and Reynolds, 2001):

- There is an enhanced focus upon the importance of pupil outcomes. Instead of the earlier emphasis upon changing the processes of schools, the focus is now upon seeing if these changes are powerful enough to affect pupil outcomes.
- The learning level and the instructional behaviours of teachers are increasingly being targeted for explicit attention as well as the school level. Specifications of curriculum and teaching are being adopted that extend current practice and that focus directly on the student learning goals that have been set.
- There is the creation of an infrastructure to enable the knowledge base, both 'best practice' and research findings, to be utilised. This involves an internal focus on collaborative patterns of staff development that enable teachers to enquire into practice, and external strategies for dissemination and networking.
- In addition there is an increasing consciousness of the importance of 'capacity building'. This includes not only staff development, but also medium-term strategic planning, change strategies that utilise 'pressure and support', as well as the intelligent use of external support agencies.
- The adoption of a 'mixed' methodological orientation, in which bodies of quantitative data plus qualitative data are used to measure quality, effects and deficiencies, is becoming more common. This includes an audit of existing classroom and school processes and outcomes, and comparison with desired end states, in particular the educational experiences of different pupil groups.
- Authentic school improvement stresses the importance of ensuring reliability or 'fidelity' in the programme implementation across all the organisational members within schools, a marked contrast with the past when improvement programmes did not have to be organisationally 'tight'.
- There is an appreciation of the importance of cultural change in order to embed and sustain this approach to school improvement. There is a careful balance between 'vision building' and the adapting of structures to support those aspirations.

Much of the rest of this book is devoted to elaborating the various aspects of this framework. The task is begun in the following chapter where the focus is on powerful learning and teaching.

5   Powerful learning and powerful teaching

One of the threats to authentic school improvement is the narrowing of the conventional definition of effective student learning. As compared with even ten years ago, 'effective student learning' is commonly equated with a range of test scores or examination results, rather than something broader. Although the shift of focus to student outcomes is to be applauded – schools in particular, and the system in general, are now taking more responsibility for student learning – there are some dangers too. The emphasis on target setting in many educational systems puts pressure on schools and teachers to raise levels of achievement in the short term. This widespread tendency often results in a tactical response such as homework clubs or teaching to the test, and leads to a reductionist and impoverished interpretation of what constitutes learning. Powerful learning is more than just results and scores, it subsumes a range of cognitive and affective processes and outcomes. The challenge is to find ways of raising levels of attainment while at the same time helping students become more powerful learners, by expanding and making articulate their repertoire of learning strategies.

A key focus for authentic school improvement is high quality teaching. This reflects the teacher's ability to create powerful learning experiences for her students. Successful teachers are not as Joyce and Showers note, simply charismatic, persuasive, and expert presenters; rather, they provide their students with powerful cognitive and social tasks and teach them how to make productive use of them (Joyce and Showers, 1991: 10). Powerful learning does not occur by accident, it is usually the result of an effective learning situation created by a skilful teacher. As Joyce and Showers (1991: 12) say again:

> Effective teachers are confident that they can make a difference and that the difference is made by increasing their own teaching repertoires and the learning repertoires of their students. Put simply, powerful teachers believe that all children can learn and that they can teach all children. More pertinently, they convey this message to their students.

Powerful learning and powerful teaching is the heartland of authentic school improvement. Yet the lack of a sufficiently robust and sophisticated language for teaching is a major impediment to achieving powerful learning. Despite the contemporary emphasis on the importance of classroom practice, the language of discourse about teaching remains in general at a restricted level. Even in those instances where more precision of language is achieved, say in the debate on whole class teaching, there are few operational definitions against which teachers can assess their own practice and thereby develop and expand their range of classroom practices.

A key task for those committed to enhancing the learning of pupils, therefore, is to expand the vocabulary of teaching. It is not just the words that are lacking, but also the frameworks and specifications necessary to inform action and reflection. The vocabulary of teaching needs to be expanded, and expanded in a systematic and intelligent way. In addressing the language of powerful learning and teaching, in this chapter, the following issues will be discussed:

- the creation of powerful learning experiences
- perspectives on the research on curriculum and teaching
- a framework for thinking about teaching
- the nature of teaching style.

Creating powerful learning experiences

The teacher's task is not simply to teach, but to create powerful contexts for learning. It is a truism that no one can teach anyone anything: the best that can be done is to help another to learn. In *Models of Learning: Tools for Teaching* (Joyce *et al.*, 1997: 7) the idea is expressed in this way:

> Learning experiences are composed of content, process and social climate. As teachers we create for and with our children opportunities to explore and build important areas of knowledge, develop powerful tools for learning, and live in humanising social conditions.
>
> Our toolbox is the models of teaching, actually models for learning, that simultaneously define the nature of the content, the learning strategies, and the arrangements for social interaction that create the learning environments of our students.
>
> Through the selection of appropriate models, content can become conceptual rather than particular, the process can become constructive enquiry instead of passive reception, and the social climate can become expansive not restrictive. Our choices depend on the range of our active teaching repertoire and our efforts to expand it by developing new models and studying those developed by others.
>
> Interestingly, the most powerful models of teaching adapt flexibly to a wide spectrum of curriculum areas and types of learners. They work when teaching phonics and physics. They help both the 'gifted' and those most 'at risk' of failure. They do not tolerate socio-economic or gender

differences as inhibitors of learning but, instead, capitalise on them. Their effects are enhanced by variety in cultural and linguistic background.

It is the integration of 'content, process and social climate' that puts the 'power' into the powerful learning experience. Bruner has written evocatively about the dialectic between curriculum, teaching and learning. In his book, *Towards a Theory of Instruction* (Bruner, 1966: 21) he wrote:

> Let me conclude with one last point. What I have said suggests that mental growth is in very considerable measure dependent upon growth from the outside in – a mastering of techniques that are embodied in the culture and that are passed on in a contingent dialogue by agents of the culture . . . I suspect that much of growth starts out by our turning around on our own traces and recoding in new forms, with the aid of adult tutors, what we have been doing or seeing, then going on to new modes of organisation with the new products that have been formed by these recodings . . . It is this that leads me to think that the heart of the educational process consists of providing aids and dialogues for translating experience into more powerful systems of notation and ordering. And it is for this reason that I think a theory of development must be linked to a theory or knowledge and to a theory of instruction, or be doomed to triviality.

There is a similarity between Bruner's notion of 'mental growth' and what has been referred to here as 'powerful learning'. He argues convincingly for an integration of the ways in which individuals develop and grow, the ways in which they are taught, and what it is that they are taught. Teaching is more than just presenting material, it is about infusing curriculum content with appropriate instructional strategies that are selected in order to achieve the learning goals the teacher has for her students. This is the basis of Bruner's famous if provocative hypothesis, 'that any subject can be taught effectively in some intellectually honest form to any child at any stage of development'. It is this 'holy trinity' of constructs that is of central relevance to authentic school improvement. Their relationship can be expressed diagrammatically as seen in Figure 5.1.

There is now an increasingly sophisticated literature on how learning occurs and on the ways in which the learning experience can be organised to make a positive difference to students. The impact is not just on test scores and examination results, but also on the students' learning capability. This is the heart of the matter. If the teacher can teach the student how to learn at the same time as assisting them to acquire curriculum content then the twin goals of learning and achievement can be met at the same time. The literature on how children learn (Wood, 1998), the different types or 'multiple intelligences' (Gardner, 1993) and the descriptions of a range of learning styles (Kolb, 1984) is helpful in designing increasingly effective learning experiences within authentic school improvement contexts.

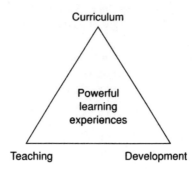

Figure 5.1 The 'holy trinity' of the constructs of powerful learning experiences

Although a discussion of these literatures is beyond the scope of this chapter, it is instructive to show how they have influenced the approach to 'powerful learning' described here. Powerful learning refers to the ability of learners to respond successfully to the tasks that they are set, as well as the tasks they set themselves – in particular to:

- integrate prior and new knowledge
- acquire and use a range of learning skills
- solve problems individually and in groups
- think carefully about their successes and failures
- evaluate conflicting evidence and to think critically
- accept that learning involves uncertainty and difficulty.

The deployment of such a range of learning strategies is commonly termed meta-cognition, which can be regarded as the learner's ability to take control over their own learning processes. The key point is that within whatever context learning takes place, it involves an 'active construction of meaning'. This carries implications for the management of learning opportunities, in particular that an active construction of meaning requires practical, cognitive and other learning approaches. As learning is interactional it can occur only as the learner makes sense of particular experiences in particular contexts. This 'making sense' involves connecting with an individual's prior knowledge and experience. Thus, new learning has to relate to, and ultimately 'fit with', what individuals already understand. Learning should therefore be seen as a process as much as producing end results.

Glaser (1991) has neatly and comprehensively summarised this approach to learning in the following quotation:

> learning is an active, constructive, intellectual process that occurs gradually over a period of time. It is not simply an additive process. Knowledge cannot, to use a common metaphor, be poured into learners' heads

with the hope that learning will automatically occur or accumulate. Understandings of new knowledge can only take place, or be constructed, in the minds of individual learners through a process of making sense of that new knowledge in the light of what they already know. In other words, learning is a process of constructing new knowledge on the basis of current knowledge.

This interactive view of learning is mirrored in the following sections of this chapter by an approach to teaching that is similarly optimistic.

Three perspectives on the research on curriculum and teaching

There is an extensive research literature on teaching and curriculum and its impact on student learning (for an authoritative summary see Wittrock, 1986). The following three perspectives provide a way of illustrating some of the key lessons for authentic school improvement that can be summarised from this evidence base (adapted from Joyce, 1997: 43):

- There are a number of well-developed models of teaching and curriculum that generate substantially high levels of student learning than does normative practice.
- The most effective curricular and teaching patterns induce students to construct knowledge – to enquire into subject areas intensively. The result is to increase student capacity to learn and to work more effectively.
- The most effective models of curriculum and teaching increase learning capacity for all students, greatly reducing the effects of gender, socio-economic status, linguistic background, and learning styles as factors in student learning.

Perspective 1: there are a number of well-developed models of teaching and curriculum that generate substantially high levels of student learning than does normative practice. Support for the veracity of this statement is found in a study conducted in the Motilal Nehru School of Sports about 30 miles north-west of New Delhi, India (Baveja, 1988, cited in Joyce *et al.*, 1997). The study was designed to test the effectiveness of an inductive approach to a Botany Unit compared with an intensive tutorial treatment. All of the students were given a test at the beginning of the unit to assess their knowledge before instruction began, and were divided into two groups equated on the basis of achievement. The control group studied the material with the aid of tutoring and lectures on the material – the standard treatment in Indian schools for courses of this type. The experimental group worked in pairs and was led through inductive and concept attainment exercises emphasising classification of plants. Figure 5.2 shows the distribution of scores for the experimental and control groups on the post-test which, like the pre-test, contained items dealing with the information pertaining to the unit.

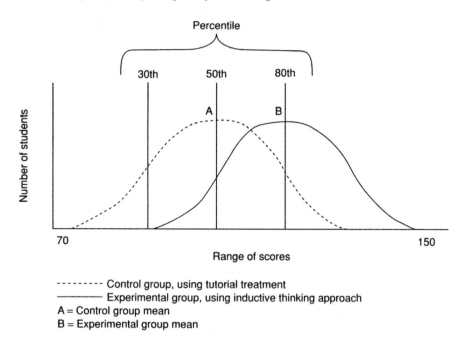

Figure 5.2 Distribution of student scores on post-test for a botany unit (Baveja, 1988)

The difference between the experimental and control groups was a little above a standard deviation. Essentially, what that means is that the experimental group average score was approximately where the 80th percentile score was for the control group. The difference increased when a delayed recall test was given ten months later, indicating that the information acquired with the concept-oriented strategies was retained somewhat better than information gained via more traditional teaching.

Although substantial in its own right, learning and retention of information was modest when compared with the effect on the students' ability to identify plants and their characteristics. The scores by students from the experimental group were eight times higher than the scores for the control group. Students, using the inductive model, were able to apply the information and concepts from the unit much more effectively than were the students from the tutorial treatment.

Besides illustrating the power of the inductive model of teaching to enhance student learning, the Baveja study also illustrates the use of 'effect size' data in interpreting the research on curriculum and teaching. 'Effect size' provides a means of gauging the effect of a particular school, change in teaching method, or classroom organisation on learning and achievement. It describes the magnitude of gains from any given change in educational practice in terms of its impact on the normal curve of distribution. By the same token, it can also be used to predict what can hope to be accomplished by using that practice (adapted from Appendix One *Models of Learning: Tools for Teaching*, Joyce *et al.*, 1997; see also Glass, 1982).

A research study by Benjamin Bloom (1984) illustrates the point further. Bloom (1984: 4) and his colleagues compared student learning under the following three conditions of instruction:

- conventional teaching in a class with about 30 students per teacher
- 'mastery learning' in a class with about 30 students per teacher
- tutoring, with a good tutor for each student.

For the purposes of the research the students whose previous achievement and attitudes were similar were randomly assigned to one of the three learning/teaching groups. The amount of instructional time was the same in all three groups – eleven periods over three weeks. Bloom (1984: 4) concluded:

> Most striking were the differences in final achievement measures under the three conditions. Using the conventional class as a control, it was typically found that the average student under tutoring was about two standard deviations above the average of the control class (i.e. the average tutored student was above 98 per cent of the students in the control class). The average student under mastery learning was about one standard deviation above the average of the control class (i.e. the average mastery learning student was above 84 per cent of the students in the control class).

It is now well established that as a result of tutoring *most* students do have the potential to reach high levels of learning. The important task is to seek ways of accomplishing this under more practical and realistic conditions than one-to-one tutoring, which is obviously too costly for most societies to bear on a large scale. The implications for authentic school improvement are:

- That most students have the potential to reach impressively high levels of learning.
- That the challenge is to search out those 'models of teaching' that can approach the effect on learning and achievement realised by tutoring.

Perspective 2: the most effective curricular and teaching patterns induce students to construct knowledge – to inquire into subject areas intensively. The result is to increase student capacity to learn and to work more effectively.

The example used to illustrate this proposition is the 'Cognitive Acceleration through Science Education' (CASE) project, based at King's College in London. CASE has reported some striking long-term effects on secondary school children's academic achievement (Adey and Shayer, 1994). The researchers, Philip Adey and Michael Shayer, claim successful intervention for

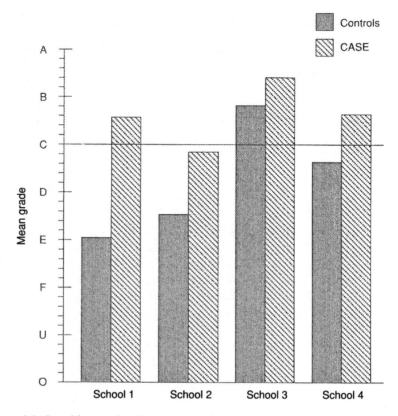

Figure 5.3 Cognitive acceleration in science education (CASE): mean grades in GCSE science obtained in four schools

between 25 and 50 per cent of children taught using CASE teaching strategies. The results indicate that, through CASE, it is possible to increase significantly the proportion of children passing not only GCSE science, but also by extension GCSE mathematics and English. Groups of children who participate in the CASE intervention programme during Key Stage 3 are found to achieve significantly higher grades at GCSE examinations in science, mathematics and English than matched control groups. New data becoming available replicates and exceeds (on a larger scale) the originally reported effects of immediate cognitive acceleration and longer-term academic improvement.

The central tenet of CASE is that a particular set of teaching strategies can accelerate children's intellectual development, their ability to think and, in the longer term, can serve to improve their academic achievement. CASE provides a 70-minute activity in science every two weeks for two school years. Teachers are given in-service training to run and implement these activities. The lessons involve children in problem-solving activities aimed at developing their capacity to find their own solutions and increase their awareness of how they reached these solutions. Adey and Shayer (1990: 268) argue that it is the process of constructing their own meanings which enables children to develop their general thinking skills or intellectual abilities:

> If effectiveness of learning is determined by the general strategies available to the child, then training in those strategies will allow a child to leapfrog over the detail into a higher level of abstraction, from which rapid assimilation of detail becomes possible.

By creating such powerful learning situations, CASE teachers are instrumental in raising the levels of achievement and learning capability of their students. The general point being made here is that it is the meta-cognitive elements in the CASE approach that gives it its power.

A comparable effect is achieved in most situations where the teaching strategy has an explicit meta-cognitive component. This is a very similar message to that of Stigler and Hiebert (1999) whose highly influential book *The Teaching Gap* is focussing the debate on school improvement in America on the quality of teaching. Using videotape data from the Third International Mathematics and Science Study (TIMSS) they compared the teaching practices of a random sample of American, German and Japanese teachers. In the TIMSS study, the students of Japanese teachers out-performed their German counterparts, who in turn had higher test scores than those of American students.

Stigler and Hiebert found little within culture variation in the tapes they examined. Most American teachers, for example, taught in the same way but they did find profound differences between cultures. This they argue should mean that the debate on educational standards needs to focus on the quality of teaching rather than on the quality of the teacher. Stigler and Hiebert (1999: 10) maintain that: 'Although variability in competence is certainly visible in the videos we collected, such differences are dwarfed by the differences in *teaching methods* that we see across cultures.'

Interestingly, the format of lessons was similar between cultures. Most lessons followed the typical four phases: teachers begin a lesson with a review, they then present the key ideas in some form of presentation, this is followed by an individual or group activity, and the lesson concludes with a summary and possibly the setting of homework. The difference was not with the format, but with the quality of teaching within this broad framework.

Stigler and Hiebert characterise American teaching as extremely limited focussing mainly on a very narrow band of procedural skills. This is irrespective of whether students are working individually in rows or are sitting in groups, or whether they are using pencil and paper or have access to the latest technology. American students, they claim, spend most of their time acquiring isolated skills through repeated practice. Japanese teaching however is distinguished not so much by the competence of Japanese teachers, as by the way in which they teach for *conceptual understanding*. Students in the

Japanese classrooms Stigler and Hiebert observed, spent as much time solving challenging problems and discussing mathematical skills as they did practising skills. This was the major difference between the quality of teaching in the two cultures (Stigler and Hiebert, 1999: 11). (The style of teaching in German schools came some way between the other two, with more teaching for conceptual understanding than American teachers, but less than the Japanese.)

There is much of importance in this richly detailed study to inform the practice of authentic school improvement. This includes the nature of teaching, teacher preparation, in-service training and curriculum development. The unmistakable conclusion however was that it was the teaching, not the teacher, that made the difference, and that difference was relentlessly related to the level of problem solving and conceptual content that pervaded the lesson.

Perspective 3: the most effective models of curriculum and teaching increase learning capacity for all students, greatly reducing the effects of gender, socio-economic status, linguistic background, and learning styles as factors in student learning.

There are many research studies that support this general conclusion, and some that demonstrate that such powerful learning contexts can also compensate for social disadvantage (for a review see Joyce and Weil, 1996). For example, in a research study of learning through group investigation, Shlomo Sharan and Hana Shachar (1988) illustrated, like Adey and Shayer, that students can rapidly accelerate their learning rates. In addition, their study focussed on a problem that exists in many societies: that students whose families are regarded as socially and economically disadvantaged frequently display low achievement.

Sharon and Shachar prepared social studies teachers to organise their students into learning communities and then compared the classroom interaction and academic achievement with classes taught by the customary 'whole class' method. In Israel, where the study was conducted, Middle Eastern origin students generally belong to the 'disadvantaged' population, whereas European origin students generally are more advantaged. In their study students from both origins were mixed in classes. The research design compared the achievement of the students who were taught using group investigation with the students taught by the 'whole class' method most common in Israeli schools.

The Middle Eastern students taught with group investigation methods achieved average gains nearly two-and-a-half times those of the Middle Eastern students taught as a whole class. These normally disadvantaged students also achieved larger average gains than did the European origin students taught by the more typical 'whole class' method and actually exceeded them on the post-test by about half a standard deviation. In other words, the 'socially disadvantaged' students taught with group investigation learned at rates above those of the 'socially advantaged' students taught by teachers

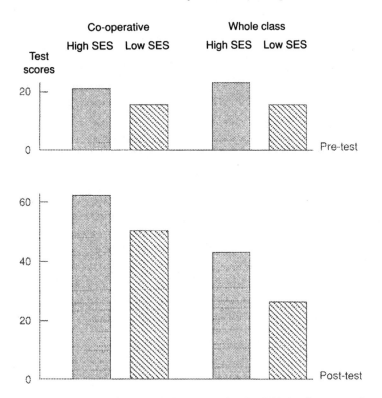

Figure 5.4 Effects of complex co-operative learning by SES (socio-economic status)

who did not have the repertoire provided by group investigation. The use of that specific teaching approach had enabled them to become more powerful students immediately. The average gain by the western origin students taught with group investigation was twice that of their 'whole class' counterparts. Thus the model was effective for students from both backgrounds and by a large margin.

A framework for thinking about teaching

The framework for powerful teaching proposed in this book revolves around three aspects of teaching that are often regarded as being contradictory rather than complementary (see Hopkins *et al.*, 1994: chapter 4; Hopkins, 1997, 2000b; Hopkins and Harris, 2000). The diagram in Figure 5.5 summarises the relationship between:

- teaching skills
- teaching relationships
- teaching models.

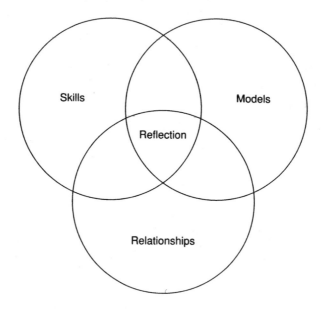

Figure 5.5 Three ways of thinking about teaching

Teaching skills

There is an extensive research literature on teaching effects. Consistently high correlations are achieved between student achievement scores and classroom processes (see Brophy and Good, 1986; Walberg, 1990; Creemers, 1994). One general conclusion stands out: 'The most consistently replicated findings link achievement to the quantity and pacing of instruction' (Brophy and Good, 1986: 360). The amount learned is as Good (1989) subsequently noted, determined in part by opportunity to learn, which is determined by four broad teacher behaviours:

- First, the extent to which teachers are businesslike and task-oriented, emphasise instruction as basic to their role, expect students to master the curriculum, and allocate most classroom time to those activities that have relevant academic objectives.
- Second, teachers whose students make reasonable academic progress frequently use classroom organisation and management strategies that maximise the time students spend engaged in academic activities.
- Third, effective teachers allow students to move through the curriculum briskly but also relatively successfully.
- Fourth, these teachers were found to spend most of their time actively instructing their students in group lessons or supervising their work on assignments rather than allowing students to spend inordinate time on individual seatwork practice without supervision or feedback.

It is naive to assume, however, that the amount of time spent teaching is in itself a sufficient condition for student achievement. The literature on teaching effects is replete with the cues and tactics necessary for effective teaching (Hopkins *et al.*, 1994: 57–8). For example, Doyle (1987: 96) argues that classroom studies of teaching effects have generally supported a direct and structured approach to instruction. That is, students usually achieve more when a teacher:

- emphasises academic goals, makes them explicit, and expects students to be able to master the curriculum
- carefully organises and sequences curriculum experiences
- clearly explains and illustrates what students are to learn
- frequently asks direct and specific questions to monitor students' progress and check their understanding
- provides students with ample opportunity to practise, gives prompts and feedback to ensure success, corrects mistakes, and allows students to use a skill until it is thoroughly learned and automatic
- reviews regularly and holds students accountable for work.

Brophy's (1983) review of the research on teaching behaviours most closely associated with student achievement gains comes to the following conclusions:

- *Content coverage* Students learn more when their teachers cover more material.
- *Time allocated to instruction* Students learn more when teachers allocate available class time to academic activities.
- *Engaged time* Students learn more when they are on task a high proportion of class time.
- *Consistent success* Students learn more when their success rates (responses to questions, answers to written work at desk) are high.
- *Active teaching* Students learn more in classes where their teachers spend most of their time actively teaching them rather than having students work on their own without direct teacher supervision.
- *Structuring information* Students learn more when teachers structure information using such techniques as advance organisers, reviewing objectives, outlining content, signalling transitions between lesson parts, drawing attention to main ideas, and reviewing main ideas. Clarity of presentation and enthusiasm in presenting material, are also associated with achievement gains.
- *Effective questioning* Students learn more when questions are asked frequently and are relatively easy. Waiting for responses, acknowledging correct answers and working with students who give partial or incorrect answers to give them a chance to improve their answers are all associated with achievement gain.

At the heart of the teacher's work is classroom management. If classrooms are to be places where students can feel safe to concentrate on the tasks they are set teachers have to be skilled in organising and managing large groups of students within a relatively confined space. Evertson and Harris (1992: 76) for example, have identified the following highlights of research on classroom management:

- use time as effectively as possible
- implement group strategies with high levels of involvement and low levels of misbehaviour
- choose lesson formats and academic tasks conducive to high student engagement
- communicate clearly rules of participation
- prevent problems by implementing a system at the beginning of the school year.

Similarly, Kounin (1970) in his classic study identified several strategies that teachers use to elicit high levels of work involvement and low levels of misbehaviour:

- *Withitness:* communicating awareness of student behaviour
- *Overlapping:* doing more than one thing at once
- *Smoothness and momentum:* moving in and out of activities smoothly with appropriately paced and sequenced instruction
- *Group alerting:* keeping all students attentive to a whole group focus.

From this perspective, a teacher promotes student learning by being active in planning and organising his or her teaching, explaining to students what they are to learn, arranging occasions for guided practice, monitoring progress, providing feedback, and otherwise helping students understand and accomplish work. Despite the impressive gains associated in the research literature with the range of teaching skills described above, they should be regarded as a necessary but not sufficient condition for effective teaching. They do however provide the essential foundations for powerful teaching.

Teaching relationships

There is another set of factors that characterise quality teaching; they are less technical and are more related to the teacher's 'artistry'. Here there is a recognition that teaching involves creativity and is carried out in a highly personalised way. While this need not deny the potential value of considering particular models of teaching or examining the impact of specific skills, it draws attention to the fact that once in the classroom each teacher has the sole responsibility for creating the conditions within which each student can expect some success. This must involve a degree of previous planning, but it also requires a capacity to improvise. Even the best-defined lesson plan has to be adapted to take account of unforeseen happenings. Indeed the artistry of a very successful teacher involves this ability to engage with, and turn to advantage, events and responses that could not have been anticipated.

It is much more difficult to report research evidence that arises from this frame of reference. The evidence does not lend itself readily to specifications or lists of features. Yet this perspective on teachers' work is one that is immediately recognised by practitioners and, indeed, others in the wider community. It is not uncommon for teachers to be told by friends from outside the profession of the 'teacher who made a difference'. The personality and flair of the individual teacher is increasingly receiving belated attention. The idea of artistry in teaching is well summed up by Rubin (1985: v) when he comments:

> There is a striking quality to fine classrooms. Students are caught up in learning; excitement abounds; and playfulness and seriousness blend easily because the purposes are clear, the goals sensible, and an unmistakable feeling of well-being prevails.
>
> Artist teachers achieve these qualities by knowing both their subject matter and their students; by guiding the learning with deft control – a control that itself is born out of perceptions, intuition, and creative impulse.

The 'artistry' of teaching lies in the teacher's ability to generate and sustain high quality relationships with her students. For example, one of John Gray's (1990) three performance indicators of an 'effective' school is the proportion of pupils who 'have a good or "vital" relationship with one or more teachers'. An essential aspect of this is for the teacher to have high expectations of her students. A supportive, rigorous and optimistic learning environment is fundamental for high levels of student achievement.

The influence of expectations is often a subtle one, and is felt within a myriad of classroom interactions. The ways in which the teacher sets tasks, arranges groups, locates the responsibility for learning and provides feedback are all illustrations of how teacher behaviour consistently gives messages and conditions student behaviour. Teacher expectation, behaviour and relationships are all vital contributions to learning. As Good and Brophy comment in *Looking in Classrooms* (1994: 97):

> Expectation effects on student achievement are likely to occur both directly through opportunity to learn (differences in the amount and nature of exposure to content and opportunities to engage in various types of academic activities) and indirectly through differential treatment that is likely to affect students' self-concepts, attributional inferences, or motivation.

The notion that the relationship between pupil and teacher is at the centre of the learning process is however by no means new. Indeed, as long ago as

1961, MacMurray observed that 'The first priority in education . . . is learning to live in personal relation to other people. Success or failure of the teaching depends very largely on the character and quality of this relation.'

Richard Peters (1974) called for close personal relationships with individual learners, advocating 'receptiveness and outgoingness' towards each as individual human beings; and Carl Rogers' work in psychology and education also support this notion (see for example his *Freedom to Learn*, Rogers, 1983). In this and other publications Rogers identifies some conditions that facilitate 'learning to be free' such as 'a trust in the human organism', 'realness in the teacher', 'unconditional acceptance' and 'empathy'.

This is what is referred to in the following chapter as the need to establish *authentic relationships* within the classroom. It implies establishing the classroom as a safe and secure learning environment in which pupils can expect acceptance, respect and even warmth from their teachers, without having to earn these – they are intrinsic rights that are extended to pupils because they are there.

Teaching models

There is a further and equally strong body of research and practice that suggests that student achievement can be additionally enhanced by the consistent and strategic use of specific teaching models (Joyce and Weil, 1996; Joyce et al., 1997). As Joyce and Weil (1996) point out, there are many powerful models of teaching – each with their own 'syntax', phases and guidelines – that are designed to bring about particular kinds of learning and to help students become more effective learners.

In *Models of Learning: Tools for Teaching*, and the 'Creating conditions for teaching and learning' handbook based on experiences in IQEA schools, a range of contrasting and complementary teaching strategies are described (Joyce et al., 1997; Hopkins and Harris, 2000). These are drawn from Joyce's original four families of teaching models, namely the information processing, the social, the personal, and the behavioural families (Joyce and Weil, 1996). An illustration of the range of teaching models contained in the four families is listed in Table 5.1.

These models of teaching (actually models for learning) simultaneously define the nature of the content, the learning strategies, and the arrangements for social interaction that create the learning environments of students. All of the models are research based in so far as they have been developed and refined through cycles of development and evaluation and have proven effectiveness. They are defined and described in terms of their structure or syntax, which refers to its major elements, core principles and phases, as well as its main instructional and nurturant effects.

It is important to be clear about what is meant by a 'model of teaching'. One can regard the research on teaching effects or teaching skills as providing the teacher with say tactical knowledge. The research on 'models of teaching'

Table 5.1 A selection from the four families of models of teaching

Model	Developer (redeveloper)	Purpose
Information processing models		
Inductive thinking (classification)	Hilda Taba (Bruce Joyce)	Development of classification skills, hypothesis building and testing, and understanding of how to build conceptual understanding of content areas.
Concept attainment	Jerome Bruner Fred Lighthall (Bruce Joyce)	Learning concepts and studying strategies for attaining and applying them. Building and testing hypotheses.
Advanced organiser	David Ausubel (and many others)	Designed to increase ability to absorb information and organise it, especially in learning from lectures and readings.
Mnemonics	Michael Pressley Joel Levin (and associated scholars)	Increase ability to acquire information, concepts, conceptual systems and meta-cognitive control of information processing capability.
Social models		
Group investigation	John Dewey Herbert Thelen Shlomo Sharan Rachel Hertz-Lazarowicz	Development of skills for participation in democratic process. Simultaneously emphasises social development, academic skills and personal understanding.
Role playing	Fannie Shaftel	Study of values and their role in social interaction. Personal understanding of values and behaviour.
Structured social enquiry	Robert Slavin and colleagues	Academic enquiry and social and personal development. Co-operative strategies for approaching academic study.
Personal models		
Non-directive teaching	Carl Rogers	Building capacity for personal development, self-understanding, autonomy and esteem of self.
Behavioural models		
Direct teaching	Thomas Good, Jere Brophy (and many others)	Mastery of academic content and skills in a wide range of areas of study.

Source: Joyce *et al.* 1997, chapter 2

on the other hand gives teachers more strategic knowledge, about how to create whole classroom settings to facilitate learning.

A well known, if dated example, of a model of teaching is that of the Humanities Curriculum Project (HCP). In this curriculum, discussion was the main mode of enquiry and the teacher acted as a neutral chairperson. Discussion was informed and disciplined by evidence, such as items from history, journalism and literature. This particular curriculum approach inevitably placed new kinds of demand on both teachers and pupils (Rudduck, 1984: 57). For example:

New skills for most teachers:

- discussion rather than instruction
- teacher as neutral chairperson
- teacher talk reduced to about 15 per cent of the total talking done in the classroom
- teacher handling material from different disciplines
- new modes of assessment.

New skills for most pupils:

- discussion, not argument or debate
- listening to, and talking to, each other, not just the teacher
- taking initiatives in contributing – not being cued by the teacher.

Models of teaching are also models of learning. How teaching is conducted has a large impact on students' abilities to educate themselves. In Table 5.1, a selection of models for teaching were described each with its own core purpose. These purposes relate not only to how to organise teaching, but also to ways of learning. So for example, if in whole class teaching the teacher uses the advance organiser model to structure a presentation, the student can use the same method as a means of extracting information and ideas from lectures and presentations. The relationship between the model of teaching and of learning most commonly used in IQEA schools is seen in Table 5.2.

As students acquire information, ideas, skills, values, ways of thinking, and means of expressing themselves, they are also learning how to learn. In fact, the most important long-term outcome of teaching may be the students' increased capabilities to learn more easily and effectively in the future both because of the knowledge and skill they have acquired, and because they have mastered learning processes (Joyce *et al.*, 1997: 15).

When these models and strategies are combined, they have even greater potential for improving student learning. Thus imagine a classroom where the learning environment contains a variety of models of teaching that are not only intended to accomplish a range of curriculum goals, but are also designed to help students increase their competence as learners.

In such classrooms the students learn models for memorising information, how to attain concepts and how to invent them. They practise building

Table 5.2 Relationship between model of teaching and learning skills

Model of teaching	Learning skill
Advanced organiser	Extracting information and ideas from lectures and presentations
Group work	Working effectively with others to initiate and carry out co-operative tasks
Inductive teaching (classification)	Building hypotheses and theories
Mnemonics	Memorising information
Concept attainment	Attaining concepts and how to invent them
Synectics	Using metaphors to think creatively

hypotheses and theories and using the tools of science to test them. They learn how to extract information and ideas from lectures and presentations, how to study social issues and how to analyse their own social values. These students also know how to profit from training and how to train themselves in athletics, performing arts, mathematics and social skills. They know how to make their writing and problem solving more lucid and creative. Perhaps most importantly, they know how to take the initiative in planning personal study, and they know how to work with others to initiate and carry out co-operative tasks. As students master information and skills, the result of each learning experience is not only the content they learn but also the greater ability they acquire to approach future learning tasks with confidence and to create increasingly effective learning environments for themselves.

The models of teaching are therefore simply tools that teachers can use to create more powerful learning experiences. But such research and strategies should not be regarded as panaceas to be followed slavishly. Research knowledge and the various specifications of teaching can have limitations, especially if they are adopted uncritically. Such knowledge only becomes useful when it is subjected to the discipline of practice through the exercise of the teacher's professional judgement. For, as Lawrence Stenhouse (1975: 142) said in the quotation cited at the beginning of the book, such proposals are not to be regarded 'as an unqualified recommendation, but rather as a provisional specification claiming no more than to be worth putting to the test of practice. Such proposals claim to be intelligent rather than correct.' It is in this way that the use of 'teaching models' forms part of an overall strategy for authentic school improvement.

A brief note on the nature of teaching style

The concept of 'teaching style' has been well documented in the literature (see for example the series of studies by Bennett, 1976, 1988, and Galton and his colleagues 1980, 1999). Instead of focussing on discrete teacher behaviour, as does the 'process–product' research associated with specific teacher effects, this research explores the relative effectiveness of different teaching styles or collections of teacher behaviours. An attempt has been made in the analysis of teaching given in this chapter to reflect the contribution of both schools of research to an understanding of effective teaching and learning.

The three perspectives on high quality teaching described in this chapter are not discrete. As was illustrated in Figure 5.5 it is the practice of fine teachers to combine these elements through a process of reflection to create an individual style. Consequently, it may be that critical systematic reflection is a necessary condition for quality teaching. This is not reflection for reflection's sake, but in order to continue to develop a mastery of one's chosen craft.

There are no ceilings to the performance of quality teachers. Outstanding teachers take individual and collective responsibility to base their teaching on the best knowledge and practice available. But they then take those ideas and strategies and critically reflect on them through practice in their own and each other's classrooms. It is through reflection that the teacher harmonises, integrates and transcends the necessary classroom management skills, the acquisition of a repertoire of models of teaching, and the personal aspects of her teaching into a strategy that has meaning for her students.

Ultimately, however, effective teaching and learning has to be seen within a holistic framework. The comparative study of policies aimed at improving teacher quality that we conducted for the OECD identified six characteristics of high quality teachers (Hopkins and Stern, 1996):

- commitment
- love of children
- mastery of subject didactics
- a repertoire of multiple models of teaching
- the ability to collaborate with other teachers
- a capacity for reflection.

Although it is convenient to group teachers' desired capacities and behaviours into categories, these attributes all interact in practice. For example, one French teacher elegantly defined teacher quality as 'savoirs, savoir-faire, et savoir-être', this is translatable perhaps as 'knowledge, knowing how to do, and knowing how to be' (Hopkins and Stern, 1996: 503).

Commentary

A vision for authentic school improvement is of students engaged in compelling learning situations, created by skilful teachers in school settings designed to promote learning for both of them. The achievement of this aim is, however, severely inhibited by the lack of a sufficiently sophisticated language and coherent frameworks within which to consider teaching. It is such a framework for reflecting on teaching and learning that has been presented in this chapter. In concluding the discussion however three caveats need to be entered.

It should now be obvious that evidence from research on teaching can help teachers become more creative in providing effective learning environments for the students. There is a danger that centrally designed curricula can become blueprints that inhibit autonomy in teaching and learning. In that respect the models of teaching presented here are *specific* rather than *prescriptive*. Although they define the nature of the educational encounter, they do so in order to encourage teachers to experiment with the specificity rather than being bound by the prescription. Within the spirit of the process model of curriculum, as described by Stenhouse (1975), this approach is liberating or emancipatory because it encourages independence of thought and argument on the part of the pupil, and experimentation and the use of judgement on the part of the teacher. When teachers adopt this experimental approach to their teaching they are taking on an educational idea, cast in the form of a curriculum proposal and testing it out within their classrooms.

Second, it is imperative that any teaching strategy is fully integrated within the curriculum. Too often 'thinking skills' or 'study strategies' are presented in isolation outside of the curriculum. As a consequence the application to learning capability is minimal, because it is left to the student to transfer the strategy to real settings and the opportunity of cross-curriculum reinforcement is not exploited. As Bruner implied, the power of any teaching strategy to accelerate learning and achievement is most effectively realised when the teaching strategy is integrated and embedded within a curriculum context. In the UK there has been a tradition, notably associated with the Schools Council curriculum projects, of linking curriculum to teaching styles (Stenhouse, 1980; Hopkins, 1987a). The future success of authentic school improvement efforts lies in the rigorous integration of pedagogy and curriculum content, disciplined by clear educational objectives, and formulated within materials that are accessible to teachers. The curriculum approach adopted in this respect by 'Success For All' is exemplary, and the Key Stage 3 Thinking Skills project in England holds similar promise.

Finally a comment on the debate around whether 'whole class' or 'group activity' should dominate, or what should be the balance between whole class, small group, and individual activities. Settling that question leads to the broader question of what will work best for children, because it is the models of learning and teaching that are chosen, rather than the grouping arrangements adopted, that will directly affect student achievement. In these classes, students are taught directly models for learning that they use when working as members of the class community, when working in small collaborative groups, and when working as individuals. The more efficient models of teaching assume that the whole class will be organised to pursue common learning objectives within which individual differences in achievement are comfortably accommodated. Thus, their creators have a vision of the whole class and a vision of small group work and individual work as part of the overall educational scheme (Joyce *et al.*, 1997: 16).

Thus, as Bruce Joyce elegantly phrased it, the operational repertoire of the teacher is the critical element in the calculus of effects. For one can teach whole classes well or badly, organise collaborative groups well or badly, and provide direct individual instruction well or badly. Yet powerful teaching and learning occurs in powerful schools. As Lawrence Downey (1967) once put it: 'A school teaches in three ways, by what it teaches, by how it teaches and by the kind of place it is.' It is a consideration of the context and conditions that support effective teaching and learning that provide the focus for the following chapter.

6 Creating the conditions for school improvement

It is classroom practice that has the most direct impact on student learning. If the enhancement of student achievement and learning is to be taken seriously however, then work on the internal conditions of the school has to complement the focus on teaching and learning. Authentic school improvement is best achieved when a clear and practical focus for development is linked to simultaneous work on the internal conditions within the school. Conditions are the internal features of the school, the 'arrangements' that enable it to get work done. Without an equal focus on conditions, even initiatives that directly address classroom practice quickly become marginalised.

Authentic school improvement designs emphasise the importance of enhancing the internal conditions of the school while undertaking innovations in curriculum and instruction in the pursuit of enhanced levels of student achievement. Much of the research associated with the 'Improving the Quality of Education for All' (IQEA) project has focussed on developing and testing a strategy for school improvement based on such a twin focus. The conditions identified during the early phases of the project were related to school level conditions, or the school's management arrangements, although of course many of the schools' priorities were classroom based (Hopkins *et al.*, 1994).

In line with contemporary school effects research, it was found necessary to modify the conditions within the classroom as well as those at the level of the school, if school improvement strategies are to fully impact on student achievement (Scheerens, 1992; Creemers, 1994; Joyce and Showers, 1995). More recently therefore a set of classroom conditions that enable teachers to facilitate the learning of all students have also been elaborated (Hopkins *et al.*, 1998).

This chapter focusses on creating the conditions for authentic school improvement. Although the discussion draws on the research conducted within the IQEA project it is presented here on the assumption that it has some generalisable applicability. In describing the conditions for school improvement:

- the rationale for the emphasis on 'enabling conditions' is presented
- the set of 'school level conditions' is outlined
- a complementary set of 'classroom conditions' is briefly reviewed

- the evidence on the 'conditions' profile of IQEA schools is discussed
- a strategy for authentic school improvement based on the conditions approach is described.

Rationale

The research on both school and teacher effects draws on similar epistemological models to generate knowledge. Put (over-) simply, they follow a process–product research design. High levels of student achievement are identified and 'backward mapped' to identify those school and teacher characteristics that correlate with high levels of student outcome.

School and classroom   ⟨   *'Correlational*   ⟩   *High levels of*
effectiveness   *relationship'*   *student achievement*
characteristics

This research effort has over the past 20 years yielded impressive results and given us rich and detailed descriptions of the characteristics of effective schools and classrooms. Yet for those committed to improving, as well as understanding, the effectiveness of schools and classrooms, the research on school and classroom effects has one major weakness. Because the relationship between these characteristics and student outcomes is one of association, it says little about how the one affects the other. The argument being presented in this chapter is that there are a set of intervening variables operating at the school and classroom level that mediate between the characteristics of effectiveness on the one hand and enhanced levels of student achievement on the other. It is this emphasis on the *enabling conditions* that allows the 'process' to affect the 'product'.

Innovations in teaching   ⟨   *'Enabling conditions'*   ⟩   *High levels of*
and learning designed   *or 'capacity building'*   *student achievement*
to enhance student   *in the school*
achievement, e.g.,
co-operative group work

A simple example illustrates the point. It is now well established that co-operative group instruction has a positive impact on student achievement (e.g., Joyce *et al.*, 1987; Johnson and Johnson, 1989; Slavin, 1993). Knowing this, however, is not enough. We also need to know what conditions have to be in place inside the school to allow the one to impact upon the other. These conditions will obviously vary from school to school. It is fair to suggest that the full impact of this teaching strategy will not be achieved without a degree of school and classroom based *staff development*, some *enquiry and reflection* on progress made, and the *involvement of students* in the teaching and learning process. In order for this teaching strategy to have a whole school impact, then there would also be a need for *leadership* at all levels in order to initiate and sustain the momentum, some *collaborative planning* to ensure direction, and *co-ordination* of the activity throughout the school. It is these six enabling conditions (in italics) that provide an operational definition for the school's capacity to manage change and to work effectively on strategies that enhance student achievement.

Besides the focus on capacity building, there is another characteristic of the enabling conditions that needs mentioning. If the concern is to help teachers modify their behaviour in order to enhance the learning of their students then it is necessary to use the language and frames of reference that reflect the experience of teachers. Although this may appear an obvious point, Brown and her colleagues (1995: 6) argue on the basis of their research that 'the ways in which teachers conceptualise pupils' progress, and the kind of classroom support that is required to promote that progress, are much more complex and rich than the conceptions of progress and support implicit [in the] school effectiveness research.'

The disjuncture between the language of research and the language of teachers is a major barrier to innovation and development in schools. Unless a school improvement strategy reflects the implicit theories of practitioners, then it is doomed to failure. This is not to argue that the teacher's view is necessarily correct or complete; if it were then there would be little need for school improvement. But it is to argue that change efforts need to reflect the experience of teachers, and to work out from there.

Fullan (1995) makes a similar point in his critique of 'Schools as Learning Organisations'. If schools as learning organisations are not to be a distant dream, he argues, teachers need to expand their notions of teaching within the context of capacity building and action enquiry. Changes in teaching practice only occur when there is clarity and coherence in the minds of teachers. This clarity needs to be at the 'receiving end rather than at the delivery end'. In other words, researchers and policy makers may have very clear strategies for change and improvement, but unless these connect with the understanding of realities of teachers then this increasing clarity at the top will only increase incoherence at the bottom.

It is for these reasons that in the IQEA project a rating scale has been developed that is used by schools to estimate their 'conditions profile' (Ainscow *et al.*, 1994). The scale is easily administered and the items relate to the daily experience of teachers. It thus acts as a research tool as well as a staff development activity. Through using the scale, teachers are given a practical understanding of the need to build 'capacity' while enhancing the teaching–learning process, in language and images that are very much part of their normal ways of working. Taken together these conditions result in the creation of opportunities for teachers to feel more powerful and confident about their work.

The six conditions for school development

Difficulties often occur for both individual teachers and the school when initially embarking on school improvement. Teachers may be faced with acquiring new teaching skills or with mastering new curriculum material, and the school, as a consequence, may be forced into new ways of working that are incompatible with existing organisational structures. It is therefore often necessary to work on some aspect of the internal conditions within the school at the same time as achieving the curriculum or other priorities the school has set itself.

As a consequence of our work on the IQEA project we have begun to associate a number of 'conditions' within the school with its capacity for sustained development. Broadly stated these conditions are:

- a commitment to *staff development*
- practical efforts to *involve* staff, students and the community in school policies and decisions
- 'transformational' *leadership* approaches
- effective *co-ordination* strategies
- serious attention to the potential benefits of *enquiry and reflection*
- a commitment to *collaborative planning* activity.

Staff development

A systematic and integrated approach to staff development, that focusses on the professional learning of teachers and establishes the classroom as an important centre for teacher development is central to authentic school improvement. Staff development is the central strategy for supporting teachers as they engage in improvement activities. Attention to teacher learning has direct spin-offs in terms of pupil learning. The research evidence that is available on the effectiveness of staff development initiatives is, however, far from encouraging. Despite all the effort and resources that have been utilised, the impact of such programmes in terms of improvements in teaching and better learning outcomes for pupils is rather disappointing (Fullan, 1991; Joyce and Showers, 1995).

As a result of his review of available research evidence, Fullan (1991) provides a bleak picture of in-service initiatives that are poorly conceptualised, insensitive to the concerns of individual participants and, perhaps critically, make little effort to help participants relate their learning experiences to their usual workplace conditions. In stark contrast to this gloomy analysis, the research evidence from schools with high levels of student and teacher engagement and learning, demonstrates how they build infrastructures for staff development within their day-to-day arrangements (see for example Joyce and Calhoun, 1996). Such infrastructures involve portions of the school week being devoted to staff development activities such as curriculum development and implementation, discussion of teaching approaches, regular observation sessions, and on-site coaching.

Joyce and Showers (1995) identify a number of key training components which, when used in combination, have much greater power than when they are used alone. The major components of training are:

- presentation of theory or description of skill or strategy
- modelling or demonstration of skills or models of teaching
- practice in simulated and classroom settings
- structured and open-ended feedback (provision of information about performance)
- coaching for application (hands-on, in-classroom assistance with the transfer of skills and strategies to the classroom).

Joyce (1992) has also distinguished between the locations in which these various forms of staff development are best located – either in the 'workshop' or the 'workplace'. The *workshop*, which is equivalent to the best practice on the traditional INSET course, is where teachers gain *understanding*, see *demonstrations* of the teaching strategy they may wish to acquire, and have the opportunity to *practice* them in a non-threatening environment. If the aim is to transfer those skills back into the *workplace* – the classroom and school – then merely attending the workshop is insufficient. The research evidence is very clear, that skill acquisition and the ability to transfer vertically to a range of situations requires 'on-the-job-support' (Joyce and Showers, 1995). This implies changes to the workplace and the way in which staff development is organised. In particular this means the opportunity for *immediate and sustained practice, collaboration and peer coaching*, and *studying development and implementation*.

The paradox is that changes to the workplace cannot be achieved without, in most cases, drastic alterations in the ways in which schools are organised. Yet the transfer of teaching skills from INSET sessions to classroom settings will not occur without them. Consequently staff development is perhaps the most crucial of the enabling conditions for school improvement.

Involvement

In the literature on effective schools, there is strong evidence that success is associated with a sense of identification and involvement that extends beyond the teaching staff. This involves the pupils, parents and, indeed, other members of the local community. It does seem that those schools that are able to create positive relationships with their wider community can create a supportive climate for learning.

Referring to a series of studies carried out in Wales, Reynolds (1991) refers to the existence of what he calls an 'incorporative approach'. This he notes has two major elements: incorporation of pupils into the organisation of the school, and incorporation of their parents through supportive roles. In many improving schools this approach is widened to include members of the local community (Gray *et al.*, 1999). In the UK it is also important to fully involve school governors.

Pupil involvement is a particularly important factor in school improvement. This can occur at an organisational level, by involving pupils in decision making and encouraging them to take responsibility for day-to-day routines. At the classroom level, students can be encouraged to take responsibility for their own learning and, through involvement, to learn organisational, planning, discussion, decision-making and leadership skills (Stoll, 1991; Rudduck *et al.*, 1996). When pupils are less involved, it is likely that their attitudes to school will be much more negative. Then, when innovations are introduced, they may well become barriers to change. Their resistance may not be open and tangible, but nevertheless their intuitive reactions may create the negative atmosphere that discourages staff from pursing their goals.

The incorporative approach can be extended beyond the school gate to *involve parents*, members of the local community, and of course, school governors. Here the attitudes of staff are a major factor. Unfortunately some staff still see parents as a hindrance. Similarly, parental views of schools and teachers vary. Often parents' views of teachers are based on their own experience in school. This may have been negative, and the parents may see the school as an institution that fails people. The whole issue of communications between school and parents therefore needs to be handled effectively, particularly through careful planning and skilful interviewing techniques.

One research project asked parents to describe the kind of information professionals should be giving families (Ainscow and Muncey, 1989). The parents wanted it to be honest, concise and useful. They want practical advice directed towards immediate problems and some indication of the likely long-term outcomes for their child. Asked to give advice to professionals on how best to deal with parents, they suggested the following:

- *Be frank and open* Excuses or vague explanations are often interpreted by parents as a defensive attitude or simple evasion of the truth on the part of the professional.
- *Listen* Teachers must recognise that all parents have knowledge of their child that they cannot possibly have. This knowledge may well be valuable in helping the child overcome some difficulty.
- *Do not be afraid to say 'I don't know'* Parents often appreciate the honesty of the response, and this may well help to foster a sense of partnership between home and school.
- *Encourage* Parents feel that they need encouragement and reassurance from teachers, rather than attempts to lay blame.

Leadership practices

Studies of school effectiveness affirm that leadership is a key element in determining school success (Mortimore, 1999). Recently, studies of leadership in schools have moved away from the identification of this function exclusively with the headteacher, and begun to address how leadership can be made available throughout the management structure and at all levels in the school community (Gronn, 1999). This shift in emphasis has been accompanied by a shift in thinking about leadership itself. As is seen in the following chapter, there is an increasing call for 'transformational' approaches which distribute and empower, rather than 'transactional' approaches which sustain traditional, and broadly bureaucratic, concepts of hierarchy and control (Hallinger, 1992; Leithwood, 1993).

Schools that are successful with their improvement efforts not only regard leadership as a distributed function, they also deliberately set out to promote discussion about leadership style and to help staff from different levels in the school to share perceptions about how leadership operates. In IQEA schools, such discussions tend to identify a number of key aspects of the leadership role (Hopkins *et al.*, 1996):

- The first underlines the responsibility of school leaders in establishing a clear 'vision' or set of purposes for the school. The methods through which the vision is developed seem to be as important as vision itself in generating staff commitment. There is clear concern in the literature over the imposition of a vision at the expense of 'vision building'.
- The second relates to the way individual knowledge, skills and experience are harnessed, and the extent to which the school is able to transcend traditional notions of hierarchy or role in bringing together the 'best team for the job'. Leadership that arises from relevant knowledge or experience seems to be more successful than leadership stemming from authority.
- A third aspect is the way leadership is used in group or team meetings. Leader behaviour is obviously an important determinant of group effectiveness. A strong commitment to the quality of relationships within the group can however sometimes lead to over-cohesiveness, with a corresponding decline in the quality of critical thinking which individuals bring to the group. The dangers associated with 'group think' are well known.
- Fourth, the more effective schools seem to explore opportunities for 'spreading' the leadership function throughout the staff group. This means accepting that leadership is a function to which many staff contribute, rather than a set of responsibilities vested in a small number of individuals or jobs.

Co-ordination strategy

The characteristic of schools as 'loosely coupled systems' has already been referred to (Weick, 1976). Loose coupling occurs because schools consist of units, processes, actions and individuals that operate in isolation from one another. Loose coupling is also encouraged by the goal ambiguity that characterises schooling. Despite the rhetoric of curriculum aims and objectives, schools often consist of groups of people who may have very different values and, indeed, beliefs about the purposes of schooling. Although there are some advantages to this way of working, most school improvement efforts attempt to 'tighten' the loose coupling as part of the overall strategy. The importance of achieving this is highlighted by the characteristic of consistency that pervades effective schools.

The school's capacity to co-ordinate the action of teachers behind agreed policies or goals is therefore an important factor in promoting change. At the core of such strategies are communication systems and procedures, and the ways in which groups can be created and sustained to co-ordinate improved effort across a range of levels or departments. Of particular importance are specific strategies for ensuring that *all* staff are kept informed about development priorities and activities, as this is information vital to informed self-direction. Awareness among staff of one another's responsibilities can not always be assumed.

Communication is vital to overall school co-ordination. In order for a school to organise itself to accomplish its goals, maintain itself in good working order and, at the same time, adapt to changing circumstances, sound procedures for communication are essential. Meetings must be scheduled, reports from task groups distributed, departmental meetings organised, and summaries of various activities written and sent round to all staff. All of these responses are structured communication opportunities. The communication network thus created determines the amount and type of information a member of staff will receive from colleagues.

Fullan (1991) stresses the importance of effective communication within a school during improvement initiatives. He notes that no amount of good thinking by itself will address the ubiquitous problem of faulty communication. Since change is a highly personal experience, and since schools consist of numerous individuals and groups undergoing different (to them) experiences, no single channel of communication is going to reassure or clarify the meaning of change for people. A cardinal fact of social change is that people will always misinterpret and misunderstand some aspect of the purpose or practice of something that is new to them. The theory of change indicates the importance of frequent, personal interactions as a key to success.

A further factor is the 'informal' organisation – all schools are made up of a number of informal or self-selected groupings that rarely coincide with formal work units. The attitudes and behaviour adopted by these groups often have a profound effect on the individual's willingness to undertake formal tasks. As a consequence, it is important not to overlook the impact of informal organisation on formal structures, and a co-ordination strategy needs to take account of informal contacts which influence (and can often contribute directly to) the quality of effort.

Establishing a co-operative way of working is not a simple matter, not least because it is necessary to do so in ways that do not reduce the discretion of individual teachers. Teachers must have sufficient autonomy to make instant decisions that take account of the individuality of their pupils and the uniqueness of every encounter that occurs. What is needed is a well co-ordinated, co-operative style of working that gives individual teachers the confidence to improvise in a search for the most appropriate responses to the situations they meet. In other words, the aim is to create a more tightly coupled system without the loss of loose coupling benefits.

Enquiry and reflection

The unprecedented pressures for change at the level of the school created by national reforms is a continuing theme in this book. Changes in curriculum context, processes and assessment have been enshrined in legislation – requiring adoption at a pace that many schools feel is beyond their capacity. In addition to creating a potentially de-skilling context in which individual teachers must work, the logistics of implementing these changes has proved a severe test for even the most confident of school management teams. So much so, it may appear perverse to be arguing that schools should actively adopt a focus upon school improvement activities at a time when many teachers are finding that all their time and energies are consumed in trying to assimilate the range of 'unavoidable' changes currently required.

Paradoxically, those schools that recognise enquiry and reflection as important processes in school improvement find it easier to sustain improvement effort around established priorities. They are also better placed to monitor the extent to which policies actually deliver the intended outcomes for pupils, even in times of change. There is growing evidence of the importance of systematic collection and use of school-based data (Wilson and Corcoran, 1988: 20): 'The Californian Study (Overcoming the Odds: Making High Schools Work) found that more effective schools were clearer about their indicators of success, and used data to assess their progress more frequently, and conducted diagnostic assessment of students more regularly.'

There is another irony here. Information gathered by outsiders, be they inspectors or consultants, is often seen as having more significance than information that is routinely available to those within the school community. Yet schools that understand the potential of internally generated information about progress or difficulties are better placed to exploit opportunities and to overcome problems. It is routine data collection within the school that is likely to provide a more useful and enduring basis for decision making than is commissioned external investigation. Nevertheless, simply collecting data, however systematically and routinely, will not of itself improve schools. There needs to be a commitment to scrutinise such data, to make sense of it, and to plan and act differently as a result.

Schools that recognise that enquiry and reflection are important processes in school improvement find it easier to sustain improvement effort around established priorities, and are better placed to monitor the extent to which policies actually deliver the intended outcomes for pupils (Ainscow *et al.*, 1994). Central to the conditions that promote the effective use of enquiry and reflection as developmental tools are:

- systematic collection, interpretation and use of school-generated data in decision-making
- effective strategies for reviewing the progress and impact of school policies and initiatives
- widespread involvement of staff in the processes of data collection and analysis
- clear ground rules for the collection, control and use of school-based data.

Some schools are much better organised than others and have clear systems and procedures for collecting, analysing and interpreting information relevant to particular aspects of the school or particular decisions. Even in these cases, however, a more general commitment to enquire into and reflect on the school's progress is rare – more often it is the issue that is identified then the information collected, rather than data being collected to help identify what the issue should be. It is the habits of enquiry and reflection, particularly about the *impact*, rather than the implementation, of improvement programmes, that are the important forces for improvement.

Collaborative planning

During the 1990s development planning established itself as a key strategy for school improvement. In England, development planning was regarded as a means of helping schools manage the extensive national change agenda, and to enable the school 'to organise what it is already doing and what it needs to do in a more purposeful and coherent way' (DES 1989: 4). Given the amount of change schools and teachers were expected to cope with in the late 1980s and early 1990s such a strategy was welcomed by many (Hargreaves and Hopkins, 1991). Planning was also being widely advocated in many other western educational systems. The 'school based management' approach that originated in Tasmania, Australia (Caldwell and Spinks, 1988), and the 'school growth plans' strategy of the Halton school board in Canada (Stoll and Fink, 1992), are but two well known examples.

There is rather more to planning however than simply producing a development plan. Indeed, often the quality of the 'plan' as a written document is a very misleading guide to its influence, it is the link between planning and action which in the end justifies the effort put into planning activities. Working through the planning cycle however is likely to involve the school in generating a number of 'priorities' for action, often too many to work on. This means that decisions about 'priorities' must be made – moving from the separate, perhaps even conflicting priorities of individuals or groups, to a systematically compiled set of priorities which reflect the overall needs of a whole school community. Previously, it was suggested that two principles should guide this process of choice among priorities (Hargreaves and Hopkins, 1991: 42):

- *Manageability:* how much can we realistically hope to achieve?
- *Coherence:* is there a sequence that will ease implementation?

It has since been noted that a third principle can help to guide schools through what is often a difficult series of choices (Hopkins *et al.*, 1994):

- *Consonance:* the extent to which internally identified priorities coincide or overlap with external pressures for reform.

There is evidence to suggest that those schools which understand consonance, and therefore see externally generated change efforts as providing opportunities, as well as (or instead of) problems, are better able to respond to external demands. It is through such an understanding of how to approach planning that schools begin to see the potential in adapting external change for internal purpose.

Ongoing research into school improvement during the 1990s has indicated that during this decade the use of development planning itself has changed in many schools (MacGilchrist *et al.*, 1997; Hopkins and MacGilchrist, 1998). One research study in particular (MacGilchrist *et al.*, 1995), has shown that schools that exhibit best practice in development planning now use it as a strategy to enhance directly the progress and achievement of students. The crucial difference between this and previous approaches to development planning is that it is rooted in classrooms. The focus is on students' learning, their progress and achievement, and what is needed to improve it and how this is best supported. The plan begins with learning goals for students. A teaching strategy for achieving them is then produced. This strategy is supported by any necessary adjustments to the school's management arrangements: for example, modifications to curriculum policies and schemes of work, changes to the staff development programme and the timetable and any re-allocation of budgets, roles and responsibilities needed to achieve the goals set. This is radically different from the type of plan that simply focusses on the implementation of external change, however important that is, or on the development of school-wide policies and practices, which may not have a direct impact on classroom practice.

Experience suggests that although not all schools find development planning easy, collaboration is the key to successful planning. Involvement in planning is more important than producing plans. It is through collective planning that goals emerge, differences can be resolved and a basis for action created. The 'plan' is really a by-product from this activity, and will almost always need to be revised, often several times. The benefits of the planning activity, however, will often outlast the currency of the plan. More detailed advice on the development planning process is found in *The Empowered School* (Hargreaves and Hopkins, 1991).

Some propositions

Through the experience of working with IQEA schools on the building of 'capacity' in these areas, a number of factors influencing how particular conditions can best contribute to a 'moving school' ethos have been observed. As a consequence, a series of propositions about the relationship between the way in which a school approaches a particular condition and the impact of that condition on the school's capacity for improvement have been developed (Hopkins and West, 1994). These propositions hold the key to the establishment of a school culture that can meaningfully empower all teachers within the school community (Figure 6.1).

Proposition 1
Schools will not improve unless teachers, individually and collectively, develop. While teachers can often develop their practice on an individual basis, if the whole school is to develop then there need to be many staff development opportunities for teachers to learn together.

Proposition 2
Successful schools seem to have ways of working that encourage feelings of involvement from a number of stake-holder groups, especially students.

Proposition 3
Schools that are successful at development establish a clear vision for themselves and regard leadership as a function to which many staff contribute, rather than a set of responsibilities vested in a single individual.

Proposition 4
The co-ordination of activities is an important way of keeping people involved, particularly when changes of policy are being introduced. Communication within the school is an important aspect of co-ordination, as are the informal interactions that arise between teachers.

Proposition 5
We have observed that those schools which recognise that enquiry and reflection are important processes in school improvement find it easier to gain clarity and establish shared meanings around identified development priorities, and are better placed to monitor the extent to which policies actually deliver the intended outcomes for pupils.

Proposition 6
Our experience alongside that of colleagues in IQEA schools suggests that through the process of planning for development the school is able to link its educational aspirations to identifiable priorities, sequence those priorities over time, and maintain a focus on classroom practice.

Figure 6.1 Creating the conditions for school improvement: some propositions (from Hopkins and West, 1994: 192–3)

The conditions for classroom development

The six school level conditions and the related propositions were the initial focus of work with IQEA project schools. Subsequently a set of conditions within the classroom to complement those at the level of the school was developed (Hopkins *et al.*, 1997, 1998). The aim of the classroom conditions is to enable teachers to facilitate and enhance the learning of all students. They are:

- *Authentic relationships:* being the quality, openness and congruence of relationships existing in the classroom.
- *Rules and boundaries:* being the pattern of expectations set by the teacher and school of student performance and behaviour within the classroom.
- *Planning, resources and preparation:* being the access of teachers to a range of pertinent teaching materials and the ability to plan and differentiate these materials for a range of students.
- *Teacher's repertoire:* being the range of teaching styles and models internalised and available to a teacher dependent on student, context, curriculum and desired outcome.
- *Pedagogic partnerships:* being the ability of teachers to form professional relationships within and outside the classroom that focus on the study and improvement of practice.
- *Reflection on teaching:* being the capacity of the individual teacher to reflect on his/her own practice, and to put to the test of practice, specifications of teaching from other sources.

This brief outline of the conditions for classroom development provides an example of how a specific research activity within the IQEA project contributes to the aspiration of elaborating a more specific approach to authentic school improvement. It is also interesting to note that current conceptualisations of the 'school as a learning organisation', as was seen earlier, lack a sufficiently robust link between the school and classroom levels. The defining characteristic of a learning organisation is the way in which it establishes and maintains an organisational memory. The importance of reflection therefore at both school and classroom levels, and the connections between them cannot be underestimated. The articulation of the classroom conditions provides that connection. The role of the teacher in this is crucial. In that respect, the classroom conditions comprise a practical curriculum for teacher development that links whole school improvement to those modifications in classroom practice that are necessary for enhanced levels of student learning and attainment.

Research on the school level conditions in the IQEA network

The research programme within the IQEA project has three main foci. In relation to the theme of this chapter they are:

- *Conceptual issues:* i.e., what are the school and classroom conditions that can help facilitate the learning of all pupils?
- *Methodological issues:* i.e., how can teachers within a school establish the extent to which these conditions are in place?
- *Strategic issues:* i.e., how can teachers be helped to improve these conditions?

These complementary tasks are characteristic of the way in which the research agenda is taken forward in the IQEA programme. This combination of functions reflects the commitment to the integration of research and development in authentic school improvement projects. In terms of the 'conditions of school improvement', the *conceptual* issue has been dominant in this chapter, the focus is now more briefly on *methodological* and *strategic* concerns.

The methodological focus has resulted in questionnaire scales that measure teachers' perceptions of the quality of the school and classroom conditions existing in the school (see Ainscow *et al.*, 1994; Hopkins *et al.*, 1994, 1997). The rating scales can be used by a school staff to estimate their profile at school and classroom levels, and more generally by researchers interested in 'mapping the process of change' (Cambridge University, 1994; Ainscow *et al.*, 1995). The virtue of these rating scales is that they not only provide an estimation of the school's current conditions profile, but it also gives teachers an increasingly sophisticated language in which to discuss school improvement issues.

Over the years data has been systematically collected on the school level conditions to such an extent that there are now fairly well established norms against which schools can compare their own positions. The following figures illustrate some of the data collected for a selection of IQEA schools for the three-year period 1997–9. This data is presented for illustrative and heuristic purposes rather than as a comprehensive analysis.

Figure 6.2 shows the perceptions of staff in two schools in the Nottingham Project over a period of three years. It shows the percentages of staff who have felt that the management conditions outlined above have been in evidence 'often' or 'nearly always' in their schools. In that sense, the responses are affirmative of the capacity of the school to develop. The data suggests that the respective staffs feel that, while the schools have been in the project, the conditions of enquiry, planning, staff development and leadership have generally been enhanced. Staff are less confident about the involvement in the school of other groups in the school community. Our experience has been that staffs initially have a low estimation of their ability to involve such groups in the running of the school, and often choose as an improvement focus the involvement of students. This has a dual effect: students become more involved, for example in the evaluation of teaching and learning in the school, but schools become more critical of their failure to involve other groups more, for example parents and governors. In that respect, the conditions

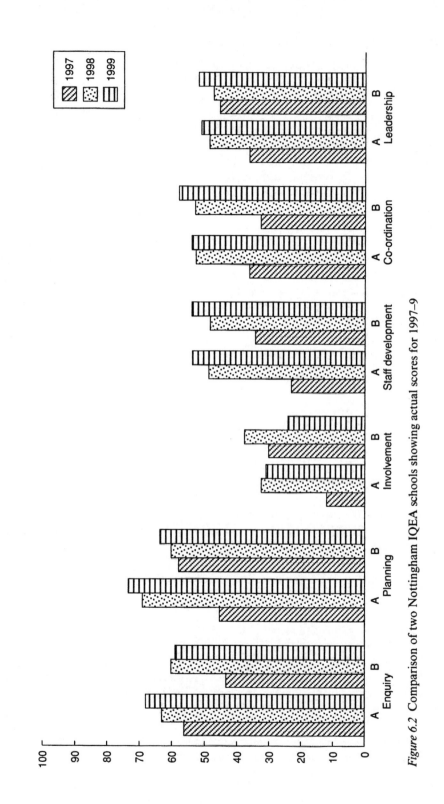

Figure 6.2 Comparison of two Nottingham IQEA schools showing actual scores for 1997–9

survey is a heuristic, inasmuch as it raises staff awareness about issues relating to the development of the school's capacity for development.

The low estimation of their ability to involve other school stakeholders by many schools is confirmed in Figure 6.3. This shows the average level of affirmative responses to the conditions survey in the Nottingham IQEA cohort schools over a period of three years. While the other conditions show a steady degree of enhancement over the three-year period (notwithstanding a slight hiccup in Co-ordination in 1998), the Involvement condition demonstrates the volatility shown in Figure 6.2.

Figure 6.4 compares responses between different cohorts of schools from different areas. The staffs in Bedfordshire Upper Schools, were surveyed on their entry to BUSIP (Bedfordshire Upper Schools Improvement Project). They show a similar range of responses as the Nottingham cohort, but are clearly more affirmative (though by no means ecstatic!) in their views on staff development than their Nottinghamshire colleagues.

Figure 6.5 shows that 6 of the 15 schools who joined the Nottingham Project in 1998 had better GCSE scores in the year after they joined than they had in 1997. Four had worse results, and a further 5 have stayed at about the same level. While we would expect (and have evidence) that schools in the project would gradually improve their results over a period of time, this data would suggest that IQEA does not provide a 'quick fix'!

Towards a strategy for authentic school improvement

It is on the basis of such analyses that the 'Strategy for Authentic School Improvement' was developed (Hopkins, 1996; Hopkins *et al.*, 1996). Figure 6.6 provides the setting for a series of assumptions upon which this generic approach to school improvement is based. There are essentially two major components – the 'capacity building dimension' and the 'strategic dimension'.

The *'capacity building dimension'* relates to the conditions at both the school and classroom levels. Through sustained work on the conditions for development the school enhances its capacity for managing change. It is important that the conditions be simultaneously worked on with the school's chosen priority for development, which is usually some aspect of teaching and learning or classroom practice.

Improvement strategies are organised around the conditions for a number of reasons. First, because they identify those key areas where management arrangements influence the school's capacity to engage in improvement activities. Second, in many cases it is necessary to start by focussing on one or more of these conditions before any substantial improvement in classroom practice is possible. Third, each school is unique in the way in which it addresses a particular condition in procuring its own improvement initiatives. This means, in practice, that both sequence and emphasis varies from school to school, according to their own priorities. It also means that conditions

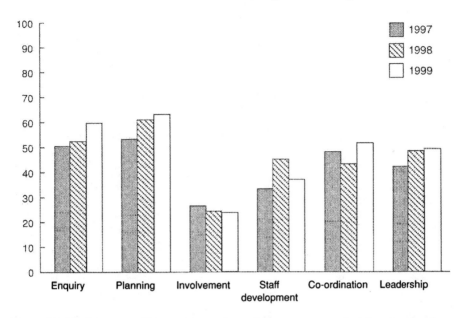

Figure 6.3 Median scores for management conditions surveys undertaken in schools in Nottingham IQEA projects, 1997–9

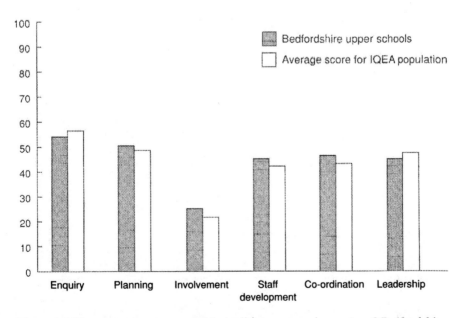

Figure 6.4 Responses to management conditions survey in group of Bedfordshire upper schools, October 1999

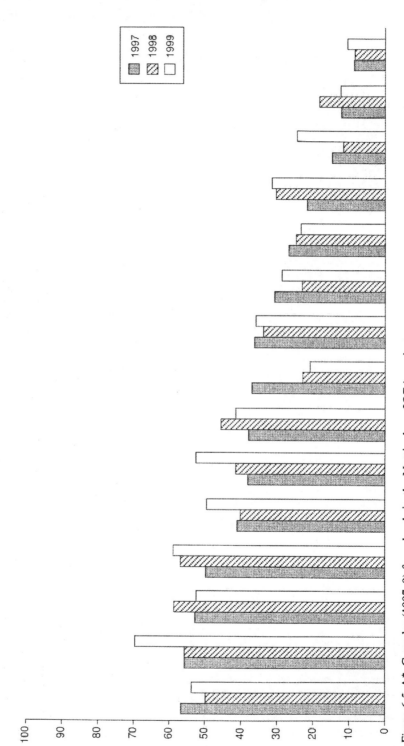

Figure 6.5 A*–C grades (1997–9) for schools in the Nottingham IQEA project

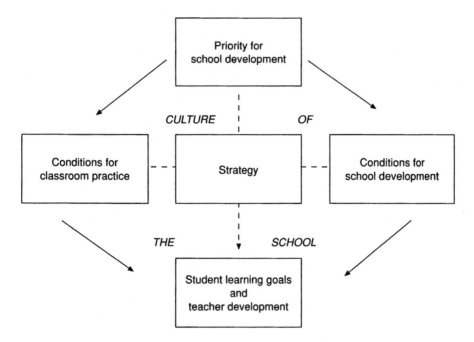

Figure 6.6 A strategy for authentic school improvement

need to be addressed in combination, as it is not often that increasing the school's 'capacity' in relation to a single condition will serve meaningful development.

The *strategic dimension* reflects the ability of the school to plan sensibly for improvement efforts. The process is depicted by the vertical links in the diagram, between:

- priorities
- strategy
- outcomes.

Most schools are by now familiar with the need to establish a clear and practical focus for their improvement efforts. In England, the experience of school development planning coupled with the demands of accountability and inspection has helped them understand the need for priorities and priority setting. Within the IQEA project, the school's *priorities* are normally some aspect of curriculum, assessment or classroom process that the school has identified from the many changes that confront it. In this sense, the choice represents the school's interpretation of the current reform agenda. Although the balance of activities varies from school to school, the more successful schools set priorities that:

- are few in number – trying to do too much is counter-productive
- are central to the mission of the school
- relate to national reform requirements
- link to teaching and learning
- lead to specific outcomes for students and staff.

The school improvement *strategy* is the deliberate actions or sequence of actions taken by a school staff in order to implement identified curriculum or organisational priorities. The strategy will need to be more or less powerful depending on the relative 'strength' of factors that might militate against this particular development. When circumstances exist that are less supportive of change, it is necessary to concentrate much more in the initial stages on creating the internal conditions within the school that facilitate improvement. Work on the priorities is limited until the conditions are in place.

There is a clear assumption that such school improvement efforts will result in enhanced *outcomes* for students and staff. 'Outcomes' in the IQEA project are defined broadly, and vary according to the focus of improvement effort. For students, 'outcomes' could relate to the enhancement of critical thinking, learning capacity, self-esteem and so on, as well as improved examination or test results. For staff they could, for example, include increased collegiality, better opportunities for professional learning or increased responsibility.

Many schools quite reasonably regard the sequence that has just been described as the logical way to plan their school improvement activities, and in many ways it is. Some schools however, and those that appear to be more successful than most at managing school improvement, begin at the other end of the sequence – with student learning goals. It is as if they ask, 'what changes in student performance do we wish to see this year?' Having decided these, they then devise a strategy for bringing them about. Often they also translate them into priorities within the development plan and articulate the explicit links between them to external changes or opportunities.

The final element in the framework is *school culture*. A key assumption is that school improvement strategies will lead to cultural change in schools through modifications to their 'internal conditions'. It is this cultural change as is seen in chapter 8 that supports innovations in the teaching–learning processes that lead to enhanced outcomes for students.

It is in these ways that the most successful schools pursue their improvement efforts. While focussing on the learning needs of students in the context of systemic and environmental demands, they also recognise that school structures must reflect both these demands as well as offering a suitable vehicle for the future development of the school. In this sense the structure of the school provides the *skeleton* that supports cultural growth, rather than the framework which constrains it.

Commentary

There are four key messages from those schools that are raising student achievement through focussing on the quality of teaching and learning in classrooms, and the conditions that support it (Hopkins and MacGilchrist, 1998).

1   *They keep the focus on student learning* The increasing emphasis on student academic outcomes is very welcome. Achievement at whatever level however, is based on pupils' ability to respond effectively to the tasks they are set; and this depends on how well they can take control over their own learning. It is these skills and strategies, as well as the focus on academic outcomes that are integrated into the targets set for pupil progress and achievement.

2   *They clarify the link between effective teaching and student learning outcomes* Effective teachers and effective schools take seriously the link between classroom practice and student learning outcomes. This is particularly in terms of what the child learns, how the child learns, the pace of learning and the high expectations existing in the classroom. Teaching strategies reflect not just the teacher's classroom management skills, but also the ability of the teacher to help students expand their learning capability.

3   *They make certain that the school's management arrangements keep the focus on student learning* These schools identify any modifications that are needed to the school's current arrangements, for example, the timetable, the budget, staffing and staff development. They plan for any changes that may be needed in their curriculum policies, schemes of work and assessment arrangements in order to make a difference where it matters most – namely – in classroom for pupils.

4   *They maintain consistency across the school* Schools that add value to the learning, progress and attainment of their pupils are consistent in their teaching practices, the educational values that they hold, the high levels of expectation that they maintain, and their low tolerance of failure. Pupils in highly effective schools are clear about what is required from them, feel secure in their learning and school environment, and respond positively to the academic and social demands placed upon them.

Evidence of good practice and the lessons of research suggest that authentic school improvement needs to focus on both classroom practice and the organisational conditions within the school. The role of leadership in establishing this way of working is the focus of the next chapter.

7 Instructional leadership and staff development

It is now more than 20 years since leadership was identified as one of the key components of 'good schools' by HMI who stated that, without exception, the most important single factor in the success of these schools is the quality of the leadership of the headteacher (HMI, 1977: 36). Since that time the changes imposed upon the UK education system, and indeed most other 'developed' educational systems, have radically altered the role and responsibilities of the headteacher or principal. In particular, the devolution of responsibility for local management of schools in many systems has resulted in the headteacher or principal becoming a manager of systems and budgets as well as a leader of colleagues. Also, the increasingly competitive environment in which schools operate has placed a much greater emphasis upon both the managerial and the leadership qualities of headteachers. On the one hand, the skills of marketing, public relations, orchestrating boundary roles and coping with multiple accountabilities are at a premium; on the other, headteachers need to become increasingly strategic and creative and to have the leadership skills to raise standards and to improve the school's outcomes. One of the major growth areas in education in recent years has been in the field of leadership training. While most of this could be criticised as being too narrowly focussed, competency-driven and de-contextualised, it has reinforced the centrality of the headteacher's role in leading school development and improvement.

The theme pursued in this chapter is that, although leadership is essential for successful school improvement, the leadership function in those schools which are most successful in adopting school improvement values and approaches does not necessarily rest exclusively with the headteacher or principal. It will also be argued that the prime function of leadership for authentic school improvement is to enhance the quality of teaching and learning. 'Instructional leadership', as this approach has been termed, is about creating learning opportunities for both students and teachers – hence the link in the title of this chapter to staff development.

It has not ever been thus. The history of educational leadership tells of a much more conventional evolution. Murphy (1991), for example, suggests that the thinking about leadership falls into a number of phases – building towards the current interest in the links between leader behaviour and organisational culture – as follows:

- Initial interest in the personal qualities and characteristics of 'successful' leaders which result in personality or trait theories of leadership.
- Increasing focus on what it is that leaders actually do – are there some behaviours and approaches which are consistently associated with successful leadership? Such enquiries support the development of behavioural theories of leadership.
- Growing awareness that task-related and people-centred behaviours may be interpreted quite differently by different groups and in different contexts, prompting explanation of how the particular context might best be accounted for within a general theory, and resulting in a variety of situational approaches to leadership.
- Most recently, emphasis on the links between leadership style and the culture of the organisation – a movement towards the notion of leadership as transformational, having the potential to alter the cultural context in which people work.

During the past decade the debate about educational leadership has been dominated by a contrast between the (so-called) 'transactional' and 'transformation' approaches. As we noted elsewhere, there seems to be a preoccupation with 'transaction' models in systems where strong central control has been retained, while in those systems where de-centralisation has been most evident considerable interest in 'transformational' models has emerged (West *et al.*, 2000). It is worth briefly contrasting these two 'stereotypes' of the leadership role.

In the more stable system, where 'maintenance' (by which is meant a focus upon effectiveness and efficiency issues) has a higher priority than 'development', and the headteacher is seen as playing a major role in protecting and promoting the interests of the system, a transactional approach is frequently found. In such an approach, the emphasis will tend to be on the management of the school's systems and structures. It may be an effective method for bringing about a certain kind of organisational change – those where parameters are very clearly identified, where conformity rather than creativity is valued, where assuring quality is a priority and where it is hoped to retain organisational structures and relationships despite changing (say) education content or method. Transactional models of leadership therefore seem best suited to static school systems and communities.

It has been widely argued that complex and dynamic changes, such as the 'cultural' changes and the organisational redesign that are required for sustained school improvement, are less likely to occur as a result of transactional leadership (Beare *et al.*, 1989; Stoll and Fink, 1996). A model of leadership more congruent with the requirement of cultural change is that of transformational leadership. This style of leadership focusses on the people involved, their relationships, and requires an approach that seeks to transform feelings, attitudes and beliefs. Transformational leaders not only manage structure, they also purposefully seek to impact upon the culture of the school in order to change it. Consequently, transformational leadership would appear to be consistent with a desire to bring about school improvement, rather than simply 'change' the school.

It will be further argued that transformational leadership approaches that focus on culture change are necessary, but not sufficient, for authentic school improvement. There also needs to be a focus on student learning and achievement which is more specifically the domain of 'instructional leadership'. In this chapter therefore:

- a model of leadership that builds on both the 'transformational' and 'instructional' styles will be outlined
- confirmation for this proposal will be sought from the research conducted on headteachers and principals
- a concept of 'dispersed' leadership, particularly in regard to the school improvement group or 'cadre' will be argued for
- an illustration of how this process works in an IQEA school will be provided
- it will be maintained that a key task of leadership for authentic school improvement is in promoting and sustaining collaborative forms of staff development.

Transformational and instructional leadership

Leithwood *et al.* (1999) begin their recent book on leadership with the question, 'Do we need another book on leadership?' They comment that one of them already has 213 different such books on their shelves already, and answer their rhetorical question by saying that 'Times change'. Well of course they do, and this is part of the problem. Any dominant theory of leadership at a point in time tends to reflect the mores and conventional wisdom of the day. The brief historical review provided by Murphy (1991) in the introduction attests to that. So, instead of models of leadership being cumulative, they tend to be relative and possess a distinct historical flavour.

All this is to argue that leadership is a relative concept that is contextually bound. The dominant leadership construct for our times is, as has already been intimated, 'transformational leadership'. Unfortunately there is a problem when reviewing the literature on educational leadership. It is that most commentators, certainly those writing during the past ten or 20 years, tend to conflate their own views about what leadership should be with their descriptions of what leadership actually is and fail to discipline either position by reference to empirical research. This can lead us towards a somewhat mythical view of leadership that is often embellished by rhetoric. Consequently transformational leadership is, as with many concepts in education, a somewhat plastic term. In order to capture the range of conventional wisdom on trans-formational leadership that has some empirical support, a selection of research studies have been selected for a brief review.

From the research evidence, the cited advantages of transformational leadership are:

- An improved capacity to respond to change and achieve effective school restructuring (Strodl and Johnson, 1994). This is particularly so in connection with urban schools, where complex and diverse cultures and increased levels of potential conflict are an issue.
- Geijsel, Sleegers and Berg (1998), in a qualitative study of schools in the Netherlands, argue that transformational leadership is needed in a context where schools are becoming more and more responsible for the successful implementation of large-scale innovations initiated by govern-mental policy.
- The concept of the learning organisation has also been connected with transformational leadership. Leithwood *et al.* (1998), looking at the conditions fostering organisational learning in schools, conclude that collegial atmosphere and transformational principal leadership are essential conditions.
- Enhanced teacher efficacy through transformational leadership has been proposed as a means of linking leadership to outcomes. Hipp (1996) claims that three of Leithwood's transformational leadership behaviours: modelling behaviour, inspiring group purpose and providing contingent rewards, are significantly related to general teaching efficacy.
- Innovation, inclusion and conflict management have all been linked to transformational leadership behaviours. Berg and Sleegers (1996) found that transformational school leadership plays a 'particularly crucial' role in the development of the innovative capacities of schools.
- On the issue of change, Cheng (1997) claims that transformational leader-ship is critical to meeting educational challenges in a changing envir-onment, and Turan and Sny (1996) argue that strategic planning, like transformational leadership, is vision-driven planning for the future. Both transformational leadership and strategic planning, they say, are necessary for an organisation to respond to the changes and uncertain-ties of organisational life.
- Also, Fisher and Koch (1996), writing about US university presidents, argue that transformational leadership, in terms of a strong charismatic president that transforms the university through the power of his or her own vision for the future, is far more effective than the transactional leader-ship style, which emphasises collegial leadership based upon consensus.

In looking at the effects and scope of transformational leadership, a number of studies have associated transformational leadership behaviours with lead-ers judged to be successful and with features of the perceptions and social organisation of followers. These studies illuminate both the scope of the claims made for transformational leadership and, perhaps, also the limits that are likely to apply to such claims. Evans (1996), for example, in a study of the perceptions of principal leadership style and school social organisation, found a significant correlation between teachers' reports of principals' transformational leadership and their schools' social organisation.

Leithwood (1997) looked at the extent to which perceptions of teacher leadership were influenced by factors similar to those that influence perceptions of transformational principal leadership. Overall, principal leadership seemed to be about a third stronger than teacher leadership. Principal leadership exercised its strongest independent influence on planning, structure and organisation, as well as on school mission and school culture. In contrast, the independent influence of teacher leaders was strongest (and stronger than the principal's influence) with respect to school planning, and the structure and organisation of the school. Further, a portrait of the composite teacher leader emerged from interview data as warm, dependable, self-effacing with a genuine commitment to the work of colleagues and the school, and with well-honed interpersonal skills – a finding which resonates interestingly with the view of instructional leadership articulated later in this chapter.

Finally, Mannion (1998) in a study looking at the relationship between transformational leadership and trust in schools found a significant correlation between a 'Trust in Principal' score and a 'Transformational Leadership' score. This relationship did not hold between the Trust in Colleagues and the Transformational Leadership. The relationship was also not present between the Trust in Organisation score and the score on Transformational Leadership. Apparently, the relationship existing between trusted principals who are transformational leaders and faculty does not necessarily translate into a trusting relationship among colleagues or a trusting relationship between teachers and the school organisation.

Given the centrality of transformational constructs to current debates on leadership, this review has been as wide as possible, given constraints on space. There is obviously a heuristic appeal to such an image of leadership that is empowering, and seems to be positively related to both school culture and student achievement. It is obvious, however, that the term is open to different conceptual interpretations, which are often based on the particular writer's values, is difficult to operationalise in behavioural terms, and the empirical support for it is not overwhelming.

A perspective on instructional leadership

As already intimated, the transformational approach to leadership is a necessary but not sufficient condition for authentic school improvement. It lacks a specific orientation towards student learning that is a key feature to this specific approach to school improvement. For this reason the complementary notion of 'instructional leadership' is attractive. Leithwood and his colleagues (1999: 8) define it as an approach to leadership that emphasises 'the behaviours of teachers as they engage in activities directly affecting the growth of students'. Once again the term is subject to conceptual pluralism by the many commentators who are attracted to the notion (see for example Duke, 1987; Geltner and Shelton, 1991; Sheppard, 1996).

The most fully tested approach to instructional leadership is that of Hallinger and his colleagues (see for example Hallinger and Murphy, 1985). They propose a model for instructional leadership that consists of three broad categories:

- defining the school mission
- managing the instructional programme
- promoting school climate.

Hallinger has articulated over 20 more specific functions related to the construct and there is considerable empirical support for this model, particularly in relation to student outcomes (Hallinger, 1992; Sheppard, 1996).

It would seem, therefore, that in terms of a leadership model appropriate for authentic school improvement, a conceptual combination of transformational and instructional orientations would seem most appropriate and practically helpful. Although definitions and studies of transformational and instructional leadership are informative, what is really needed is a leadership model that synthesises existing approaches while providing sufficient scope to capture how leaders encourage and manage school improvement in action.

The 'Moving schools' project (West *et al.*, 1997) was a research study focussing upon five IQEA schools perceived to have made the most substantive and long-lasting improvement journey. They also had school leaders who had grappled with the complexities of leadership for school improvement; who had wrestled with the structural and cultural shifts implicit to the authentic school improvement model, and who engaged with the enquiry processes as a means of studying leadership as well as teaching and learning issues.

What emerged from this research was a set of understandings about a dispersed leadership model that is opportunistic, flexible, responsive and context-specific, rather than prescribed by roles, inflexible, hierarchical and status-driven. It is a model that encourages and provides support for a broadly based instructional leadership approach. In these schools in which sustained school improvement has been maintained, and which have learned from the questioning of fundamental assumptions to which collaborative enquiry gives rise, a new paradigm of leadership seems to have emerged. The thoughts, findings and reflections are structured under the following subheadings (the following discussion is based on Jackson, 2000):

- multi-level leadership built around shared values
- empowerment and active democracy
- collaborative learning as a source of leadership capacity.

Multi-level leadership built around values

In contrast to transformational leadership, the model evolving from our school improvement work offers a far more sustainable conceptualisation of leadership for a profession which, by the nature of the personnel it recruits, has leadership potential widely spread among its members. If this potential is to be realised, then it will need to be grounded in a learning that is rich in the school context itself. This view of leadership, then, is not hierarchical, but federal (Handy, 1990).

As long ago as 1976, Weick portrayed schools as loosely coupled systems. He proposed that schools need to become tight in ways other than visible accountabilities – through consensus on values. It is a view that is both tight and loose; tight on values, but loose on the freedom to act, the opportunity to experiment, and the authority to question historical assumptions. It is this tightness on values, which is the critical precursor to the sort of dispersed leadership required to sustain authentic school improvement.

This theme of values leadership is crucial to the concept of leadership capacity for school improvement. It involves building an evolving consensus around higher order values that will unite and excite members of the school community. It means moving from the lowest common denominator of school aims to the highest common factor of shared values and beliefs. It incorporates being articulate about these beliefs and holding action accountable to them – by those leading at all levels. It follows that leadership for authentic school improvement is not perceived as being inextricably linked to status or experience. It is available to all. In this way, coaching and mentoring are the central leadership qualities, designed to support individuals and, in so doing, to expand leadership capacity. Such a process leads to the evolution of shared understandings about leadership through school development work – as schools research their own practice and generate their own knowledge.

There is now a good deal of evidence from studies around the world that is compatible with this view of a learned leadership capacity, most particularly from the literature in the field of learning organisations (Louis and Leithwood, 1998). Here, leaders are stimulators (who get things started); they are storytellers (to encourage dialogue and add understanding); they are networkers and copers; and problem-scavengers, too (Louis, 1994). They tend to have wider social repertoires than has been customary in hierarchical educational settings, so as to encourage openness and to perpetuate relationships while wrestling with ambiguity. They will be improvisational and comfortable with spontaneity (Joyce *et al.*, 1993). They care deeply, about teachers, about students and about education.

It will be evident, then, that in the most successful IQEA schools leadership is not invested in hierarchical status, but experience is valued and structural characteristics (mixed-aged teams, cross-institutional collaborations, etc.) encourage all actors to be drawn in and regarded for their contribution. Such structural arrangements provide the context within which leadership capacity for authentic school improvement is expanded and leadership characteristics are naturally learned.

Empowerment and active democracy

The concept of multi-level leadership is descriptive of an organisational culture involving collaborative learning. It implies active participation at all levels, which can be termed 'active democracy'. This implies all participants, rather than 'representative democracy'; that is un-elected leaders in hierarchical roles. Such a formulation both requires and provides pervasive staff development systems. Some of the more advanced IQEA schools are evolving such systems located around mutual learning and the opportunity for growth inherent within collaborative processes. The partnership with university staff, and their access to knowledge sources, brings learning drawn from outside the school to support enquiry processes, to expand repertoires and to assist understandings about leadership, the implementation of change and so on. This, in itself, further expands leadership capacity, integrating theory with practice.

Once again, IQEA findings are compatible with those of Louis and Miles (1990), Joyce and Calhoun (1996) and Joyce *et al.* (1999) in that collaborative work has been found to increase the involvement, engagement and affiliation across all staff. Both professional potential and human need are satisfied – as is the moral purpose that can be rendered dormant by the stultifying constraints of traditional hierarchical school structures. Teachers are motivated through seeing their professional skills valued and by being offered opportunities to share with and to lead others; by having their capacities continually expanded, and by feeling that their school is making a difference to the lives of young people.

In a nutshell, top-down direction and institutional hierarchies are antithetical to democracy in action. Multiple partnerships, with variable leadership, offer a more appropriate set of structural norms, and are more likely to impact upon classrooms and student learning. There is also a further powerful leadership capacity emerging in some IQEA schools. As teacher expectancy of students rises, it is not only in the domain of academic achievement, but also about students' capacities to share in the actively democratic process itself – to research their own environments and to become active participants in school improvement.

Collaborative learning as a source of leadership capacity

Learning is a change process. By implication it is transformational, both in human and organisational terms. Transformational learning involves the creation of socially (mutually) constructed interpretations of information and knowledge (data), which either enters the organisation from the outside or is generated from within. If the human learning is shared, collaboratively acquired and commonly understood, then it has much greater potential for organisational improvement – and it makes the leadership of improvement teams much easier, too. This makes sense. In fact, it makes so much sense that it is surprising that schools have not restructured to accommodate collaborative professional learning long before now!

In terms of building leadership capacity, the evolving professional relationships between staff are vital, and it is here where collaborative learning is so significant. There are three interconnecting elements which are crucial: the generation of contextual knowledge (and its associate learning) through enquiry; the utilisation of that knowledge to challenge organisational development dysfunctionalities; and the internal (and external) transfer and utilisation of knowledge as a vehicle for developing leadership capacity.

While this internal development is important for all organisations, it is even more critical for schools. Schools cannot (unlike other organisations) engage in massive personnel and leadership change to effect improvement. Schools that wish constantly to evolve will need to harness their human and social capital that is their richest potential, creating and sharing the leadership opportunities that provide the process capacity to achieve this. Fortunately, schools are uniquely well placed to develop their professional, human and intellectual capital because they recruit adults motivated by learning who also wish to make a difference for young people.

Regrettably, though, many schools are structured in ways that are antithetical to teacher learning and in which collective norms of shared learning are not culturally embedded. It is both ironic and wasteful that the generous creative potential and goodwill of teachers is so often frustrated by patterns of organisation that owe more to control than development. This need not be the case. The school improvement journey can help us to view structure as something that should derive from, rather than determine purposes. And within restructuring the teacher can be nurtured as the most vital and renewable resource.

These three reflections on leadership in IQEA schools have similarities with the analysis of leadership in schools committed to school improvement elsewhere. In concluding this section it is worth comparing in a little more detail the experience of some 44 schools in the USA who were actively engaged in successful restructuring. In these schools Wohlsetter and her colleagues (1994: 24) noted that they:

- Establish many teacher-led decision-making teams (in which many subgroups were formed to work on specific tasks with lots of communication and dialogue).
- Focus on continuous improvement with school-wide training in functional and process skills and in areas related to curriculum and instruction (in which professional development was a very high priority for all, and was deliberately tied to specific school reform objectives and to developing a school-wide capacity for change).

- Create a well-developed system for sharing school-related information with a broad range of constituents (in which many forms of information were collected and shared among the school, the community, and the district).
- Develop ways to reward staff behaviour that helps achieve school objectives (in which work well done is regularly recognised including differentiated staffing, extra compensation for administrative duties, professional development grants and the like).
- Selected principals who can facilitate change (in which, principals 'played a key role in dispersing power, in promoting a school-wide commitment to learning, and in expecting all teachers to participate in the work of the school').

This similarity between improvement efforts in very different contexts is, on reflection, reassuring. How these relationships are sustained in IQEA schools through a specific approach to dispersed leadership, is the focus of the following section.

Dispersed leadership and the role of the 'cadre'

The role of dispersed leadership is crucial to the development of a sustained capacity for school improvement. For reasons that are now well established school improvement needs to affect all *levels* of the school. Specifically, the focus needs to be on the three levels outlined in Figure 7.1, and the ways in which these levels interrelate. The *school level* is to do with overall management and the establishment of policies, particularly with respect to how resources and strategies for staff development can be mobilised to support school improvement efforts. At the level of *working groups* the concern is with the

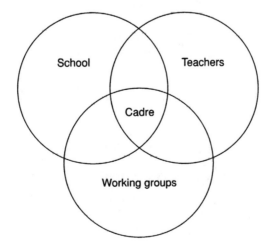

Figure 7.1 Integrating the levels

details of and arrangements for supporting improvement activities. Finally, at the *individual teacher* level the focus is on developing classroom practice.

In schools with high levels of internal capacity, these three levels of activity are mutually supportive. Consequently a specific aim of authentic school improvement is to devise and establish positive conditions at each level and to co-ordinate support across these levels. It is in this connection that a team of co-ordinators is established in each school, whose task includes the integration of activities across the various levels. These co-ordinators are referred to as *the cadre group*, a term borrowed from Schmuck and Runkel's (1985) organisational development cadres in Oregon who fulfilled a similar role in those schools. They are responsible for the day-to-day running of the project in their own schools, and for creating links between the principles and ideas of school improvement and practical action. In many schools members of the cadre establish an *extended cadre group* that serves to extend involvement in the project in a more formal way within the school.

Typically, the cadre group is a cross-hierarchical team which could be as small as three or four to six in comparatively small schools, to between six and ten in large schools. Though one of these is likely to be the headteacher, it is important to establish groups that are genuinely representative of the range of perspectives and ideas available in the school – it should, ideally, then, be cross-hierarchical, cross-institutional, have a mix of ages, experience, gender, length of time at the school, and so on. Cadre group members should also not come together in any already existing group within the school, such as the senior management team or a heads of department group, so that the problem of pooled rationalisations is minimised. The cadre group is responsible for identifying the project focus (through a consensus-building process involving the rest of the staff), and for managing efforts on a day-to-day basis within the school. They are supported through a core training programme, through networking with cadre groups from other schools, and by external consultancy support and facilitation.

In organisational terms the reason a cadre group is required is because of the tensions in schools caused by the conflicting demands of maintenance and development. One of the underpinning characteristics of authentic school improvement is the separation of maintenance activities from development work. Structurally, the formal roles and responsibilities, the committee structures and the decision-making processes of schools have evolved in relation to structural hierarchies designed to support efficiency, stability and functional effectiveness. Put another way, staff are appointed to roles which involve the management of structural units that tend to incorporate a standard set of functions, which often provide perpetual membership of committee structures, all of which relate predominantly to management and maintenance aspects of the school. Schools then tend to overburden this system by asking it also to take on development roles for which it was never designed. As an aside, the same structures create vertical communication systems, but virtually prevent lateral communication or lateral learning. Sadly, different

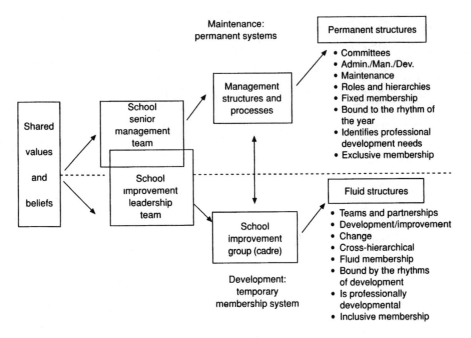

Figure 7.2 Maintenance and development: a model

organisational units within a school rarely exchange practices or learn from one another: in some schools they rarely even talk to one another!

The cadre or school improvement group is essentially a *temporary member-ship system* focussed specifically upon enquiry and development. This tempor-ary membership system brings together teachers (and support staff) from a variety of departments within the school, with a range of ages or experience and from a cross-section of roles to work together in a status-free collabora-tive learning context. The model in Figure 7.2 illustrates this separate (yet integrated) structural construct (from Jackson, 2000). One teacher has described it as the educational equivalent of a research and development group, and the traditional school as analogous to a company in which every-one works on the production line, without any research and development function. The result is stagnation, and that is how schools have been. The establishment of a school improvement group creates the research and devel-opment capacity, while retaining the existing structures required also for organisational stability and efficiency. It also unlocks staff potential often stifled within formal structures, and opens up new collaborations.

It goes without saying that staff at all levels of the school are involved, including newly qualified teachers, support staff and, in an increasing number of schools, students. Each partnership is entirely free of status positions within the more formal organisational structure of the school and offers leadership opportunities to a variety of staff. Some partnerships might be involved with significant whole-school issues (for example, assessment strategies to improve student achievement) while others may be engaged in focussed classroom research activity (questioning technique, or co-operative groupwork). The scale of the intended impact is less significant than the quality of the knowledge deriving from the enquiry. A piece of classroom research, for example, can have equally powerful whole-school impact if the knowledge (about seating arrangements, starts and finishes of lessons – or whatever) is sufficiently significant and widely owned.

Finally, in the same way that the school improvement group is mutually supportive of one another, the school community (the wider staff and the institutional support of senior management and governing body) makes a number of tacit commitments to:

- support each partnership in whatever way possible – time, resources, visits to centres of good practice, the adoption of recommendations, etc.
- agree to remain informed about the progress of each area of enquiry in order to maintain collective ownership of the directions being travelled
- support the implementation of new practices, new structures, or new ways of working
- be open to the research process by contributing ideas, responding to research instruments, opening up classrooms for observation, offering professional support in whatever way required
- engage in workshop activity within full staff meetings, staff days or other school meetings in order to contribute to the on-going knowledge creation and learning process.

This description of cadre group functioning, although based both on our original conceptualisation of the role and the experience in a number of schools, is in many ways ideotypical. Despite best efforts, in many schools, cadre group members seem unsure about how they were selected for this role, and, initially at least, unclear about what will be expected of them. Consequently, there is hesitancy in the beginning that may last weeks or even months. With hindsight, many of those involved report that during this period it is difficult to develop a sense of 'ownership' for the project, difficult to establish relationships with colleagues at the different levels in the school, difficult to resist the 'suggestions' of the headteacher – difficult, in fact, to develop the understandings and the skills to perform their leadership role.

However, they appear to grow in confidence quite quickly, particularly as the school's efforts and resources become focussed around priorities they are addressing. Progress is not uniform – even within cadre groups – and some schools seem able to 'move' to effective operational arrangements much more quickly than others do. It also appears that the stages of development through which cadre groups move can be associated not only with 'typical' behaviours for each stage, but also with the way they view the 'task' (What is school improvement about? What is our role in it?), and the way they conceive 'solutions' (What do we need to improve? How should we go about improving it?). The three phases of this cycle of development are as follows (taken from West, 2000):

Phase 1: Uncertainty about focus
- Cadre feeling its way (What is a cadre?)
- What is school improvement?
- What is the role of the cadre group?
- How can the cadre work best together as a group?
- Initial reliance on established ways of working
- Initial reliance on existing structures
- Initial reliance on key personnel/leaders within the cadre
- Start to collect data and share it
- Uncertainty about the theory
- Where is it all going? It's hard to make things happen.

Phase 2: Clearer about focus
- Using existing structures in new ways, e.g., department meetings with single item research agendas
- New ways of working
- Greater openness within the cadre group, e.g., voice of main scale teacher
- Better at making meaning from data
- Beginning to shift from staff development mode to school improvement mode
- The theory makes sense
- Seeing the connections and learning how to implement.

Phase 3: Change/renewal of the cadre group
- Research and development (R&D) establishing its own rhythm – SDP becomes more organic
- New structures emerge – e.g. for R&D
- New roles emerge:
    - HOD as facilitator of research (R&D research post)
- Establishment of research culture within the school:
    - evidence-based
    - risk taking
- Involvement of students (pupils) as researchers:
    - from data-source to partners in dialogue
- Collection of data, making meaning, and supporting research outcomes
- The school generates its own theory
- The implementation becomes growth.

This 'summary' of how the cadre group evolves is provisional, but it does give a clear indication of how a structure for dispersed leadership that relates both to instructional leadership and authentic school improvement is established. It also illustrates how it evolves over time, gradually expanding its leadership capacity and increasing its understanding about learning – organisational learning, the learning of cadre group members and other teachers and the learning of students. In the following section a brief illustration of this way of working in one IQEA school is provided.

The Sharnbrook school improvement journey

Sharnbrook Upper School and Community College was established as a 13–19 upper school in 1975 to provide comprehensive education for 32 villages situated in rural mid-England. Sharnbrook's school improvement model is now a continuous, whole-school initiative. At its heart is a fluid group (cadre) of staff committed to working in partnerships and together around areas of mutually agreed enquiry. During the ten-year involvement with IQEA there were many different modes of operation for the school improvement group, but certain characteristics remained consistent. Some of these are:

- Two staff operating in a co-leadership model lead the school improvement group.
- The school improvement group breaks down into trios of staff, each engaged in a separate enquiry designed to generate knowledge and understanding about the school's work and to indicate directions for improvement.
- Each of these partnerships undertakes a sustained process of enquiry within the school, drawing also from the knowledge-base within the field and from good practice elsewhere, and, as an outcome of this data-gathering, suggests improvement to the school's practice, supports the implementation of improvements and then enquires further into their effect upon student learning or the wider school community.
- Each partnership tries to ensure that all those who contribute towards their research are involved, too, in the process of making meaning from the data and, where feasible, in the implementation of outcomes.
- Each partnership also commits to connect with the wider constituency of staff, students, parents and governors in order that all who need to do so can share the emergent journey.
- The school facilitates opportunities for each partnership to lock into consultation and decision-making structures, as appropriate, so that findings from the enquiry will be implemented.
- The entire school improvement group commits to monitoring the value of their own work and to critiquing each other's practice.

The 1999/2000 model involved the cadre group working for much of their time as trios, and as usual has a focus specifically upon teaching and learning (see Figure 7.3). Following a workshop with the whole staff, six areas of

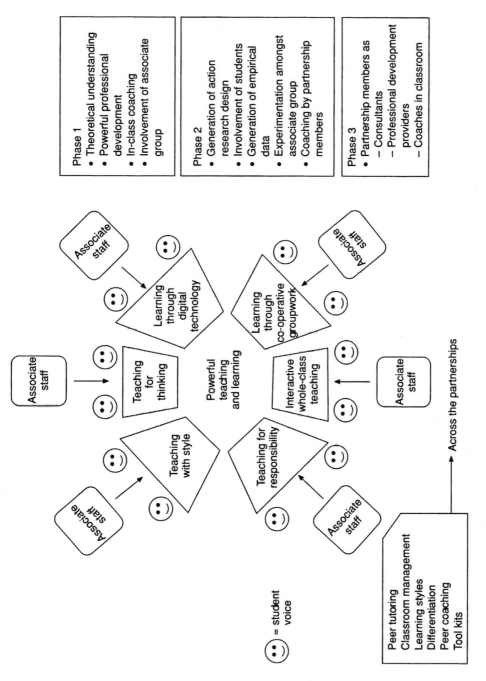

Figure 7.3 Sharnbrook IQEA 1999–2000

Phase 1
- Theoretical understanding
- Powerful professional development
- In-class coaching
- Involvement of associate group

Phase 2
- Generation of action research design
- Involvement of students
- Generation of empirical data
- Experimentation amongst associate group
- Coaching by partnership members

Phase 3
- Partnership members as
  - Consultants
  - Professional development providers
  - Coaches in classroom

Powerful teaching and learning

Learning through digital technology

Learning through co-operative groupwork

Teaching for thinking

Interactive whole-class teaching

Teaching with style

Teaching for responsibility

Associate staff

= student voice

Peer tutoring
Classroom management
Learning styles
Differentiation
Peer coaching
Tool kits

Across the partnerships

classroom practice were identified, and each of the trios adopted one of the areas mandated by the whole staff. The first 'enquiry' task for each of the partnerships was to develop a powerful theoretical understanding of their particular teaching and learning focus – by researching the knowledge-base, observing classrooms, visiting other schools, or whatever. The trio then practised and developed their skills in the classroom, providing in-house coaching for one another. The next phase was to engage in action research with students to seek to validate the impact of this approach upon learning. Throughout this process the remainder of the staff (all staff not involved in one of the partnerships) choose one of the areas, creating associate groups of about 15 staff for each partnership, who followed the course of events, engaged in workshops and generally became immersed and prepared. When the action research process validated the impact of the model, the associate staff adopted the approach in their own classrooms and were coached by the trio engaged in the original work.

This is a huge over-simplification of the approach, but even described at this level it gives indications of the changes in infrastructure and culture that have evolved as a consequence of this approach to school improvement. These include:

- The opening up of classrooms and classroom practice and the legitimisation of in-class coaching.
- The creation of a language to talk about teaching and school improvement.
- The integration of enquiry and professional development approaches.
- The value and authenticity of the student voice and the significance given to the perceptions of students as learners.
- The willingness of all staff to embrace the value of the development work emanating from the school improvement group.
- The ownership by the whole staff of the school improvement approach.
- The power of a sustained school improvement journey to win over those initially sceptical or even cynical.
- The expansion of leadership capacity.

The staff development imperative

As is seen in the previous example, the experience of working with cadre groups suggests that simply belonging to the group can be seen as a major staff development opportunity; the group's work becomes a significant part of the members' overall role in the school. Most cadre group members are busier and spend more time at school than they did. The motivation for the increase in commitment seems to spring from two sources. On one hand, there is often a very real sense of 'making an impact' – actually influencing the quality of learning opportunities in the school, seeing changes, feeling that the school is serving the needs and aspirations of its pupils better. On the other, there is a heightened sense of professionalism. Different kinds of dialogue and discussion take place, more emphasis is placed on pedagogy, more sharing of practice evolves, and a clearer sense of the professional challenges and achievements that teachers address daily develops. In this section, the explicit link between dispersed leadership and staff development, and their contribution to creating a professional learning community in the school is briefly explored.

The range of staff development activities involved in such authentic school improvement approaches is considerable and is likely to include:

- whole staff in-service days on teaching and learning and school improvement planning as well as 'curriculum tours' to share the work done in departments or working groups
- inter-departmental meetings to discuss teaching strategies
- workshops run inside the school on teaching strategies by cadre group members and external support
- partnership teaching and peer coaching
- the design and execution of collaborative enquiry activities, which are, by their nature, knowledge-generating.

In addition, cadre group members are involved in:

- out-of-school training sessions on capacity building and teaching and learning
- the pursuit of their own knowledge in support of their role – about leadership, the management and implementation of change, the design of professional development activities, etc.
- planning meetings in school
- consultancy to school working groups
- observation and in-classroom support
- study visits to other schools within the network.

This is a wide range of staff development activity and represents a fairly sophisticated infrastructure for sustained professional development. It is based on the established ideas of Joyce and Showers (1980, 1995) that were discussed in the previous chapter. A key element in all of this is the provision of in-classroom support or in Joyce and Showers' term 'peer coaching'. It is the facilitation of peer coaching that enables teachers to extend their repertoire of teaching skills and to transfer them from different classroom settings to others.

During the implementation of this approach during our IQEA school improvement projects refinements have been made in the use of peer coaching to support student learning. When the refinements noted below are incorporated into a school improvement design, peer coaching can virtually assure 'transfer of training' for everyone:

- Peer coaching teams of two or three are much more effective than larger groups.

- These groups are more effective when the entire staff is engaged in school improvement.
- Peer coaching works better when headteachers and deputies participate in training and practice.
- The effects are greater when formative study of student learning is embedded in the process.

The argument being made here is that for effective school improvement, forms of dispersed leadership are essential. The cadre group is one way of facilitating this. The links between cadre group working and the constellation of staff development activities just described makes the structural link between their work and enhanced levels of student achievement clear and achievable. The staff development focus has the potential to unite both the emphasis on teaching and learning and capacity building. Coaching in particular is so powerful because it integrates transformational and instructional leadership *and* professional development. In highly effective schools it is this that provides the essential infrastructure for school improvement.

Commentary

The purpose of this chapter has been to establish a view of leadership compatible with authentic school improvement. The two features of school improvement that have been emphasised are the focus on teaching and learning on the one hand, and capacity building on the other. Leadership within the school has therefore to evolve a style that is able to create synergy between these two constructs.

In developing the argument, transformational leadership was discussed, which is the leadership style most commonly associated with school improvement. Although transformational styles have a range of advantages, they are necessary, rather than sufficient, for the purposes of authentic school improvement. A focus on instructional leadership is necessary, given the importance of teaching and learning and dispersed leadership, and given the capacity building focus. The importance of staff development is as an activity that links together the teaching and learning and capacity building foci. Although the examples in this chapter have of necessity been drawn from IQEA, they have been presented as examples of leadership more generally, rather than as examples of a specific project.

Elsewhere, we have set out nine propositions which, when taken together, seem to encapsulate some of the key themes of this chapter (West *et al.*, 2000). They are:

Proposition 1

The focus for leadership in actively improving schools is the creation and expansion of improvement capacity – a complex blend of structural and cultural development combined with an evolving contextual and theoretical knowledge-base. Such capacity change – culture, structure and knowledge – supports continuous organisational and professional renewal.

Proposition 2

Schools seeking to develop dispersed leadership models will move from the lowest common denominator of shared aims to the highest common factor of shared values and beliefs.

Proposition 3

Leadership in actively improving schools will challenge the system pathologies, organisational dysfunctionalities and other barriers to school development that have historically inhibited school improvement work.

Proposition 4

In actively improving schools, the focus is less upon the characteristics of 'the leader' than upon creating shared contexts for adult learning about leadership. School leaders develop leadership capacity.

Proposition 5

School leaders in continuously developing schools give away leadership and coach others to be successful.

Proposition 6

Actively improving schools will have reconceptualised the nature and delivery systems for adult professional learning – both as a vehicle for pedagogic learning and as a means of generating leadership density.

Proposition 7

Leadership in continuously improving schools not only expands, but changes over time. Leadership repertoires and styles will evolve as the school's own cycle of development evolves.

Proposition 8

Post-transformational leadership operates significantly in the domains of induction and coaching, cultural transmission and values articulation.

Proposition 9

In schools with a highly developed improvement capacity, not only do staff at a variety of levels take on leadership and cultural transmission roles, but so do students. Students as a significant voice and as co-leaders of school improvement, are of course the prime focus of school improvement work.

In summary, the behaviours that leaders in school improvement settings need to display are:

- An ability to articulate values and vision around student learning and achievement, and to make the connections to principles and behaviours and the necessary structures to promote and sustain them.
- An understanding of a range of pedagogic approaches and their ability to impact on student achievement and learning.
- An ability to distinguish between development and maintenance structures, activities and cultures.
- A strategic orientation, the ability to plan at least into the medium term, and an entrepreneurial bent that facilitates the exploitation of external change.
- An understanding of the nature of organisational capacity, its role in sustaining change, and how to enhance it.
- A commitment to promoting enquiry, particularly into the 'how' rather than the 'what'.
- A similar commitment to continuing professional development and the managing of the teacher's 'life cycle'.
- An ability to engender trust and provide positive reinforcement.

The benign paradox of leadership for school improvement is that the style of leadership described in this chapter is necessary to create and develop ownership around such an approach to staff development, but it is also a mode of leadership that is sustained by such an infrastructure. In the following chapter a series of examples are given of schools that aspire to this way of working.

8   Patterns of development and the process of cultural change

The purpose of the preceding chapters has been to build the argument for 'school improvement for real'. As a consequence, in describing the various elements of the approach, the discussion has tended to be analytic and taxonomic rather than holistic. In this chapter it is important to give a flavour of the authentic school improvement experience in a small number of schools. The case studies in this chapter are intended to provide examples of 'whole school' settings where the approaches to learning, teaching and assessment described in the previous chapters are occurring. In these schools all improvement and development efforts are focussed on learning and teaching. Clear goals or targets for student learning are set, and teaching strategies based on research and good practice, are being utilised. Conditions are also being created in these schools where teachers have time to talk to each other about teaching and to work together towards improving it. These are schools where the quick fix response to target setting has been eschewed in favour of a more reflective and iterative approach to change that unswervingly focusses on the learning of students. These schools are becoming more effective over time because they are progressively adapting their organisations and classroom practices to support student learning and teacher development.

Each of the schools described in this chapter has unambiguously placed teaching and learning at the forefront of their agenda. It is surprising that it is not at the forefront of every school's agenda! In order to underscore this point it is instructive to refer again to the 'Improving schools' research project (Gray *et al.*, 1999). There are striking similarities between the description of 'rapidly improving' schools in that project, and the cameos presented in this chapter, that reinforce the importance of placing teaching and learning at the very centre of all school improvement efforts.

The classroom level provided the explicit focus for development work in the 'rapidly improving' schools. What was striking in these schools, and clearly differentiated them from the more 'slowly improving' schools, was that they were seriously interested in student learning and classroom practice. They were focussed on the 'learning level'. The clear focus throughout the school on student learning was complemented by an explicit use of the subject department, or equivalent, as the mode of delivery. In most cases, the

focus on classrooms began incrementally. It was first seen as an encouragement for teachers to talk about teaching. It was as if teachers had to be
enfranchised to discuss pedagogy with other colleagues. This talk then served
as a basis for some form of experimentation with different aspects of classroom practice. Teachers were actively encouraged to 'tinker' with their teaching to use Michael Huberman's felicitous expression (Huberman, 1992b). It
was then that achievement scores began to rise.

What was interesting about 'the rapidly improving schools', and the schools
described in this chapter, is the extent to which they display a willingness to go
beyond merely incremental approaches to change and engage in some form of
organisational restructuring to support student learning. They are specific
about how they wish to improve pupils' learning, about how to draw on
colleagues' experiences to formulate strategies, and have found ways of helping colleagues evaluate and learn from their own and other teachers' classroom experiences. The other significant point is that innovations in teaching
are conducted within a curriculum context. As will be clearly seen in the cameos,
the inductive and group work strategies, the meta-cognitive cues and meaning-
making activities, are all well embedded within a curriculum framework. In-
corporating instructional cues and strategies within schemes of work enables
consistency to be more easily ensured across the school, and allows students to
engage more directly with the learning aspect of the teaching strategy.

In their quest for higher performance all of these schools show a willingness to engage with a wide range of potential sources of advice. They encourage their staffs to pursue their own professional development, by providing
in-house opportunities for development and support, seeking out help from
their LEAs, as well as finding ways for higher education to support their
school improvement efforts.

The examples of 'real' school improvement programmes reviewed in this
chapter reflect many of the characteristics of effective school improvement
initiatives as described by other commentators (Joyce *et al.*, 1993: 72). This is
in so far as they:

- focus on specific outcomes which can be related to student learning,
  rather than succumbing to external pressure to identify non-specific goals
  such as 'improve exam results'
- draw on theory, research into practice, and the teachers' own experiences
  in formulating strategies, so that the rationale for the required changes is
  established in the minds of those expected to bring them about
- recognise the importance of staff development, since it is unlikely that
  developments in student learning will occur without emphasising the
  instructional behaviour of teachers
- provide for monitoring the impact of policy and strategy on teacher
  practice and student learning early and regularly, rather than rely on
  'post-hoc' evaluations
- pay careful attention to the consistency of implementation.

In the first section of the chapter four brief examples of schools will be presented. At best, they will only be vignettes or cameos, fuller accounts demand another and different book, but at least they provide a glimpse into the day-to-day reality of school improvement. In the second section of the chapter four of the more common patterns of development and examples of cultural change associated with authentic school improvement and reflected in the cameos will be discussed. The school contexts described are:

- 'Success For All' in the Meadows family of schools, Nottingham
- 'Just Read' in Hempshill Hall School, Bulwell, Nottingham
- establishing a 'language for teaching' in Swanwick Hall School, Derbyshire
- building a focus on teaching and learning in Big Wood School, Nottingham.

The SFA pilot in Nottingham

The 'new' Nottingham City LEA with its challenging literacy targets was ideally suited to piloting 'Success For All' in the UK. The challenges facing the Nottingham City schools in terms of raising literacy levels are considerable. The government set, and the LEA accepted, a target of 72 per cent of Year (Grade) 6 students reading at Level 4 Key Stage 2 by the year 2002, as compared with 36 per cent in 1996. The initial pilot was based in the Meadows family of schools.

The components of 'Success For All' implemented in Nottingham involved a regular 90-minute reading period, reading tutors (in the Nottingham SFA Pilot, the Boots company provided some 200 tutors to support this aspect of the programme), eight weeks assessments of students' progress, a pre-school and reception programme, a programme facilitator in each school, as well as teacher and in-service training.

Here are some glimpses of a typical 90-minute 'Roots' lesson:

It's 10.30 am and the children are moving from their normal classroom into their SFA base where they will be taught for the next 90 minutes as part of an ability matched group. In this particular group there are 24 children drawn from Years 1, 2 and 3. The children immediately take their reading books and sit on the floor ready to begin.

The lesson begins with 'STaR' (Story Tell and Retell). A new book is introduced today. The teacher begins by drawing the children's attention to the front cover. Having shared the title, author and illustrator with the children she asks them to think for a moment and consider what the story may be about. After a few seconds she asks them to share their ideas with their partner, only then does she ask the children to put up their hands. She does not however ask the children for their own ideas, but rather asks them to tell her about their partner's prediction. The children are then shown key pictures in the story and are asked to revise their predictions again using the 'Think/Pair/Share' strategy.

After this the children move to their seats with their partner. Before they record their predictions in writing they first orally draft what they are going to write with the active support of their partner. Once the predictions have been written the children once again turn to their partners and read their predictions aloud. Together they practice the 'monitoring for meaning' strategies. The main questions they ask each other today are: 'Does my writing make sense?' 'Do I understand what I have just read?' The children revise their writing in light of the discussion.

After 20 minutes it is time to move on to the 'Reading Roots' lesson itself. They return to the carpet for 'Showtime'. They adopt the partner reading position (ear-to-ear, facing in different directions) and re-read a familiar story chosen from their guided reading books. Before beginning the children scan the text to remind themselves of the details of the story and to identify those words they need help with. By re-reading familiar texts the children master the flow and phrasing of reading necessary to comprehend what is being read. 'Showtime' also involves letter formation review. The children use two different strategies for learning to read these words. For the phonetically regular words they use 'Stretch and Read'. For the sight vocabulary they use a repetition procedure known as 'Say–Spell–Say'. The children rapidly run through the reading of these familiar words.

Now 25 minutes into the lesson, the teacher introduces a new group story. As she picks up her big book version, she glances quickly at the teacher's script in her Level 1 Handbook to remind herself of the suggested introduction and then distributes the children's books so that they have one each. The children then preview the book in the same way as they previewed the 'STaR' story, the teacher asks some background questions, and then reads the story. She reads slowly and with expression, stopping at the end of every page to ask the predictive questions provided and encouraging the children to use evidence from the text to support their predictions. At the end, she asks the children to reflect on the main ideas in the story. She then tells them that they are going to learn all the letters and words they will need to know in order to read the story by themselves.

This session continues for ten minutes. It includes regular work on using context and grammar to decode unfamiliar words and also an activity called 'Quick Erase' where children change one letter of a word at a time to create new words. The teacher then reviews the previewing strategy. She reads the introductory script and the story again and then says, 'Right, children, I think you're ready to have a try yourselves.'

The children turn again into the partner reading positions. They take it in turns, reading a page each of their new book. The partner acts as a support with difficult words and as a constant reminder to each other to *use the monitoring for meaning strategies* they have been taught. The children use the partner strategies to help them with their next tasks, story comprehension and sentence reading, and 'story related writing', having planned their writing carefully with their partner. Then the children review their spelling, using cards with the letter sounds they need and are encouraged to *stretch and spell* the words orally.

Sixty-five minutes after the lesson started it is time for celebration. Today it's Joseph's turn to read a story to the rest of the class. He is a little nervous but the rest of the children offer encouraging comments and his voice grows stronger as time goes on. There is a spontaneous round of applause as he finishes. The teacher invites the children to make positive comments about Joseph's reading.

The final 20 minutes of the lesson are focussed on aural language development, developing concepts and logical thinking, and to increase children's background knowledge about the world around them through using the Peabody Language Development kit.

At the end of the lesson, the children leave the classroom armed with their new stories, their share sheets and their story related writing.

These are some reflections on the first two terms' experience of SFA:

- *Headteacher's view* In reality I felt we were all ready for this. The children were not achieving and we were ready to rethink our whole strategy. I think the staff recognised that what they were doing wasn't fully working. It appeared very structured and prescriptive, but it was good to find something that was research-led, rather than relying on individual teacher intuition reflecting a school-devised policy. I knew that teachers, to a greater and lesser degree, would find giving up established methods of working difficult, but hoped they would see it as the chance to take a long hard look at reading in a new way. Now that we are seeing such positive results in the children's reading, the teachers are beginning to relax. We were particularly pleased to see such a good fit between SFA and the NLS.
- *Facilitator's view* All the children have made progress. The most able have made outstanding progress, irrespective of age, and some slow starters have really taken off. During SFA the school is calm and quiet and there are no behaviour problems. There has been a substantial increase in the children's self-confidence. The co-operative learning skills have been a real bonus and are helping children to relate to each other more effectively.
- *Teacher's view* I was quite concerned initially, but we had worked hard on reading in the past without getting very good results and were willing to give anything a go. We all had our own ways of teaching reading and it was a wrench to relinquish those. My group is now hitting the targets in reading that I would want for them at this stage of Year 2. They are matching national expectations where they had not done in the past. This is happening in spelling also. The children are starting to transfer the skills and styles of learning used in SFA to other lessons.

Hempshill Hall School, Nottingham, and 'Just Read'

Hempshill Hall Primary School, Nottingham, serves about 350 children from the working-class community of Bulwell. About 30 per cent of the children in the school receive 'free' lunches. The school has a headteacher and ten full-time teaching staff. There are four paid teaching assistants. In addition, there are five assistants-in-training under a programme developed by the head-teacher. In addition, there are usually a half-dozen student teachers working in some capacity in the school. Perhaps most important, 60 parent volunteers work in the school each week for about a half-day to two days each.

Marcia Puckey, the headteacher, has worked with the staff and parents to develop a thoroughgoing process for building a collaborative, energetic social system. One in which school staff, parents, and students share responsibility for excellence in academic, social, and personal development of the children. From the letter to parents: 'We are all equal partners at Hempshill Hall. We welcome parents who want to be fully involved in school life.'

The curriculum is academically rich and integrative. School subjects are divided into units that are approached as experiential and reading/writing enquiries. The curriculum is naturally, rather than artificially, integrated; i.e., it is organised around related concepts, not around topics. The curriculum is, still however, 'based on the programmes of study in the National Curriculum Core Subjects of Mathematics, Science, English, and Technology' (from the letter to parents).

A general enquiry model dominates teaching and learning. All teachers and all students follow a scheme where material to be mastered and problems to be solved are presented, and students, organised into groups, tackle the material and problems. Thus, collaborative enquiry is the hallmark of the process, but individual students have responsibility for many strands of learning, and individual differences in achievement are closely monitored. The school as a whole is the educative unit. In this, the school is very different from the typical setting, where schools assign students to classes in which teachers, working as individuals in miniature schools, progress through the curriculum. At Hempshill Hall, everybody is responsible for all the students, working towards common goals and using common strategies.

Every effort is made to help the students feel that they are capable and that each is responsible for the learning of all. From the letter to parents: 'We provide a warm, caring, "family style" environment where your child can feel valued, living in harmony with friends – a real extended family unit.' Within the context of the curriculum units, the students and teachers work together to plan specific activities. In a real sense, learning to co-operate, learning to live democratically, and learning to collaborate as enquirers – as scholars – fit together in a comfortable whole.

The operation of the school is relevant to contemporary discussions about 'whole class' and 'co-operative group' activity. In a very real sense, the entirety of Hempshill Hall Primary is a 'class' whose members co-operate as a whole and within which co-operative groups work within a common framework to pursue excellence. Personal, social, and academic growth are perceived to be part of a whole. From the letter to parents: 'Hempshill Hall School has a mission – that all our children shall be happy, live in harmony, and achieve success.'

Classes are not isolated educational settings. The classes operate as units where several teachers work together to plan and carry out their project plans and day-to-day enquiries. The familiar image of 'chalk-and-talk' and 'drill' is absent. Goals are made clear and the whole class is driving at common substantive objectives. On a day-to-day basis, the students work from three-quarters to nine-tenths of the time in collaborative groups and as individuals to master those goals and develop their capacity as learners.

Everything is taught as the achievement of literacy. Reading is taught through real books. Every child in the school is provided with a red vinyl briefcase, called a 'reading wallet', which they carry between home and school. The wallet contains real books and student work. Parents are encouraged to provide time for their child to read the books at home and are helped in learning how to support their child's reading.

An important communication document in each reading wallet is a 'comment book', a notebook in which teachers and parents write back and forth to each other on a weekly basis. If either makes a comment, the other responds. The comments discuss aspects of the students' academic and social progress and ways of helping them move forward.

To get the flavour of the interaction, let's look at the comments between the parents and teacher of a five-year-old student.

September 4 (first day of school)
Teacher: 'Jessica has chosen some books to share with you, *The Greatest Show on Earth*, *Brown Bear* and *Not Now, Bernard*. She could just concentrate on one or read them all equally. She can keep these as long as she wants – I will probably next share them with her next Monday.' (This last is a reference to the twice-weekly conference with individual students about books they are reading.)

September 4
Father: 'I read *The Greatest Show* with Jessica and her brothers, Jeroen and Dylan. We discussed the story and tried to find out what was happening from the pictures. Jessica enjoyed the story and understood all the pictures.'

September 5
Mother: 'Jessica read Dylan and me the *Brown Bear* book without much help. She also read Jeroen's book *The Red Fox*.'

Over time, the interchange becomes relatively dense as parents and teachers try to talk to one another over the common objective – helping the child become a successful reader. The teachers feel that the interchanges help extend the influence of the school into reading/writing activities in the home. The parents feel that the process keeps them in close touch with the student/teacher/parent triad that makes education work.

Reading and writing are pervasive activities at Hempshill Hall. So much so, that when the headteacher heard about an American approach to supporting reading throughout the school community, she adopted it enthusiastically. The 'Just Read' programme is designed to increase the number of books read by students in and outside of school (Joyce and Calhoun, 1996: chapter 4). The research on 'Just Read' suggests that community involvement in encouraging students to read has multiple benefits. This ranges from increased ability in literacy on the part of students, through an enhanced involvement in schooling on the part of parents, to an increasing commitment to education from the community (Joyce and Calhoun, 1998: 154–70).

In Hempshill Hall Primary School the results were similarly encouraging. The number of books read by students each week almost doubled following the first two months of implementation, and remained consistent at that level thereafter. The total number of books read by students in the school increased from a total of 1,093 in March 1998, to 48,882 in December 1998, to 89,370 in July 1999, and 112,320 and 148,177 in January and July 2000 respectively – a remarkable increase by any standard. More recently, the 'Just Read' programme is being used by the school not simply to increase the number of books read, but also in consultation with parents to set individual targets for students and to help focus their reading in order to enhance mastery and enjoyment.

The commitment to creating the school as an educational centre for the community and as a positive social and learning environment for students has been widely recognised. The school is one of 50 outstanding primary schools participating in a national school-based teacher training programme, it was formally identified by OFSTED as an excellent school in 1995. In addition, an analysis of test scores for the past three years at ages of 7 and 11 illustrates a consistent upward trend in the key curriculum areas at a level of at least 10 per cent above national averages.

In the school's most recent OFSTED inspection (November 1999), the inspectors described Hempshill Hall as a 'very good, highly effective school' with only 'minor weaknesses'. The school does 'better than average when compared with similar schools', levels of attainment are increasing, and teaching is satisfactory or better in over 90 per cent of lessons. The summary of the inspection points to: outstanding leadership; excellent pupil behaviour, attitudes and work; and high quality teaching in all parts of the school. These judgements endorse the commitment of the headteacher and staff to creating a social system of the entire school – including parents and the community – that encourages students to excel academically, socially and emotionally.

Swanwick Hall School, Derbyshire

Swanwick Hall School is an 11–18 comprehensive school in eastern Derbyshire with a fully comprehensive intake but a skew to the less able. The school joined the East Midlands IQEA partnership three years ago because many of the 'school improvement measures' used in school prior to that time were not classroom based. The emphasis on teaching and learning since has meant:

- a better deal for pupils in terms of interest and variety, which caters for a greater range of learning styles
- most staff development time has been concentrated on teaching and learning which pleased virtually all staff
- the impetus for change belongs to a volunteer group of staff ranging across departments and experience (it includes the headteacher and several NQTs this year) working collaboratively with the heads of faculty group. This means that the staff does not feel driven by senior management or external pressures as much as they did previously.

After extensive discussion, the IQEA group decided that all staff should concentrate on the 'inductive' model of teaching for the first year of development. The main reasons for this decision were:

- The model is applicable to all departments.
- No one understood it previously so all staff were learning together and sharing ideas across departments.
- The different phases cater for different styles of teaching, including individual and group work, so there is variety in the lessons.
- The six phases make it quite a complex model, which requires understanding, so the staff had something to talk about. Comments like 'Phases 1–4 are fine but then I struggle with phases 5 and 6. Any ideas?' were often heard in the staffroom.
- The latter phases involve higher order thinking skills, which were underdeveloped in school.
- Though the data for inductive teaching often requires considerable time in planning, it can be used from year to year, once it exists. This meant that building the teaching model into schemes of work was not too difficult.

Once the volunteer group had practised the model and videoed themselves, they were ready to organise a whole school in-service day with time to learn about the model and then prepare work for inductive teaching in departments. Volunteer staff, who had never done any INSET work before, talked to the staff during the day. This produced a much more powerful message than an expert from outside school.

Over the next 12 months a variety of ways were found to share ideas on inductive teaching:

- More half-INSET days to report back on progress and develop more data sets for new lessons.
- Lots of co-planning and co-teaching while the volunteer IQEA group covered colleagues' lessons.
- Sharing ideas via videos.
- After every staff development session, each department completed a questionnaire for the IQEA group who published a 'State of inductive teaching' report for staff.
- Lists were produced of topics taught inductively, with lists of the year groups involved. These ranged from Year 7 to Year 13 with no obvious bias to any particular key stage.
- Heads of faculty meetings were used as a way of sharing ideas and problems e.g., how to include reluctant staff, building the model into schemes of work.
- Pupils were questioned about their perceptions and the results were published.
- During the in-service day 12 months later a curriculum tour was organised. All departments put on a 20-minute workshop on topics they had taught inductively. This again proved to be a highly successful staff development session.

The IQEA group accepted some flexibility during the year. The languages department, for example, decided that many of their Key Stage 3 pupils needed more vocabulary in order to maximise the advantages of inductive teaching. They made a decision to start with mnemonics, a memory model of teaching, prior to moving into using the inductive approach. This worked very well for them. One or two departments were slower to start than others for internal reasons but, on the whole, staff felt that inductive teaching was an ideal way to start school improvement at Swanwick Hall.

The pattern for the second year of IQEA was very similar to the first. It was decided to focus on co-operative group work and mnemonics in the second year, while remembering that it was still important to check that inductive teaching was well embedded into schemes of work. Virtually all departments engaged in co-operative group work, especially pairs/fours, jigsaw techniques and numbered heads. Pupils quickly got used to sitting where the teacher decided, so that it was far easier to organise group work than previously. Some very committed staff moved pupils round so often that they now always ask, 'Where do you want us to sit today?' as they enter the room. Staff worked hard to establish co-operative learning standards, with an ethos of acceptance of all contributions.

Mnemonics was the other new model of learning for the second year. It was quicker to learn than inductive teaching and co-operative group work. It was used extensively in the Languages and Science (and other) departments. Sometimes the pupils were better than the staff at producing mnemonics!

The third year of IQEA was more open-ended. More departments felt self-confident in developing their own variety in teaching and learning. Several departments used synectics, and concept attainment worked well in 'content heavy' courses. The maths department improved its approach to investigations in maths. The languages department was heavily involved in preferred learning styles with techniques for ensuring there is more kinaesthetic learning. Some of the science department began using accelerated learning techniques.

As the focus on teaching and learning continued, the cadre group:

- developed the use of some of the newer models across more staff
- linked work on behaviour for learning more specifically with other IQEA initiatives
- used the guidelines for co-operative learning across the school
- collected more data from staff and pupils about progress and perceptions.

Big Wood School, Nottingham

Situated on the northern boundary of the city, Big Wood School serves an area described as 'one of serious social need'. Eight years ago Big Wood faced possible closure. Demographic trends coupled with a poor image in the community meant that the school had been steadily losing pupils and staff for several years. In January 1993 a new headteacher was appointed with a brief to arrest the decline.

A rapid period of research – interviews with staff, questionnaires to pupils/parents/local community, and meetings with feeder school staff – produced a picture of a school that was seen as caring but which lacked rigour. Three clear aims were quickly established:

- to improve the school's image in the community
- to develop the links with the feeder schools
- to tackle the underachievement culture.

The threat of possible closure, replaced after the first twelve months with the 'threat' of an OFSTED inspection, proved to be powerful factors in focussing people's minds. A new staffing structure, clear policies, new uniform, well-structured Code of Conduct, mentoring programmes all began to show positive effects. Pupil numbers began to rise, examination results improved and the 'what-can-you-expect of . . .' culture was being successfully challenged. The OFSTED report was, in the main, positive, but the quality of teaching and learning emerged as a major issue.

A start had been made. The school had begun to develop the capacity to accept change. However, the initiatives outlined above were, in many ways, only peripheral. It was recognised that for lasting improvement the school needed to bring about more sustainable change focussed on the classroom.

At the critical moment the school learned of the IQEA project. The project's emphasis on teaching and learning at the heart of sustained improvement was felt to be in total accord with where Big Wood was in its particular stage of development.

This approach to school improvement called for, among other things, the establishment of a cadre group to act as the initial change agents. The first cadre group consisted of the headteacher and seven volunteers – a deputy headteacher, two heads of department and four MPG teachers. Interestingly, and purely by chance, all areas of the curriculum except one were represented. During this time, several members of the cadre attended a summer school on models of teaching run by the university and soon realised that the inductive model offered a possible way to address the issues facing the school. It seemed an ideal place to start, partially because it was a new approach, and therefore offered exciting possibilities, and also because it was applicable across the whole curriculum.

For the cadre group, the first stage was to learn more about the model, to practise it and to observe each other. Lessons were then videoed and, when they felt ready, a day's INSET session was prepared for the whole staff. The model was explored inductively, videos shown and opportunities created for staff to begin to practise using the model in a safe environment, i.e., with other groups of staff.

In order to encourage other people to adopt this approach, staff were clustered into small groups with a member of the cadre attached to each one to provide support and guidance. Opportunities were created for people to observe each other and some notable successes were recorded, when, for example, a member of staff, known more for his competence than his charisma, found himself surrounded by a group of eager pupils at the end of an inductive lesson wanting to continue with their work. As well as working with their support groups, staff also worked within their departments, reviewing schemes of work to see where the inductive approach might be used to greatest effect and planning lessons accordingly.

By the end of the first year the whole process was reviewed and several clear 'messages' emerged.

- Time was an issue:
    - the importance of creating a regular time for the cadre group to meet
    - the need for time for staff to learn new models, to prepare new materials, to observe each other and visit other schools to observe good practice
    - the fact that interviews/questionnaires all required time.
- The power of the pupil voice. A 14-year-old pupil's calm statement on video that, 'copying is a waste of time because the words go from the board down your pen and onto the paper without going anywhere near your brain' is a more arresting message that any amount of exhortation and analysis from the headteacher on ineffective methodologies.

- In the same way, showing in-house videos and persuading a particular member of staff, not normally seen as the most inventive of teachers, to demonstrate effective approaches, had a powerful impact especially on the dissenting few.
- The value of residentials and other twilight sessions in helping to develop a real group ethos among the members of the cadre.
- The difficulty of maintaining momentum. It was not always easy to find regular development time.

In the second year a more structured model was developed. Creating more time required a radical rethinking of the way time was currently used in the school. The problem was resolved in the following ways:

- The existing meeting structure was reviewed, and staff meetings, for example, were replaced by staff development time, and alternative methods were used to disseminate information. All remaining meetings, such as departmental meetings, were to devote 50 per cent of the time to development issues relating to teaching and learning.
- Staff were encouraged to 'bank' some non-contact time by covering other colleagues. This time was then pooled so that all staff, either as individuals or departments, were given half-day slots for development.
- Members of the senior management team were to provide a percentage of the cover time each fortnight, which could be booked by staff.
- Adults other than teachers were to be used to supervise exams and thus free departments.

The careful positioning of INSET, twilight and staff development meant that staff were now meeting approximately every four weeks to look at development issues focussed on teaching and learning. It was also agreed, following consultation with the staff, to broaden the range of activities.

It was during the second year that the real benefits of this approach to school improvement became apparent. Working in pairs and triads, the cadre used the expertise of university and LEA staff plus their own reading and research to develop their expertise in areas as diverse as the major components of a well-structured lesson, co-operative group work, whole class teaching, formative assessment, creating the learning classroom. The aim was to encourage staff to develop at their own pace, while providing the necessary expertise and support within a climate that encouraged risk taking.

As the school was preparing to enter its third year of the IQEA project the inevitable brown envelope arrived and, while not totally subsuming everything else, it would be fair to say that the prospect of an imminent OFSTED inspection led to a period of consolidation rather than breaking new ground.

The inspection results were better than the headteacher and staff had hoped for. In a term with four NQTs having had very little time to settle in and when two members of staff were off with long-term illness and being covered by supply staff, OFSTED deemed that, 'teaching is a strength of the school': 97 per cent of lessons were judged satisfactory or better, 64 per cent were good or better and 28 per cent were very good or excellent. This was in sharp contrast with the picture four years earlier when only 75 per cent of lessons were judged satisfactory and less than 30 per cent were good or better.

As compared with three years ago, Big Wood School is now moving forward from a position where:

- teaching and learning is acknowledged by all as fundamental and is at the heart of the development agenda
- classrooms are more open and people are more willing to observe and be observed
- staff are developing a language to talk about teaching and learning
- people feel part of the development process; they are involved in making it happen, not just the unwilling recipients.

Obviously this is just part of a wider picture, but in working to improve education for all, the following comment from OFSTED encapsulates everything the headteacher and staff have been working towards: 'The school is successfully challenging the non-achievement culture, noted in the previous OFSTED Report, through its major focus on raising the quality of teaching. This is having a major impact on pupils' attainment and progress.'

Patterns of development

The purpose of including these cameos has been to give a flavour of 'real' school improvement efforts, to provide a feel for the process of change. The criteria for inclusion were simply that they provided examples of some of the schools that we work with on a variety of school improvement programmes. The claim is not being made that they are particularly challenging or exemplary schools. It should be noted however that each of the schools are well prized by parents, are regarded locally as 'good' schools, and have increased their examination and test scores year-on-year over the past five years. They have all also received excellent OFSTED reports on both of the occasions that they have been inspected, with the second report being better than the first. Apart from giving a range of examples, one other criterion was used to select them. It is that taken together, they reflect some of the major themes in authentic school improvement that illustrate different patterns of development and cultural change. These are the themes that are discussed below:

- the learning focus
- balancing 'capacity building' and 'teaching and learning'
- the phases of school improvement
- the process of cultural change.

The learning focus

The phrase 'learning focus' refers to two aspects of the work of the schools reflected in the cameos as well as a prime characteristic of all authentic school improvement programmes. The first is the focus on the learning and achievement of the students in the school. The success of the schools in achieving this aim is evident even from the brief accounts given earlier. The second focus is less tangible, but equally important. It is how the learning focus is sustained over time and embedded in the way in which the school carries out its day-to-day work. Glimpses of this have been seen in each of the cameos; in this section of the chapter the issue is addressed more analytically.

Figure 8.1 contains an illustration of the activities that contribute to a capacity for learning within a school. It represents an attempt to capture how schools such as the ones described earlier, establish the 'learning focus' and how a number of the elements of authentic school improvement come together in practice. It begins from two assumptions. The first is that all students have a potential for learning that is not fully exploited. The second is that the students' learning capability refers to their ability to access that potential through increasing their range of learning skills. The arguments supporting these assumptions have been made in earlier chapters, particularly in the discussions on teaching and learning. Given these assumptions, the goal of authentic school improvement is to realise as much of that potential as possible.

The experience of the schools in the cameos, is that this potential is best realised, and learning capability enhanced, through the range of teaching and learning models that the teacher uses with her students. It is the deliberate use of a range of teaching and learning strategies that are rich in meta-cognitive content that is one of the clearest features of the cameos. But as has already

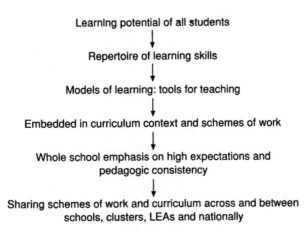

Figure 8.1 Models of learning: tools for teaching

been stressed, the teaching and learning strategies are not 'free-floating', but embedded in the schemes of work and curriculum content that teachers use to structure the learning in their lessons. These schemes of work also have the potential to be shared between schools and be available for wider dissemination.

Finally, this way of working assumes a whole school dimension through the staff development infrastructure the school has established, the emphasis on high expectations, and the careful attention to consistency of teaching and the discussion of pedagogy that pervades the cultures of these schools.

There is an interesting parallel here with the experience of school improvement in Japan, reported in the *Teaching Gap* (Stigler and Hiebert, 1999). Much was made in that study of the professional development activities of the Japanese teachers who adopted a 'problem solving' orientation to their teaching. According to Stigler and Hiebert, the dominant form of in-service training is the lesson study. In lesson study, groups of teachers meet regularly over long periods of time (ranging from several months to a year) to work on the design, implementation, testing, and improvement of one or several 'research lessons'. By all indications, report Stigler and Hiebert (1999: 110), lesson study is extremely popular and highly valued by Japanese teachers, especially at the elementary school level. It is the linchpin of the improvement process.

Stigler and Hiebert (1999: 111), maintain that the premise behind lesson study is simple:

> If you want to improve teaching, the most effective place to do so is in the context of a classroom lesson. If you start with lessons, the problem of how to apply research findings in the classroom disappears. The improvements are devised within the classroom in the first place. The challenge now becomes that of identifying the kinds of changes that will improve student learning in the classroom and, once the changes are identified, of sharing this knowledge with other teachers who face similar problems, or share similar goals, in the classroom.

It is the focus on improving instruction within the context of the curriculum, using a methodology of collaborative enquiry into student learning that provides the similarity of experience with the English schools reported in the cameos. The broader argument is that it is this form of professional development, rather than short courses, and one-off lectures and workshops that provide the basis for the problem solving approach to teaching adopted by Japanese teachers. The further implication is that it is this form of teaching that explains the higher levels of performance of Japanese students.

The learning focus is the key to authentic school improvement. It is the ability to focus on enhancing student learning, while building the capacity for sustaining learning throughout the school that, as is seen in the following section, provides the crucial strategic challenge.

Balancing 'capacity building' and 'teaching and learning'

Establishing the appropriate balance between 'capacity building' and 'teaching and learning' is essential if authentic school improvement is to be realised. Without the former, changes in classroom practice will not become school wide or be sustained into the medium term; without the latter, there will be little significant impact on student achievement and learning. Unfortunately many school improvement initiatives have focussed on either one or the other. Each of the cameos in the earlier part of the chapter found ways to balance the two. They also exhibited the ability to progress on these two levels at once.

Figure 8.2 illustrates the way in which this balance can be achieved in different types of school. Three possible starting points for improvement efforts are noted for different types of schools. Type 1 schools are those that have little experience of school improvement efforts. They are schools where the internal conditions or management arrangements are relatively weak particularly in the way in which they relate to developmental activities. In such circumstances it is difficult to develop the school by focussing solely on classroom practice, it is also important to build the 'capacity for sustained improvement'. The school improvement team will need to look at how management arrangements can be put in place which facilitate sustained attention to the school's priorities. Once this way of working has been established then these schools can take on more ambitious classroom development and innovations.

This is the case in Type 3 schools where the internal conditions are sufficiently robust and established to allow a high level of classroom change. In these circumstances the way the school is being managed and the goals it is pursuing are common and mutually supportive.

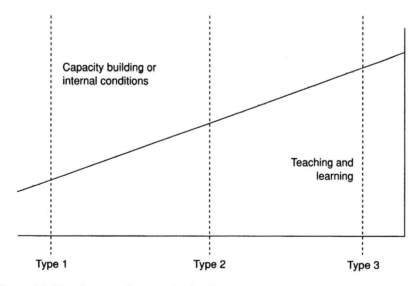

Figure 8.2 Development focus and school type

Experience would suggest that at any one point in time, a Type 1 school is more likely to be struggling, whereas a school at Type 3 is more likely to be successful. This observation leads to the speculation that the approach (in the short term) most likely to lead to improvement in schools which are experiencing difficulties, will be one which ties action on management arrangements into the identification of development priorities. Similarly, in already successful schools, it is likely to be the further development of classroom practice that needs to be linked into improvement priorities. By the same token Type 2 schools will need to pay fairly equal attention to both 'capacity building' and 'teaching and learning'.

This discussion leads to two conclusions that are further explored in the next chapter. First, that different improvement strategies are needed in schools that exhibit different levels of success. Second, that it is probably easier to improve a school which is moderately well managed and has moderately developed classroom practice than it is to help a struggling school improve or to make a successful one even more successful.

A final comment needs to be made on the importance of 'timeframes'. Figure 8.2 offers a reasonable description of how the improvement focus may vary across schools at any point in time. However, over the longer term schools are unlikely to remain stable as, for example, Type 1 or Type 3 communities. Rather, they will develop over a series of cycles, each cycle building on the progress of the previous one. Over time, therefore, one would anticipate that a Type 1 school that worked hard on capacity building initially, may well in the next cycle, be a Type 2 or a Type 3 school. The process of real school improvement is therefore a cyclical one. This requires attention to different arrangements at different times, alongside the pursuit of increasingly ambitious plans for the teaching repertoires of staff and the learning capacity of students.

The phases of school improvement

Looking across the case studies one sees images of schools that are increasingly:

- taking student learning outcomes as their developmental focus
- focussing on medium-term and strategic planning
- becoming more skilful in managing staff development and school improvement
- adopting specifications of curriculum and teaching that extend their current practice and that focus directly on the student learning goals that have been set
- managing the change process by using a combination of pressure and support
- monitoring progress and gathering appropriate research data on student learning
- modifying their culture and developing a 'capacity for change'.

All these characteristics are features of authentic school improvement. Yet they are realised in different ways. In the cameos as it so happens, the primary schools have tended to adopt programmes developed elsewhere, while paying careful attention to the development of the school as a social system. The secondary schools however represent a different style of development. They chose to become part of a school improvement network in order to pursue their commitment to enhancing the teaching and learning process. One of the features of the IQEA approach to authentic school improvement is the use of dispersed leadership in the form of a cadre group to support school improvement. Although the cadre group drive the school improvement work they do this at least initially within a relatively structured approach. The experience of the IQEA project is that working through the following phases provides a secure foundation for capacity building and sustained school improvement.

Phase 1: introducing IQEA into the school

As IQEA is not a 'quick fix' school improvement approach, it is important that careful deliberation is given to the decision to embark on this way of working. Preparing for the project involves generating commitment, planning and gathering data on the school level conditions. This involves:

- school level conference with headteacher and/or significant others
- school's introduction to IQEA and conditions survey
- whole school decision to embark on IQEA.

Phase 2: working with the cadre group

Although it is important to move into action as soon as is practicable, it is vital that the cadre group is fully established and *au fait* with management of change and teaching/learning strategies, and have carefully planned the whole school improvement strategy. This involves:

- selection of cadre and co-leaders – school and LEA
- the principles of IQEA
- understanding your school
- designing the whole school programme – visioning and timeline
- cadre preparation and development
- seeding the whole school approach.

Phase 3: going whole school

The initial cycle of activity will last up to two terms and begin and end with a whole staff day. In the first the curriculum and teaching focus and learning teams will be established; in the second, the staff will share with each other on a curriculum tour around the school the progress they have made. The activities involved in this phase are:

- the initial whole school INSET day(s)
- establishing the curriculum and teaching focus
- establishing the learning teams
- the initial cycle of enquiry
- sharing initial success and impact on student learning – curriculum tour.

Phase 4: sustaining momentum

It is in this phase that the capacity for change at school and classroom level is fully established. Learning teams become an established way of working and there is an expansion of the range of teaching strategies used throughout the curriculum. This activity includes:

- establishing further cycles of enquiry
- encouraging differentiation
- building teacher learning into the process
- sharpening the focus on student learning
- finding ways of sharing success
- reflecting on the culture of the school and department.

Phase 5: establishing the school as the centre of enquiry

During this phase some eighteen months to two years after embarking, the school will begin to feel confident about its ability to conduct school improvement and increasing efforts are made to establish enquiry as a continuous process of professional learning. This involves:

- creating school improvement networks within and between schools
- listening to the student voice
- continuously involving stakeholders
- integrating enquiry and implementation
- establishing action research as the focus of development work
- orientating new staff to the school
- moving from experimentation to mastery.

One of the problems with previous approaches to school improvement is that they have taken a short-term view of change and focussed on the implementation of a single issue or a given curriculum development at the expense of 'capacity building'. In order to cope with a 'change-rich' environment, where multiple policy initiatives and innovation overload can easily oppress schools, there is a need to adopt a medium- or at times long-term perspective. In focussing on the management of change in general, on the creation of effective and flexible structures and on the empowering of individuals, as well as on the implementation of specific changes in curriculum and instruction the secondary schools in the cameos embarked on a systematic approach to school improvement. This description of the phases they passed through, mirrors the earlier discussion of 'capacity building' and modifications to 'teaching and learning', as well as to the focus in the following section on culture change.

The process of cultural change

There have been in this book many references to the term 'school culture', and there is evidence in the cameos of significant culture change. The common view is that the culture of the school is best thought of as the procedures, norms, expectations and values of its members. The popular phrases that describe the culture of the school as 'the way we get things done around here' or 'what keeps the herd moving west' (Deal and Kennedy, 1983: 4), provide an image with which most are comfortable.

In reflecting on the process of culture change it is helpful to heed the distinction between *structure* and *culture*. Structure and culture are of course interdependent, and the relationship between them is dialectical. Structure influences culture, but it works the other way around too. Structures are often regarded as the more basic and profound, in that they generate cultures which not only allow the structures to 'work', but also justify or legitimate the structures. On the other hand, changes in culture, i.e., value systems and beliefs, can change underlying structures. The two go hand-in-hand and are mutually reinforcing. At a practical level however, it is often easier to change structures than cultures. But if one changes structures too radically, without paying attention to the underlying culture, then one may get the appearance of change (change in structure), but not the reality of change (change in culture). Similarly it is difficult to sustain changes in culture, perhaps inspired by a charismatic leader, without some concomitant change in structure to support their ideas about curriculum or instructional innovation.

In a paper on 'restructuring', Hargreaves highlights the relationship between culture, structure and 'capacity' in the sense that the word was used earlier (1991):

> it is not possible to establish productive school cultures without prior changes being effected in school structures that increase the opportunities for meaningful working relationships and collegial support between teachers. The importance of the structural option of restructuring, therefore, may be less in terms of its direct impact on curriculum, assessment, ability grouping and the like, than in terms of how it creates improved opportunities for teachers to work together on a continuing basis.

In terms of authentic school improvement, in order to build 'capacity' there is a need to direct equal attention to both structure and culture, and to be alert to the effect one has on the other. In previous research for example, we found a positive relationship between school culture, the personality of the individual teacher, and the implementation of 'new' ideas from an exemplary in-service course (Evans and Hopkins, 1988). The actual process of use of the new ideas was found to be considerably affected by the culture in which the teacher was working. Although the results from this study point to a stronger effect for the teacher's personality than the climate of the school, in practice these factors are inseparable – it is the total effect on the process of use that is important. In short, a positive climate evolved by positive people, equals effective implementation (Hopkins, 1990).

The cameos also point to another link between school improvement strategies and the culture of the school. That change is disruptive, even on the evidence of the school's experiences that have been related in this book, is self-evident. This is the phase of 'internal turbulence' referred to earlier. Indeed many research studies have found that without a period of de-stabilisation, successful, long lasting change is unlikely to occur. But, many schools survive this period of destabilisation by either consciously or intuitively adapting their *internal conditions* in response to the new situations created by the demands of the agreed on school improvement 'priority'. As has been seen, schools are encouraged to take stock of their internal conditions *before they begin developmental work*. Then they can begin to build modifications to conditions into the strategies they are going to use.

When this is done, changes that enhance the *culture* of the school begin to occur. For example, classroom observation of teachers by colleagues becomes more common in many schools as a result of improvement efforts. When this happens, the teachers involved usually begin to talk more about teaching, and collaborative work outside of the particular project increases, as management structures are adapted to support the work. When taken together, these changes in attitudes, practices and structures create a more supportive environment within the school for managing change. The school's 'change capacity' is thus increased and the groundwork is laid for future change efforts. What might be described as a 'virtuous circle of change' begins to be established. Schools that have been through similar 'change cycles' either experience less internal turbulence second time around, or are able to tolerate greater levels of turbulence, because they have progressively enhanced their capacity for change as a result of engaging in this developmental process.

One can describe what is happening here in terms of a sequence of activities and relationships. P stands for the priority the school sets itself, S the chosen strategy for change, the brackets the period of destabilisation, Co those internal conditions that are modified in order to ameliorate the destabilisation, and Cu the resulting change in culture. The process of cultural change is not a 'one off' as may be implied by the notation, but one that evolves and unfolds over time. Often a number of such sequences have to be gone through before a radically different culture emerges in a school:

$$P > S > \{\} \; Co > Cu$$

This way of describing the process of culture change resonates with the experiences of many of the headteachers of the schools portrayed in the cameos. They agree with Schein (1985: 2) when he wrote that, 'the only thing of real importance that leaders do is to create and manage culture'. These headteachers realise that the impact of successful change falls on the culture of the school, for it is the culture that sustains the changes in teaching and learning that consequently enhance the achievement of students. It is not that they necessarily begin the development process by asking 'What cultural changes are required?' and then, 'What priorities, strategies, and changes in conditions can bring this about?' Yet, experience suggests that outstanding headteachers do manipulate priorities, strategies and conditions in order to affect school culture, for they know that ultimately this is the only way of maintaining improvements in the quality of educational outcomes and experience for all students.

Commentary

In this chapter the focus has been on the patterns of development of schools that have consciously engaged with an authentic school improvement process. In *The New Structure of School Improvement* we articulated a set of hypotheses that characterise the 'evolutionary school', one that has enquiry as its main focus. When implemented it is these ideas that provide a structure for staff development that has student achievement as its core. The six hypotheses are (adapted from Joyce *et al.*, 1999: chapter 1):

Hypothesis 1

That staff development embedded in the workplace increases enquiry into new practices and the implementation of school improvement initiatives.

Hypothesis 2

Restructuring the work patterns of teachers, so that time for collective enquiry is built into the workplace, will create the structural conditions in which the process of school improvement is nested.

Hypothesis 3

An information-rich environment will enhance enquiry. Studying classroom practice will increase enquiry into ways of helping students learn better.

Hypothesis 4

That connecting teachers to the knowledge base on teaching and learning will increase the development of successful initiatives for school improvement.

Hypothesis 5

That building small work groups connected to the school as a whole, but responsible for one another will increase the sense of belonging that reduces stress, isolation, and feelings of alienation.

Hypothesis 6

That staff development, structured as an enquiry, both fuels energy and results in initiatives that have greater effects.

Taken together, the six hypotheses define a strategy for creating an infra-structure for staff development appropriate for sustained school improvement. Some of the apparently simple structural changes, such as the provision of substantial amounts of regular time for collegial activity, will ensure a homeostasis of change rather than a homeostasis of tradition. In the following chapter a variety of capacity building strategies for schools who differ in effectiveness will be discussed.

9   Differential school improvement

Over the past fifteen years, there has been an increasing momentum in many educational systems towards decentralisation. This has been accompanied by an increase in interest in how schools are performing and how schools can improve their performance. The publication of comparative league tables and regular inspection of all schools not only informs parents and others about schools' achievements but also allows success to be identified and inadequacy identified. This in turn has led to a growing interest in the process of school change and improvement.

In the previous chapter a series of cameos of schools that were responding positively and proactively to the educational reform agenda were presented. The central focus for development in these schools was the learning and achievement of their students. They were achieving success through building the confidence and competence of staff and strengthening the organisation and culture of the school. Despite the similarities, there was also a wide variation between the schools in terms of their response. The primary schools selected previously developed innovations to address the learning needs of their students, whereas the secondary schools used a more generic school improvement strategy to enhance the range and quality of teaching strategies used in the school. Each of the schools were also coming from different starting points in their school improvement efforts. Despite this, it is clear that there is little sensitivity to context in most policy prescriptions or the range of school improvement strategies in general use.

The argument in this chapter is that authentic school improvement strategies need to pay attention to context, that a wider range of improvement options should be made available to schools, and that more intelligence be used in linking improvement strategy to school need. The experience of the recent past however, suggests that there may be some problems in realising this approach.

First, a common response to the centralised reform agenda has been to mobilise change efforts at the level of the whole organisation. This type of intervention is premised upon a view that the key to school improvement lies in management systems. Consequently, there has been an emphasis upon the systemics of schooling as the means to improvement. The reliance upon managerial and administrative change is a clear indication that the school is concerned largely with organisational maintenance and efficiency. In practice, this has led to schools defining and re-defining roles and responsibilities, introducing monitoring systems and generally concentrating their efforts upon infra-structural change. This approach underestimates the importance of teaching and learning to student achievement, and also neglects to focus on the capacity of the school for development.

Second, there has also been a commitment to 'a one size fits all' approach to school improvement. The history of school improvement in England and Wales over the past 20 years, for example, exhibits such a singularity. School self-evaluation was popular as an agent of improvement in the late 1970s and early 1980s; TVEI, a major curriculum reform, appeared in 1984; Teacher Appraisal, after a long gestation period, occurred in 1987; all were seen as policy initiatives to enhance achievement. These were closely followed by the proposals of the Education Reform Act, in the late 1980s and early 1990s, the main elements of which – a national curriculum, delegated funding, empowered governing bodies and external inspection – were regarded as somewhat free-floating initiatives or strategies that by themselves would raise standards. The rhetoric of government policy was simply, if the school has a national curriculum, or experiences an inspection, then standards would inevitably and inexorably rise. The fallacy in such an approach to school change has already been exposed.

Third, these *external* school improvement policies and strategies can also be contrasted with the *internal* strategies often advocated by advisers, academics, and consultants, such as school self-evaluation, staff development or development planning. The crucial point, however, is that in terms of school development, neither *external* nor *internal* strategies will impact upon the progress of students *unless* the strategy itself impacts *at the same time* on the internal conditions or change capacity of the school. It is clear that if a school improvement strategy is to contribute to the sustained progress of students, then it must impact on, and be integrated with, the school's capacity for development.

The argument is that if the aspiration of continual improvement is to be taken seriously, then the focus of authentic school improvement needs to be on the school's capacity for development. 'Real' school improvement strategies therefore need to be context-specific, both in terms of the learning needs of students and the organisational conditions of the school. In other words, a differential approach to school improvement needs to be developed. This is the theme of the chapter. In the following sections:

- the school's capacity for school development will be discussed
- a framework for thinking about differential strategies for school development will be presented
- a range of strategies for different growth states of schools will be explored

- a more comprehensive approach to differential school improvement will be proposed.

The school's capacity for development

The phrase, 'the school's capacity for development', has been widely used in this book, and its central importance for authentic school improvement established. Without a clear focus on 'capacity', then a school will be unable to sustain continuous improvement efforts that result in student achievement. It is therefore critical to be able to define 'capacity' in operational terms.

As has been seen, the IQEA work has demonstrated that without an equal focus on the internal conditions of the school, innovative work quickly becomes marginalised. The 'conditions' have to be worked on at the same time as the curriculum or other priorities the school has set itself. Conditions are the internal features of the school, the 'arrangements' that enable it to get work done. In chapter 6, the 'conditions' within the school that are associated with a capacity for sustained improvement were described. In terms of the IQEA project at least, it is the 'conditions' that provide a working definition of the *development capacity* of the school.

The work of Newmann, King and Young (2000) provide another perspective on building learning capacity that complements that of the IQEA project, and the cameos in the previous chapter. They argue that professional development is more likely to advance achievement for all students in a school if it addresses not only the learning of individual teachers, but also other dimensions of the organisational capacity of the school. They define *school capacity* as the collective competency of the school as an entity to bring about effective change. They suggest that there are four core components of capacity:

1 *Knowledge, skills and dispositions* of individual staff members.
2 *A professional learning community* in which staff work collaboratively to set clear goals for student learning, assess how well students are doing, develop action plans to increase student achievement, while being engaged in enquiry and problem-solving.
3 *Programme coherence* – 'the extent to which the school's programs for student and staff learning are co-ordinated, focussed on clear learning goals and sustained over a period of time'.
4 *Technical resources* – high quality curriculum, instructional material, assessment instruments, technology, workspace, etc.

Fullan (2000) comments that this four-part definition of school capacity includes 'human capital', i.e., the skills of *individuals*, but he concludes that no amount of professional development of individuals will have an impact if certain *organisation* features are not in place. He maintains that there are two key organisational features in this conceptualisation. The first are 'professional learning communities'. These are the 'social capital' aspect of capacity.

In other words, the skills of individuals can only be realised if the *relationships* within the schools are continually developing.

The other component of organisational capacity is programme coherence. Since complex social systems have a tendency to produce overload and fragmentation in a non-linear evolving fashion, schools are constantly being bombarded by overwhelming and unconnected innovations (Fullan, 1999). In this sense, the most effective schools are not those that take on the most innovations, but those that selectively take on, integrate and co-ordinate innovations into their own focussed programmes.

To this point the argument has focussed on a widely accepted but not exclusive view of the term 'capacity'. The common usage of the term refers to 'the ability to do something'. The previous discussion has identified a consensus over the key features of schools' organisation that relate to its ability to engage in authentic school improvement for student achievement.

But 'capacity', as Corcoran and Goertz (1995: 27) point out, can also mean 'the maximum or optimum amount of production'. Corcoran and Goertz argue that this definition focusses attention on the results of school reform, and raises the issue of efficiency in terms of the 'optimal amount of production that can be obtained from a given set of resources and organisational arrangements'. This in turn leads to questions about how the product of the school, that is high quality teaching and learning, can be enhanced, within 'a given set of resources', and also how the 'organisational arrangements' can be changed at the same time.

This more strategic view of capacity raises an issue that is only rarely addressed both in the research literature and in policy initiatives. Much school improvement work assumes in practice that all schools are the same, and that any strategy will work as well in one school as another. Yet evidence of the research on school effectiveness is unequivocal – schools are differentially effective (see for example, Cuttance, 1999; Teddlie and Reynolds, 2000). This leads to the conclusion that schools at different levels of effectiveness require different school improvement strategies. As was noted in the previous chapter, when circumstances exist that are less supportive of change, it is necessary to concentrate much more in the initial stages of development work on creating those internal conditions within the school that facilitate development. Work on the priorities may be limited until the conditions are in place. As is seen in the following section, this is not well-trodden territory.

A framework for thinking about differential strategies for school improvement

Put simply, schools at different stages of development require different strategies not only to enhance their capacity for development, but also to provide a more effective education for their students. Strategies for school development need to fit the 'growth state', or culture of the particular school. Strategies

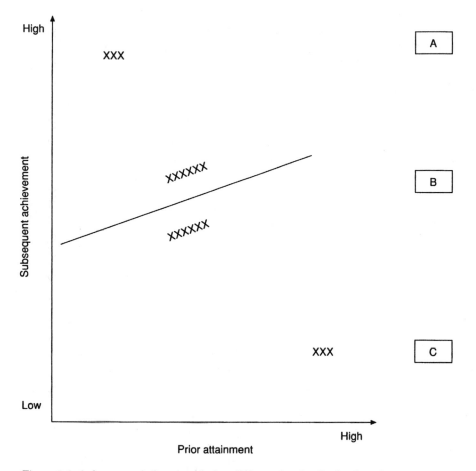

Figure 9.1 A framework for considering different levels of school performance

that are effective for improving performance at one 'growth state', are not necessarily effective at another. Strategies for school development need to be adapted according to the 'growth state' of the individual school. Little is known about how different school improvement strategies affect different schools. Previously, a framework provided by the research on school effects has been used to organise thinking around this issue (Hopkins, 1996; Hopkins *et al.*, 1997). A typical representation of the results from the research on school effects is given in Figure 9.1.

The diagonal (regression) line represents the level of achievement one would expect from a student based on their prior attainment on entry to a school, having controlled for background variables. Data sets from LEA and school district studies, where such individual student scores are available, suggest that on average most schools cluster around the line, as in B on the diagram (see for example Rosenholtz, 1989; Teddlie and Stringfield, 1993; Gray and Wilcox, 1995). Schools that are further to the right are usually those schools that have more advantaged intakes. Schools to the left have less advantaged intakes. The important point being, however, that by and large they are equally effective in terms of the value they add to a student's academic achievement. Often a pair of 'tramlines' is drawn around the distribution to illustrate the normal or expected range of performance from schools.

These data sets sometimes contain a few schools, such as those at A, which consistently 'add value' to their students in comparison with what one would expect from measures of these students' prior attainment. Unfortunately these data sets occasionally also contain schools, such as those at C, that consistently reduce the levels of student achievement one would expect. All of this is well established in the school effects literature. In chapter 3 the research of Stringfield and Teddlie, and Rosenholtz cited above, that characterised the work cultures and behaviours of schools at these extremes was discussed in more detail. Schools at A in Figure 9.1 are like Rosenholtz's 'Moving' schools, and those at C are similar to her 'Stuck' schools.

What is of central importance for those interested in authentic school improvement is not just what the capacities of schools at A, B and C are, but how do schools at C assume the characteristics of those schools at A and what strategies can be used to help them do this? Although the research base on the effects of school improvement strategies is weak, it is sensible to assume that the same strategy will not move a school directly from C to A, and that a strategy for moving a school from position C to position B would be qualitatively different from a strategy that would move a school from position B to position A. It would also make sense to assume that a strategy that helps to keep a school at A is different again.

Research by the American Quality Foundation (1992) also suggests that different management strategies are required at different phases of the performance development cycle in organisations. The message here is that there are few universal quality management strategies that are applicable across all stages of an organisation's development, and that organisations need to change their quality management strategies as they progress through their performance development cycle. The strategies that are effective for improving performance at one stage of the cycle are not necessarily effective at other stages of the cycle.

Further support for this point of view is found in our recent study of *Improving Schools* (Gray et al., 1999). The purpose of the research was to explore how schools have become effective over time, in order to complement the existing studies of effective schools that are effective at a point in time. Irrespective of a school's level of effectiveness the research has identified a number of different 'routes to improvement'. Three types in particular emerged from the analysis of the quantitative and qualitative data.

Tactics

A tactical response to improvement was evident in all of the schools involved in the case study aspect of the research. As has been seen, these initiatives or tactics include: monitoring performance, targeting students, introducing extra classes for certain groups of students, implementing 'codes of conduct', giving students greater responsibility, changing examination boards, and so on. Together they make up the 'common curriculum' of school improvement (see chapter 4). This combination of tactics is powerful enough to raise the performance of low or slowly achieving schools up towards the (regression) line, but no further. The data suggests a plateau effect after at best a couple of years.

Such a tactical response is by no means a panacea, and for at least four reasons. First, there appears to be a ceiling on the amount of improvement such a collection of tactics can deliver: at best it can bring a school from a moderately low to an average level of performance. Second, it appears that the effect is short-lived – such effects plateau or decrease after two years. There is no evidence to suggest that there is a medium-term effect. Third, and by definition, these effects, as moderate and short-lived as they are, are confined to schools in the 'slow improving' category. Fourth it is worth noting that, particularly in the case of 'slow improvers', the amount of resistance inside the school appears to be in inverse relation to sustained improvement. So even the relatively small effect of such a tactical response can be negated by the amount of resistance evident and being experienced within the school. In summary, a tactical response may be necessary, but it is by no means a sufficient condition for school improvement.

Strategies

There was another group of schools in the sample who seemed to be able to do more and progress further than those who only responded to the challenge of school improvement tactically. The level of response that we are characterising 'strategic' was not related to any level of prior effectiveness, but was expressed as a general response across the three effectiveness levels. Schools employing this level of response were, as is evident from the data previously reported, doing all that the other schools were doing, but with two major differences.

The first is that they were all engaged in a co-ordinated response to the challenge of school improvement. The leadership of the school and many of the staff were not content with just doing something; they wanted to do it with a purpose. Second, the focus of their work was explicitly at the classroom or 'learning' level. Serious efforts were being made in these schools to co-ordinate and deliver a whole school response – to ensure some consistency of practice from one department to another. What was striking in these schools, and clearly differentiated them from schools that employed a tactical response, was that they were clearly interested in student learning and classroom practice.

Capacities (for further improvement)

The sample contained few if any schools in this category. Evidence from this research, coupled with what is already known from other experiences and studies, suggests that there are schools that regularly transcend the strategic improvement dimension. These are schools that are already at relatively high levels of effectiveness and build on this by employing a far more sophisticated approach to change. These are schools that collectively understand the causes of positive change and the areas of resistance in the school. They know when change is happening and understand the reasons why, and are able to find ways to sustain positive change into the medium and long term. Above all, they have developed a willingness to go beyond the incremental approach to restructuring and genuinely see school improvement as a way of life.

Evidence from the *Improving Schools* study supports the contention that schools at different levels of performance use different tactics and strategies to promote and sustain their improvement efforts. These have been examples, however, of individual schools' own improvement trajectories. As they stand they do not offer a coherent approach of how to support schools through the process of change. This is the focus of the following section.

Strategies for improving different types of schools

The framework illustrated in Figure 9.1 focussed on three contrasting school types: the 'failing' or 'ineffective school', the 'low achieving' school and the 'good or 'effective' school. In this section, an initial list of strategies that schools of each type could use to improve their effectiveness is outlined. This discussion is based on our original conceptualisation of school growth states and strategies for development (Hopkins *et al.*, 1997).

The 'failing, or ineffective school'

By definition these schools cannot improve themselves. They are 'stuck' schools that need a high level of external support. Within these schools a number of early interventions and changes need to be made which have a direct focus upon basic organisational issues. These would include:

- *Change at leadership level* It is too sweeping to say that the headteachers of failing schools do not have the capacity to be effective school leaders. It is, though, certain that they do not have the capacity to resurrect *that* school, and therefore are potentially a part of the problem. Research suggests that leadership is, to some extent, context-related, so failing schools need new headteachers. They also need change in leadership at all levels. It is usually the case that poor management and leadership are endemic within the ineffective school, which means that the overall style of leadership needs to be changed in that particular context. New leadership opportunities will need to be created for different staff, using new models, to achieve new goals.

- *Provision of early, intensive outside support* Schools in a failing situation are likely to be isolated and in a state of cultural stasis. They are unlikely to have the potential for constructive self-analysis or evaluation, and will need support from outside to provide knowledge about school improvement strategies and models of ways of working. For failing schools, the LEA might be a part of the problem, so support might need to be sought elsewhere. It is important however, that the school has some ownership over the selection of the outside support, and should be able to choose from a range of providers considered to be most suited to their needs.

- *Survey staff and student opinion; gather and disaggregate data on student achievement* For improvement strategies to be most effective, the process of data collection is an important first step. Most ineffective schools will need to collect data to find out why they are unsuccessful, and where to direct their efforts for greatest improvement. Survey-feedback techniques have the potential to neutralise data and to de-personalise problems. Data would need to be gathered at whole school level, at departmental level and at classroom level in relation to individual students and groups of students. The purpose of this data collection exercise would be to find out if there were existing centres of good practice within the school from which it can learn. This approach has the potential to give the school community ownership of the improvement agenda and to locate the problem away from individuals to a whole school focus.

- *A short-term focus on things (relatively) easy to change, e.g., the environment, attendance, uniform* Changes to the school environment, attendance and uniform will be short-term changes, but can result in tangible gains. Following a period of low morale, such visible changes will demonstrate that things are to be different in the school. These changes should reflect the core values that the new leadership is articulating. Evidence would suggest that such early indicators of a climate change in the school are important in sustaining further improvement. They have a symbolic and real function, in so far as they show that change is taking place and that a new and different school culture is emerging.

- *A focus on managing learning behaviour, not on behaviour management* Much of the evidence concerning the improvement of ineffective, or failing schools points towards an emphasis upon managing learning behaviour rather than behaviour management. This means creating the conditions within which learners can learn most effectively. Strategies for managing learning behaviour would inevitably include a focus upon praise and positive reinforcement, rather than punishment and discipline, throughout the school.

- *Intensive work on re-skilling teams of teachers in a limited but specific repertoire of teaching/learning styles* Staff development in the ineffective school needs to be both context-specific and culturally related. There should be a preoccupation with effective teaching and learning throughout the school. Therefore, specific training and development opportunities should be made available to both teachers and students. In the first instance, the focus for staff development could be quite simple; for example: seating arrangements; classroom organisation; the phasing of lessons or active use of resources. Teachers could explore these skills in teams in order to create new partnerships. It is important that new partnerships are formed in order to replace former groupings that may have been detrimental to school development in the past.

- *Progressive restructuring to generate new opportunities for leadership, collaboration and planning* In the ineffective school any restructuring, or planning must be focussed upon what happens in classrooms. Collaboration and planning should be about enhancing pupil achievement, and about developing the potential of all staff. These areas need to be activated simultaneously as the core agenda for improvement. Time needs to be set aside for collaboration, for developmental work and for the sharing of ideas. Consequently, nothing is more important than timetabling staff together to engage in mutual learning and to plan curriculum and school improvement in a failing school. It is also the case that the gap cannot be allowed to become too large between the effective teams and the less effective teams – an intense improvement focus could produce that result. In this respect, the improvement process needs to be internally supported with expertise and time being given to those less effective teams, to ensure that the balance and momentum of change is maintained.

- *Withdraw external pressure/inspection in order to remove fear and give space to grow* Failing schools can become paralysed by the fear of imminent inspection. They dare not take the risks required to produce long-term improvement, which, as the research on school improvement shows, takes time. As suggested earlier, inspectors need to draw up a shortlist of external support agencies from which the school can choose. A school development plan and an inspection action plan need to be approved, so that everyone is secure that the structures and processes are in place for improvement – and then the pressure of inspection needs to be withdrawn in the short term.

The 'low achieving' school

The IQEA experience suggests that 'low achieving' schools need to refine their developmental priorities and focus upon specific teaching and learning issues and build capacity within the school to support this work. These strategies usually involve a certain level of external support, but it is theoretically possible for these schools to improve themselves. Developmental strategies for this type of school include:

- *Change in leadership strategies* This change incorporates both leadership styles and range. Some restructuring will be necessary in order to diversify leadership opportunities. School improvement cadres, task groups, multiple team leadership, task-related leadership are strategies which will unlock static structures and systems. Such changes will enable the process of management to become more dynamic and to be geared towards increasing the capacity for change.
- *Improve the environment* Alterations in the school environment can have a dramatic effect on teaching and learning processes. For example, the creation of work areas, enhanced display of pupils' work, improved social space all indicate to pupils that the school values them and that they should value the school. The constant reinforcement that learning is valued will contribute to raise staff morale and can affect pupil achievement.
- *Lengthen the lesson unit* Some curriculum restructuring will be needed in order to support the re-skilling of teachers. Time will be needed to focus on a wider repertoire of teaching/learning styles and on the development of learning behaviours. The longer the time unit, the more time staff will have to plan together and to practise different teaching approaches. Different lesson lengths might be necessary to support teachers in the process and practice of re-skilling.
- *Review something linked to 'standards' (e.g., uniform, homework): involve all staff, students and parents* This strategy involves focussing the attention of all 'stakeholders' upon pupil achievement and upon the development of the shared language to talk about achievement. The particular areas suggested (uniform and homework) are initial changes from which other dialogues and other strategies for improvement will evolve.
- *Target particular students at certain thresholds (across the ability range)* If achievement is to matter, then underachievement at all levels should be targeted. Data about performance will provide opportunities to generate dialogue with staff and with students – in groups and individually; by gender and by ability. Mentoring students is one effective strategy to offset potential underachievement. It is visible, relationship-building and should ideally involve all staff.
- *Talk to pupils about their aspirations; give their achievement meaning* Schools are good at internally assessing pupil effort and achievement. They are less skilled at assessing potential and it is in this gap that the potential for improvement lies. The gap between achievement and potential is only meaningful in terms of pupil life and aspirations. Achievement has to mean something, so formal mechanisms of rewarding all types of pupil achievement are important and should be built in to any school restructuring programme.

- *Harness the energy and optimism of staff new to the school* Underachieving schools will tend to have a staff who are disillusioned. Morale will be low but staff who have accepted jobs at the school within the last year or two will have done so with optimism, faith in the school and hope for what they might achieve. These staff can be used to re-energise others, and can become a catalyst for change. It is important, therefore, that the new leadership's efforts to re-ignite the values of all staff focus initially upon staff comparatively new to the school. This will provide a basis for improvement upon which further allegiances can be formed.
- *Generate an ongoing dialogue about values* The values and beliefs, both of the profession and the school, need to be articulated and re-affirmed. All staff need to be helped to be clear about the value dimension of almost everything that is done in school. For example, why do we have this assessment system? Why this homework policy? Why these rules or this code of conduct? Why did we deal with this incident in this way? All these decisions will have their roots in the values and beliefs of the school community – and they need to be shared and debated.

The 'good, or effective school'

There has been relatively little debate or research undertaken which has focussed upon improving the good, or effective, school. Most attention has been located with improving poor, or low performing schools. Yet it is imperative that those schools that are effective remain so. Consequently, in this third type of school there is a need for specific strategies that ensure the school remains a moving school that continues to enhance pupil performance. These strategies include:

- *Articulate values and disseminate eloquence* 'In effective schools, school leaders disseminate eloquence' (Weick, 1985). It is a school leader's role to articulate the school's values and to reinforce them at every opportunity. These values need to be embedded within the institution and shared by staff, and also by parents and pupils. Schools tend to be loosely coupled systems, despite the existence of a conventional chain of line management causality. Consequently, schools need to be clear about the interpretation and articulation of educational values within their individual school context.
- *Raise expectations (teacher, pupil and the wider community), define achievement and create an achievement orientation* Effective schools should constantly strive to raise expectations (teacher, pupil and the wider community) regarding potential pupil achievement ever higher. This means schools need to be explicit, eloquent and prolific in their definition of achievement. They should then celebrate it, communicate it and develop a reward system that will eliminate the need for most sanctions. Such a

process will ignite the enthusiasm of staff and generate motivation among students. It is additionally important to give pupils (and the wider community) ownership of the school's achievements too, and to involve them in organising and participating in regular celebrations of the school's success.

- *Involve and empower students in the focus on learning and develop a student charter* Once systems, structures, processes, values and professional skills have been developed within the effective school, and even when schemes of work and classroom management strategies have been refined, it is still the pupils who have to take responsibility for their own achievement. It is important that they feel involved and empowered in the process of learning. For example, they can contribute by offering an assessment of teaching and learning processes. By providing their views about how their learning can be improved in the individual classroom, within the department, and within the school pupils are contributing to the improvement process via their constructive feedback.

- *Use restructuring (and timetable) to create collaborative planning at department and classroom level* The average secondary school of a thousand pupils in England, will spend in excess of a quarter of a million pounds on teacher non-contact time. The use of this time is rarely monitored and even more rarely co-ordinated. If change could be made to the school structure to create new collaborations and new learning partnerships that included those outside traditional departmental boundaries, this time could be productively harnessed. Similarly, the timetable could be restructured to enable more teachers to share, plan, and observe one another's work. In other words, it could be used proactively as a basis for teachers to learn and grow together.

- *Engage long-term outside support focussed on developing leadership skills, team-building and models of teaching and learning* Even the most effective school will eventually become inward-looking and atrophy if it becomes too self-sufficient. Isolation from external stimulus and support can be damaging to any school, irrespective of its performance level. A school that is a learning school will seek out best practice elsewhere and will use outside support to develop the knowledge base and to initiate networks. External expertise and support can also offer alternative teaching practices and new ways of teaching and learning. Teachers can become skilled in these new processes by working alongside others both within the classroom and in functional teams.

- *Generate a common language around learning and achievement* This is more significant than it appears because teaching staff tend not to have common understandings about even basic terminology concerning pupil learning and achievement. Although many effective schools have started to focus upon developing such a common language about learning, more staff development opportunities are needed on this theme. Staff who have a shared language concerning learning and achievement are more likely to work together and to be committed to understanding and improving the processes of teaching and learning.

*   *Give teachers 'space' to experiment* Effective schools need to encourage experimentation and risk-taking. They should accept messiness and muddle rather than aim for efficiency. They should subscribe to the view that safe teaching is mundane teaching, and aim high and take joy in the successes and talk about the failures. Indeed, real learning lies in understanding the failures rather than the successes.
*   *Celebrate and share successes; reinforce the 'appetite for change'* All schools, at whatever stage in their development, should take joy in every demonstration of success. They should aim to orchestrate optimism and celebration of teacher *and* student achievement. Everyday professional and social interactions of teachers and pupils should focus upon the positive rather than the negative, upon success rather than failure to ensure that this permeates the whole school and every classroom. Cynicism about pupils, the school, the profession needs to be eroded by making it totally unacceptable within the school.

The research on these strategies is still ongoing, so these proposals should be regarded as tentative rather than authoritative. Three characteristics of these lists are, however, worth highlighting at this stage. The first is that these strategies are not homogeneous, but holistic and eclectic. The rhetoric of single school improvement is at a glance exposed. The second is that these combinations of strategies have a range of foci, they are at the same time directed at the structure/organisation of the school, the achievement of pupils, and the intangible 'culture of the school'. Third, these strategies represent a combination of external and internal strategies; the particular blend of strategies is modified to fit the 'context specificity' of the individual school.

As research progresses, it is intended to refine the conceptualisation of the culture and 'growth states' of schools, and the development strategies most suited to their particular growth state. It is this effort that is begun in the following section.

Towards a more comprehensive approach to differential school improvement

The original description of school growth states and school improvement strategies was as follows (Hopkins, 1996: 45):

> *Type I strategies* are those that assist failing schools become moderately effective. They need to involve a high level of external support. These strategies have to involve a clear and direct focus on a limited number of basic curriculum and organisational issues, in order to build the confidence and competence to continue.

Type II strategies are those that assist moderately effective schools become more effective. These schools need to refine their developmental priorities and focus on specific teaching and learning issues, and build the capacity within the school to support this work. These strategies usually involve a certain level of external support. It may also be helpful to differentiate between Type IIa and Type IIb strategies.

Type IIa strategies are characterised by a strategic focus on innovations in teaching and learning that are informed and supported by external knowledge and support.

Type IIb strategies rely less on external support and tend to be more school initiated.

Type III strategies are those that assist effective schools to remain so. In these instances external support, although often welcomed, is not necessary, as the school searches out and creates its own support networks. Exposure to new ideas and practices, collaboration through consortia or 'pairing' type arrangements seems to be common in these situations.

The original framework provides the basis for a more comprehensive way of matching school growth state with an appropriate school improvement strategy. Such an approach would enable schools to become more sophisticated in their selection of school improvement strategies and expand considerably the analysis of school improvement strategies as outlined in chapter 4 (see Figure 4.1).

In Figure 9.2 the original framework is used to illustrate how schools at various growth states could select from a range of school improvement programmes. For ease of exposition there are just three broad bands of school growth states and the familiar terms, 'moving', 'average' and 'stuck', are used to describe them. Given what is already known about school improvement programmes it may be that an IQEA type of approach may be the most appropriate for schools in the mid range. For schools at higher levels of performance, it may be that a school improvement 'club' such as may be organised by a LEA or external support agency would be the way forward. The 'Coalition of Essential Schools' in the US would be an example of this type. At the lower end of performance some form of formal intervention following an inspection may be required. Admittedly these proposals are somewhat hypothetical; in practice schools do not yet have that range of choice, and the approaches themselves are not sufficiently developed for implementation on a wide scale. The illustration does however provide a direction of the way in which school improvement programmes could be developed and disseminated.

Another illustration can be given in relation to the National Literacy Strategy (NLS) in England. Currently the NLS is prescribed for all schools, but one can imagine a situation such as in Figure 9.3 where schools had more choice in terms of their response to the NLS. It may be that 'average' schools may well use the NLS approach and materials. It may also be that

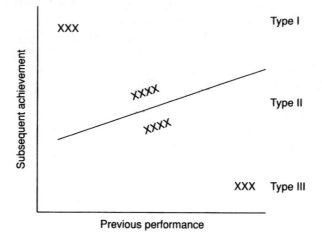

Figure 9.2 A framework for considering different school strategies

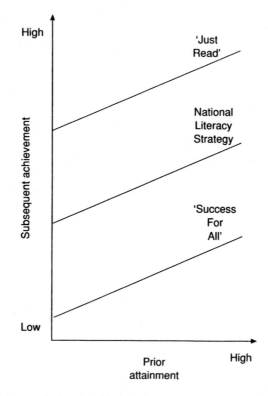

Figure 9.3 A framework for considering the relationship between literacy strategy and school performance

schools whose literacy results are already outstanding may not feel it necessary to adopt the NLS wholesale. They may choose to implement some of the
materials, and use its specifications to critique and modify their existing programme. Perhaps in addition they may adopt a supplementary programme
like 'Just Read' to increase the number of books being read by students. By
way of contrast, schools at the bottom end of the performance cycle may find
that the NLS is not sufficiently comprehensive or intense for the learning
needs of their students. They may well select a literacy strategy such as 'Success For All' as being more suitable for their purposes. As it so happens the
'Success For All' Foundation in England is currently collaborating with the
National Literacy Strategy on such an approach.

A final example applies to classrooms. Teachers in an IQEA school have
been disaggregating student achievement data for various key stages and
subjects. Having done a number of these analyses a common pattern emerged
(see Figure 9.4). In the diagram there are two contrasting groups of students
that lie outside the normal distribution and have similar test results. The
students in Group A have relatively poor learning histories, yet are performing extremely well. Conversely, Group B students came into the class with
much better learning profiles, yet appear to be under-achieving. Without this
type of analysis, the differential level of performance would not be noticed
because both groups have similar results. Staff subsequently diagnosed the
preferred learning styles of those two groups of students and modified schemes
of work accordingly.

The link between diagnosis and prescription is common across these
examples. Authentic school improvement approaches actively search out the
most appropriate strategy in response to the learning needs of students. As
was seen in chapter 5, this quest has been enhanced by the use of effect size
data. All of the models of teaching described in that chapter have strong
empirical support for their effectiveness in raising levels of student learning
and achievement (see for example, Joyce and Weil, 1996; Joyce et al., 1997;
Slavin and Fashola, 1998). The effect size will obviously vary between research studies and research settings. For the sake of illustration, some of
the models of teaching described in chapter 5 have effect sizes expressed as
standard deviations as follows:

- *inductive teaching:* 1.1 (Joyce *et al.*, 1997: 154)
- *advanced organiser:* 0.42 on higher order thinking skills, to 1.35 on lower
  order thinking skills (Joyce and Weil, 1996: 40)
- *mnemonics:* 1.91 average for transfer tasks (Joyce and Weil, 1996: 42)
- *co-operative group work e.g., Jigsaw:* 0.48 average on criterion referenced
  tests, up to 1.0 with good implementation (Joyce and Weil, 1996: 38).

These give an illustration of the power of some of the teaching strategies
discussed is chapter five. The quest for those committed to school improvement remains to seek out those teaching approaches and other classroom

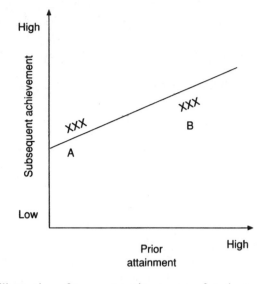

Figure 9.4 An illustration of two contrasting groups of students

practices that will move the effect size curve substantially to the right and incorporate them within their school improvement designs.

These examples illustrate context-specific strategies for differential school improvement. Although the broad strategies for improvement may be similar, the fine detail of the programme has to relate specifically to the context of the school and the learning needs of the students.

As work in this area progresses it will prove possible to describe more specifically different types of school improvement interventions and strategies. Even at present it is feasible to classify *types* on criteria such as: range and number of priorities addressed; focus, i.e., curriculum, instruction, school organisation; research knowledge/school generated knowledge; external directives/internal purpose; level of capacity building, and so on. Such a classification, when complete, would allow a more complete conceptualisation of school improvement by linking 'type' of strategy to student learning needs, various stages of school development and growth. As is seen in the following chapter, there are substantial policy implications based on the spread of programmes that have demonstrated effectiveness.

Commentary

The issues raised in this chapter have the potential to give greater insights into the dynamics of authentic school improvement. Taking seriously the school's 'capacity for development', as well as the range of strategies for school improvement provides the key to sustaining enhanced levels of student progress and achievement for all schools whatever their 'growth state' or stage in their 'performance cycle'.

In reflecting on this discussion, it appears that there are few examples of schools receiving external support from LEAs, universities or other support organisations explicitly for school improvement purposes (for some notable exceptions see Reynolds *et al.*, 1996; Stoll and Fink, 1996). Similarly there is little evidence of schools collaborating together or seeking 'off-the-shelf solutions' to the educational challenges facing them (for some other notable exceptions see Stringfield *et al.*, 1996; Slavin and Fashola, 1998). This may be one of the reasons why there is such a degree of unevenness in the impact of change on student achievement. Faced with similar demands schools respond in individual and often capricious ways. Because there is no language or technology of teaching and school improvement in most schools it is inevitable that some will be better 'interpreters' of change or better innovators than others.

This leads to an obvious question. If as seems likely that there is some form of developmental sequence schools go through in order to become more effective over time – then can this progression be accelerated in some authentic way that respects the context specificity of the schools concerned? Is there a role for LEAs, universities or other agencies in school improvement that goes beyond monitoring, conducting research, and the provision of INSET courses? Although the answers to these questions are implicit in the preceding chapters and are addressed more specifically in the chapter that follows, it is a question of such importance that it deserves at least a brief response here. Three observations are worth making at this stage.

The first is that, as has been argued here, we must move beyond the 'one size fits all' approach to school improvement. Schools are inevitably at different stages of development and/or effectiveness, and different strategies are needed to move them through their 'performance cycle'. Evidence from the examples in this chapter illustrates that different schools require different support that is quite predictable across broad bands of effectiveness or performance.

The second observation is that schools should not be 're-inventing the wheel' every time they meet an educational challenge. Boys' underachievement, the problem of students entering secondary school well below their chronological reading age, the dip in performance at the transition between elementary and high schools, the needs of the 'gifted student' are all predictable and common educational challenges. They are also challenges that are amenable to a uniform response. Unfortunately, few educational systems are developing and then disseminating well researched and proven curricula and instructional programmes that directly address these common and predictable educational challenges. As a consequence schools by and large have to find their own solutions with little guidance and inadequate resources. There is a strong case for the systematic development nationally of programmes that work and that address such predictable educational challenges. Schools could then make a choice between competing alternatives, and funding could then be attached to the implementation of these proven practices at the school level. In the United States of America for example 'Title One' funding is increasingly being attached only to those programmes that have a proven track record.

Third, will effective schools display even greater progress if they have access to appropriate support? There is growing evidence on both sides of the Atlantic that school improvement networks such as the 'Coalition of Essential Schools' or the 'Accelerated Schools' networks in the US, and the 'Improving the Quality of Education for All' (IQEA) and the 'High Reliability' school improvement projects in England can help schools to pursue more effectively and rapidly their change agendas. Unfortunately the research on these and similar projects is incomplete and not very systematic (Slavin and Fashola, 1998); but the evidence base, although fragmented and often qualitative, is growing.

These characteristics aside, it is also a moot point as to who should be providing such support – LEAs or school districts, universities, independent external agencies or commercial organisations? These are questions that link the specific experiences of the schools described and analysed in this and the previous chapter with the broader issues of policy addressed in the final chapter of this book.

10 The policy context for school improvement

In many educational systems much of what currently goes on under the label of 'school improvement' is not consistent with the principles and strategies outlined in preceding chapters. For a variety of reasons, many school improvement approaches are little more than a quick fix and expedient response to the demands for change and the setting of targets by external agencies. This is not to excuse teachers, school leaders, and governors from adopting a more authentic position, for, as has been seen, there is much they can do to improve the quality of education without reference to outside agencies. It is to argue however, that the policy context plays an important role in setting the educational agenda, and determining whether school improvement will be successful or not. It is for this reason that the final chapter of the book focusses on the policy context for school improvement for real.

Much of the debate about education in the last 20 years has been about whether schools are getting better or getting worse. This, however, is an irrelevant question. The real issue is whether current provision is good enough for the challenges now facing us as a society. If one believes that the social context is changing in important ways, then it is very likely that schools will also need to change, no matter how good the provision may have been in the past. This is of course a 'double whammy'. At the same time as society is changing so too are our school systems in, as has already been seen, unprecedented ways.

The argument of this book has been that authentic school improvement is one way of not only realising the aspirations of schooling – that is, the nurturing of students as powerful and competent learners and citizens – but also of addressing issues of social change. The hope being that if schools are able to respond to the changing educational needs of students and society, then they stand some chance of accommodating the pressures of social change as well.

To be able to even begin to do this however has major implications for policy. On a number of occasions in the book we have noted an unfortunate paradox that inhibits policy initiatives from realising their aspirations. At the time when the community of educational change researchers and practitioners has finally begun to learn something about how ongoing improvement can be fostered and sustained in schools, government policy on education has not taken adequate account of this knowledge about school development. As a consequence, an important source of synergy has been lost and student learning continues to lag behind its potential. Government efforts to improve schooling are less effective than they might be and many school improvement efforts have to swim against the current of government regulation.

Given this central irony in educational policy, the purpose of this chapter is to explore the range of policy options for authentic school improvement. This will be done by:

- documenting the failure of 'performance based' approaches to large-scale reform
- reviewing the lessons for policy from the research on school improvement
- outlining the components of a local infrastructure for school improvement
- emphasising the importance of networks in supporting school improvement
- proposing a policy framework for 'real' school improvement.

The failure of 'performance based' approaches to large-scale reform

In this section, further evidence is cited to support the contention, that in order for government policies to have the desired effect of enhancing outcomes for all students these policies must embrace the implications from the research on school improvement.

Leithwood and his colleagues (1999) have reviewed the impact of a number of 'performance based' approaches to large-scale reform. They identify seven specific properties of 'performance based' approaches to reform (Leithwood *et al.*, 1999: 8):

1   A centrally determined, unifying vision and explicit goals for student performance based on the vision.
2   Curriculum frameworks and related materials for use in accomplishing the goals set for students.
3   Standards for judging the quality or degree of success of all students.
4   Coherent, well integrated policies that reinforce these ambitious standards.
5   Information about the organisation's (especially the students') performance.
6   A system of finance and governance that devolves to the local school site responsibility for producing improvements in system and student performance.
7   An agent that receives information on organisational performance, judges the extent to which standards have been met, and distributes rewards and sanctions, with significant consequences to the organisation for its success or failure in meeting specified standards.

This approach to centralised educational change has become widespread over the past ten years. The Leithwood review examines in a comparative manner, five cases of performance-based reform that are well known and have been widely documented – Kentucky, California, New Zealand, Victoria (Australia), and Chicago. On the basis of this review two striking conclusions are reached:

- The first is that on the available evidence there was no increase in student achievement in any case except Chicago, and even that was 'slow in coming' (Leithwood *et al.*, 1999: 40).
- The second is 'the disappointing contribution that performance-based reforms have made to improving the core technology of schooling' (Leithwood *et al.*, 1999: 61–3).

In particular these reforms did not

- adequately acknowledge the local context
- take the school site seriously
- find incentives that work
- contribute to significant increases in professional capacity
- address and diagnose opportunity costs.

Although the impact of large-scale reform on student achievement is notoriously fickle, the fact that these reform strategies neglected to focus on instruction and capacity building must have contributed to their inability to impact positively on student achievement. In support of this argument, it is helpful to look at the case of Chicago where there were student achievement gains, but not until Year 7 of a ten-year initiative.

The Chicago initiative has been well-documented (Bryk *et al.*, 1998; Fullan, 1999). On examining the evidence it appears that for the first six years of the initiative, 1988–94, the 'system operated in a decentralised fashion with little functional contact between schools and the district. In other words too little structure characterised the operation' (Fullan, 2000). Since 1994 however, the central district was reorganised, with decentralised development being retained within a context of capacity building and external accountability. During this time five extra school functions were developed that may help explain why students in Chicago began to achieve more during this period (Bryk *et al.*, 1998: 279–81):

- policy making increasingly supported decentralisation
- there was a focus on local capacity building
- a system of rigorous accountability was introduced
- innovation was stimulated
- external support networks were established.

There are a number of other examples from the research on school districts in North America, that illustrate that under the right conditions, significant and rapid progress can be made in enhancing the learning of students. Three further examples support this general point. The first is the experience of the Durham School District in Greater Toronto that is part of the 'Learning Consortium' (Fullan *et al.*, 1990). The Durham district has 'pulled all the appropriate instructional and support levers' at the same time, and based their implementation strategies on those that work in practice and are supported by convincing research evidence (Bennett and Green, 1995). The second is the well-known example of the 'Schenley' project in Pittsburgh school district (Wallace *et al.*, 1990). As part of a district wide staff development programme, the Schenley School became a staff development centre where outstanding teachers were brought together. Other district teachers rotated into the school observing these teachers and studying instruction. There was an immediate rise in achievement throughout the curriculum areas. The third example is of the New York school system (Elmore and Burney, 1998; Fullan, 2000). Once again strong vision coupled to intensive staff development on instructional practices and capacity building, led to significant increases in levels of student achievement. What is impressive about these examples is that with concerted effort even inner city schools can be turned around.

The analysis of 'performance based' approaches and the school district examples are entirely consistent with previous research on the implementation of large-scale reform efforts. As we have seen, evidence from the United States of major multi-site research studies such as the Rand Study in the 1970s (see MacLaughlin, 1990), the DESSI study (see Crandall *et al.*, 1986), and the analysis of a range of restructuring programmes during the 1990s by Stringfield and his colleagues (1996), all point to the same conclusion. Unless central reforms address the context of teaching and learning, as well as capacity building at the school level, within the context of external support, then the aspirations of reform will never be realised. It is argued in the following section that this is best achieved if educational policies are based on the principles and practice of authentic school improvement.

Lessons for policy from the research on authentic school improvement

When government policy does not impact directly on student achievement and learning it is because it lacks a 'real' school improvement perspective. It matters little how 'good' the policy may be, unless it is implemented then there will be little impact on outcomes. The logic of the position is that governmental policy if it wishes to influence schools, teachers and students needs to be informed by what is known about how schools improve. The review in chapter 1 of current policy initiatives in most western countries suggested that although they may contain some of the key ingredients for a successful contemporary approach to school improvement, they are unlikely

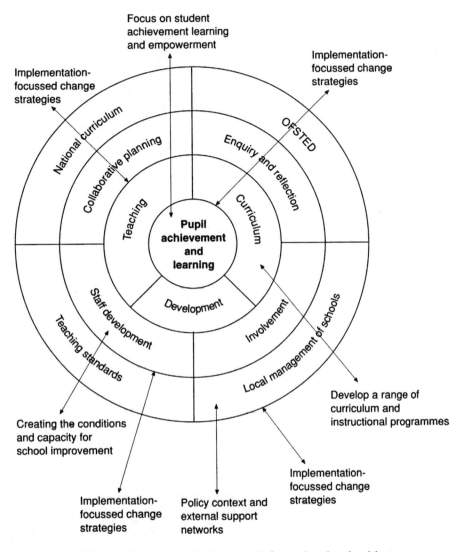

Focus on student
achievement learning
and empowerment

Implementation-
focussed change
strategies

Implementation-
focussed change
strategies

National curriculum

Collaborative planning

Teaching

Enquiry and reflection

OFSTED

Curriculum

**Pupil
achievement
and
learning**

Development

Staff development

Teaching standards

Involvement

Local management of schools

Develop a range of
curriculum and
instructional programmes

Creating the conditions
and capacity for
school improvement

Implementation-
focussed change
strategies

Implementation-
focussed change
strategies

Policy context and
external support
networks

Figure 10.1 The five elements of the framework for authentic school improvement

to deliver the promised higher levels of achievement. In general the approach being advocated is insufficiently strategic and ignores what is known about implementation and integrative and successful school improvement efforts.

It is at this point that a number of themes that have been developed in previous chapters harmonise. In chapter 2, ten principles for authentic school improvement based on an eclectic range of research, practice and theory were identified. Later, in chapter 4, following an analysis of a variety of school improvement programmes and experience, a framework for authentic school improvement was presented. In Figure 10.1 the framework

Table 10.1 Policy implications for authentic school improvement

Principles of authentic school improvement	Framework elements	Policy implications from research on educational change and school improvement
Achievement focussed Empowering in aspiration	Focus on student achievement and learning and empowerment	• Keep an unrelenting focus on student achievement and learning • Develop curriculum and teaching programmes that are based on what is known about learning
Research based and theory rich Context specific	Develop curriculum and teaching programmes that are based on what is known about learning	• Pay attention to context (one size does not fit all) – develop knowledge about what works and where • Build capacity and strengthen known capacity creating components
Capacity building in nature Enquiry driven	Creating the conditions and capacity for school improvement	• Nurture professional learning communities and provide incentives for teacher and school enquiry • Improve research and dissemination and make it practitioner relevant
Implementation oriented Interventionist and strategic	Implementation focussed change strategies	• Create a commitment to, and allow time for, effective implementation • Link pressure and support at all levels of the system
Externally supported Systemic	Policy context and external support networks	• Establish local infrastructures and networks, supported by quality external facilitation • Ensure policy coherence

has been annotated to identify its key elements; the major difference from the original is that the 'implementation focussed' style of change is portrayed as the mortar that cements the other elements together. In subsequent chapters the various elements of the framework were elaborated in relation to practice and research. Taken together these principles and key elements lead to a relatively secure set of implications for school improvement policies.

The basis of the synthesis is presented in Table 10.1. In the first column are the ten principles for authentic school improvement, in column two are the elements of the school improvement framework, and in column three, the policy implications.

As will be seen in the following section, it is salutary to compare these policy implications with the approach to school self-improvement being used by most western governments. It is reassuring however that these key findings about the implications for governmental policy is consistent with a number of recent studies of large-scale reform. (For a comprehensive review see the *International Handbook of Educational Change*, Hargreaves *et al.*, 1998; and also Crandall *et al.*, 1986; Dalin, 1994; Elmore, 1996; Leithwood *et al.*, 1999; Fullan, 2000.) Because the detail of these implications has already been discussed in previous chapters they will only be briefly reviewed here.

Keep an unrelenting focus on student achievement and learning

Little more needs to be said here about the importance of keeping an unrelenting focus on student achievement and learning. It has been a continuing and persistent theme.

The focus however needs to be on a broader range of outcome than just test scores or examination results. The learning capability and social competence of students are equally important outcomes of schooling. This point also relates to the crucial failure of most policy initiatives to impact on the 'learning level'. As has already been argued, most school improvement initiatives are poorly conceptualised in the precise ways in which they might impact upon learning in the classroom. If the aim is to raise levels of student achievement, then an explicit focus on teaching and learning needs to be at the centre of policy making.

Develop curriculum and teaching programmes that are based on what is known about learning

Much recent centralised reform places great faith in the ability of curriculum guidelines to codify and ensure consistency of practice. National governments now almost without exception outline curriculum guidelines, but require teachers to develop the detailed schemes of work involved and to select the most appropriate instructional strategies. Although guidelines ensure a degree of uniformity in the curriculum diet of students, they will not necessarily raise standards of performance. There are three key implications for policy here. The first is that educational programmes need to be sufficiently comprehensive so that they link together in explicit and concrete ways curriculum content and teaching strategies. The second is that as Crandall and his colleagues (1986: 29) have noted, 'it should not be assumed that involving teachers in developing innovations will invariably lead to better programs', 'the crucial variable is whether programs are implementable and attractive to teachers'. This leads to the third implication, the need to increase the number of comprehensive, school-wide models for school improvement that have been carefully developed and can be broadly disseminated.

Pay attention to context (one size does not fit all): develop knowledge about what works and where

Most education reforms are insufficiently differentiated to allow schools to choose or adapt programmes to fit their own particular situation, and the learning needs of their students. Some schools' performance is outstanding over a period of time, others less so. Inner-city schools may face very different challenges to rural or suburban schools. A strategy that helps to keep a school at an excellent level of performance is likely to be different again. Much also depends, of course, on what we mean by 'lower performing' and 'high performing' schools. The social context of the school has a powerful effect both on achievement levels and on strategies to improve achievement. Problems of poverty, especially, are unlikely to be managed using a strategy that focusses only on curriculum and instruction (Levin, 1995; Mortimore and Whitty, 1997). The policy implications are twofold. First, make provision for contextual differences in policy prescriptions. Do not, however, allow this to be used as an excuse by under-performing schools. Poverty may explain a certain level of under-achievement, and this may provide an argument for additional support. It is not however a reason to accept failure on a continuing basis. This links to the second implication as well as the point above, the need for a range of curriculum and instructional programmes suited to the 'contexts' of different schools and students.

Build capacity and strengthen known capacity creating components

At the same time as informed decisions are being made about appropriate teaching and learning programmes and strategies, attention needs also to be given as to how best facilitate the chosen approach within the school's organisation. This approach is neither top-down – focussed in the main on management arrangements; nor bottom-up – committed to specific changes in individual classrooms, but a combination of the two. This also has been a continuing theme throughout the book. Suffice it to say, without an explicit focus on 'capacity building', not only will classroom innovations be quickly marginalised, but also the ability of the school to sustain and manage change will be negated. The implication is to accommodate and develop a concept of 'capacity building' not just within central policy, but also in programmes for teacher and leadership training, and schemes for inspection.

Nurture professional learning communities and provide incentives for teacher and school enquiry

Recent work on staff development, in particular the peer coaching strategy, has helped challenge thinking about the conventional practice of staff development (Joyce and Showers, 1995). As we have already seen Joyce (1992) has distinguished between the two key elements of staff development: the workshop and the workplace. The *workshop* is where understanding is gained and skills are practised. If those skills are to be transferred back into the classroom then peer coaching and action research are required. In particular, peer coaching is helpful when curriculum and instruction are the content of staff development and school-based groups support each other to attain 'transfer of training' (Joyce *et al.*, 1999: 127). In short it requires a transformation to the professional culture of the school, and in most cases, as was seen in the case studies in previous chapters, will require significant alterations to the ways schools are organised. It means the establishing of the school as a professional learning community. The implications for successful policy implementation are profound, if obvious.

Improve research and dissemination and make it practitioner relevant

There are three points that relate to research and dissemination. The first is that the increasing evidence about effective practice, which comes both from formal research and from educators' experience, plays far too small a role in policy and in school development. An important role for government lies in supporting the creation and dissemination of evidence, so that schools can learn from the efforts of others. Second, and at the same time, schools need help to improve their own ability to gather and use data. Careful analysis of achievement data, both from external tests and internal evaluation, should be a key part of any school's efforts to improve. But other data is also important, including data on the nature of the student body and of the school's community, information about the post-school activities of students, knowledge of the local labour market in which students and parents live, and data on actual teaching and learning practices in the school. Third, teachers need to become increasingly well versed in the methods of action research. It is enquiry into practice that fuels the improvement process, and that contributes to the establishing of the professional learning community. Policies need to support educators in learning not just how to gather and analyse data, but also how to debate and use its implications for improvement purposes.

Create a commitment to, and allow time for, effective implementation

The focus of policy is usually on some aspect of management or the curriculum, yet as has been seen, if classroom practice is to be affected then teachers' behaviours and practices as well as their beliefs and understandings need to be addressed. It is teachers' struggles to come to terms with the technical and psychological aspects of the change process that lead to what has been called the 'implementation dip', and explains the levels of resistance characteristically associated with school improvement efforts that focus on classroom change. It is these aspects of the implementation process that are not taken account of in most policy formulations. The second issue relates to the quality of implementation. Although all policies and programmes will require some adaptation to local context, this is not a licence to dilute an innovation beyond recognition. It is the quality and consistency of implementation that eventually ensures positive impact on student achievement. Third, most effective school improvement strategies require some form of intervention or active implementation. Whether this is internally or externally initiated, it implies some break with existing practice, with all that entails. Policy therefore has to be concerned with helping teachers through the change process, as well as the quality of implementation itself.

Link pressure and support at all levels in the system

The truth in the oxymoron 'pressure and support' has increasingly been recognised in the school improvement and change literature. Without it there is little impetus to change. Interestingly, the principle works at all levels within the educational system, and it need not be as Machiavellian a strategy as it may seem on first appearance. The principle works as effectively at the level of professional collaboration ('I do not want to let my colleague down'), as it does at the national level (witness Michael Barber's [2000] advocacy for the principle of 'maximum challenge, maximum support' within the English educational system). As Fullan (2000) has noted, this works best when systems of pressure and support are *integrated,* not segmented. For example, professional learning communities incorporate pressure and support in a seamless way. In these systems, there is great 'lateral accountability' as well as support, as teachers work with each other focussing on student progress. Similarly, accountability systems are effective only when they are connected to mechanisms and processes for making changes. The integration of pressure and support at all levels in the system is the policy challenge here.

Establish local infrastructures and networks, supported by quality external facilitation

In the current 'policy epidemic' there is a tendency to ignore, neuter or abolish 'meso-level' support for schools. This is the support level – the role that local education authorities or school districts, local universities, and other agencies have traditionally played. It may well be that many (if not all) of these organisations have reached their 'sell-by date', but it is not to say that their function of supporting the improvement work of schools is equally anachronistic. What is needed are more creative and responsive structures for working with schools. These are what Fullan (2000) refers to as 'cross-over structures'. They are the variety of networks, agencies, offices, and institutions that play a vital role in implementation. In developing a policy of *systemic* educational change, a number of agencies are inevitably affected (and indeed created). Fullan's proposal is that we treat such structures as being engaged in dissemination and maximising the mobilisation of energy from the very beginning, as well as providing support once the process has been established, so avoiding the sharp distinction between initiation and implementation. This principle for policy should apply to both formal national and local agencies, as well as to the more informal networks that provide support to schools and their staff.

Ensure policy coherence

Earlier, in chapter 1, much was made of the importance of policy implementation that is both system wide and system deep. This applied both to coherence in structures as proposed above as well as to coherence at the level of values, aspirations and ways of working. There are a number of complex issues here. The key point, however, as Fullan (2000) has noted,

> is that working with systems means conceptualising strategies with whole systems in mind. Working with schools means taking into account the total set of changes facing given schools, and figuring out the best relationship with the surrounding infrastructure . . . Large-scale reform then, will require units to make connections and to synergise activities around common priorities.

The system emphasis is not to achieve control (which is impossible), but to harness the interactive capability of systemic forces. The systemic perspective also applies to the school. Changes in teaching practice only occur when there is clarity and coherence in the minds of teachers. This clarity needs to be at the 'receiving end rather than at the delivery end' (Fullan, 1995). It appears that the more coherent and collaborative the internal conditions of the school, the more knowledgeable the teachers in those schools are of national policy initiatives. In such schools, where staff commitment has been very high, the outcomes secured are unusually impressive.

If a systemic perspective is genuinely to be achieved then a high degree of consistency is required across the policy spectrum. First, policy makers continually keep the 'big picture' in mind in searching for connections and ways of exploiting potential synergy. Second, the more the school works collaboratively on improvement at the school level, the more it engages critically with external standards and policy. Third, sustained and authentic school improvement requires a high quality teaching profession that reflects both a system level commitment to upgrade the profession, as well as the nurturing of professional learning communities within the school. The role of the local level in facilitating this integration provides the focus for the following section.

Developing a local infrastructure to support school improvement

In addition to the implications for national policy described in the previous section, the role that local agencies – school districts and local education authorities – play in school improvement also needs highlighting. Although the context for the review of characteristics of successful local support will be the local education authority in England, the discussion is intended to be generalisable to other jurisdictions.

The relationship between central government and local education authorities (LEAs) in England has not been a comfortable one for the last decade or so. The election of the Labour government in 1997 gave cause for new speculation about the role and future of the LEA. It is clear that the LEA now has a more defined, if restricted, role to play in the national agenda for school improvement and in raising standards across all schools. If LEAs are to achieve the goals set for them they will need to be strategic in their planning and efficient in policy implementation. The research evidence, the upswing in interest in school improvement, OFSTED's inspection of the school improvement capacity of LEAs, and their statutory obligations, all suggest that school improvement needs to be the major focus of the LEA.

It is instructive to look at the characteristics of those LEAs that have been successful in carrying forward this agenda. Successful local education authorities and school districts such as those referred to earlier, have a very clear sense of their purpose and direction. This 'clear sense of direction' can be viewed as having six interrelated components:

- The first is a sense of vision and mission. Successful LEAs have the ability to engender and mobilise support through either a charismatic director whose values position is unequivocal, and/or clear statements of the goals for the LEA.

- Second, this vision is translated into a set of operational targets related to student learning that is achievable, limited but yet providing a clear link to the vision.

- Third, vision and targets are only one part of the equation. LEAs should also be identifying 'good practice' and providing practical strategies that enable schools to move towards these targets. Effective LEAs have mechanisms for disseminating good practice. They are able to link effective practices across the LEA and to draw good practices in from the outside. Dissemination is a very important feature of maintaining the vision of the LEA.

- Fourth, the LEA should provide high quality challenge and support to schools. This may mean a differentiated approach where one function is related to challenging and monitoring the school and the other function is supporting the change process. As part of this latter effort, curriculum consultants or advisory teachers may be employed on secondment to provide the expertise in classroom practice.

- Fifth, there are a series of other functions that effective LEAs carry out:
  - They relate OFSTED inspections to ongoing school improvement initiatives inside the school.
  - They produce value-added data that is accessible to schools and helps them define their school improvement objectives.
  - The LEA has a clear strategy for monitoring the effectiveness of schools. It knows which its good schools are and, by the same token, its poor ones.
  - The LEA also has strategies to support these different types of schools; they have 'a differential approach to school effectiveness' which links appropriate support to the various growth states of schools.
- Finally, the striking feature of effective LEAs is their ability to mobilise the community towards school improvement efforts. Many LEAs have already established School Improvement Alliances or Consortia. Such alliances however should extend beyond the educational community and link to other support agencies, media, business and the general community and galvanise support across the city for the learning targets that the LEA has set itself. Such alliances need to be broad rather than narrow in scope.

These features of the 'new' role of the LEA are illustrated in Figure 10.2, the 'Skeletal model of school self-evaluation and improvement'. This diagram gives an overview of the whole process. It is most probably the case that the LEA itself will not provide all of those functions, but that they will be delivered by a variety of agencies. It may be that over time the LEA role will change again or even disappear altogether. What is important is that these functions are still carried out, irrespective of the agency responsible for, or contributing to, provision. Increasingly in England the distinction is being made between the challenge and support functions. The challenge function is provided by the LEA, and the support by an independent support agency.

The challenge function involves:

- establishing a trusting and professional relationship with a group of schools that can be sustained over time
- having access to high quality data on performance, value added and other key dimensions with which to engage the school in dialogue
- identifying well in advance those schools that have weaknesses and alert support agencies to those ranges of needs
- being able on the basis of data to engage the schools in medium-term planning.

The support function involves:

- providing support for the school's plans either from its own resources and curriculum consultants or through some form of brokerage

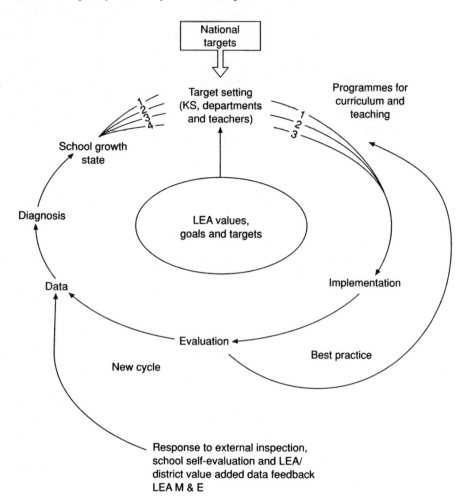

Figure 10.2 Skeletal model of school self-evaluation and improvement

- continuing to support schools in specific ways, for example with literacy, numeracy and other curriculum and instructional initiatives
- assisting schools with their own enquiry-based school improvement efforts
- being a source of leadership for school improvement through keeping the focus on student learning and achievement.

Such models of local support bring together many of the key functions related to successful school improvement that have already been identified. The evidence also suggests that networks or clusters of schools need to be established to support this process (see for example Lieberman, 1995). As is seen in the following section, these networks would:

- represent a coherent and geographically distinct set of schools
- identify a lead school that could facilitate the school improvement agenda
- provide support for each other both horizontally, i.e., across the curriculum to support consistency in teaching practices, and vertically, i.e., between phases of education to provide the continuity in learning practices
- be the focus for inter-agency and community support.

There is great potential for the lead school in such a network to contribute significantly to a range of school improvement purposes. A number of educational systems have identified roles for such schools. In England there is the development of 'Training Schools' or 'Beacon Schools' to fulfil this function. The 'Professional Development School' in North America is another more established example. These schools are ones where collaborations or partnerships have been established between schools, local agencies and university schools of education that focus on high quality education, the preparation of student teachers, continuing professional development for school staff, and continuous enquiry into improving practice. These are medium-term relationships characterised by reciprocity and parity, and by commitments to shared beliefs about teaching and learning and issues of equity.

The model of school improvement implied by this definition encompasses a commitment to focus on all pupils, all teachers and their professional development, teaching and learning strategies and the building of a professional learning community. The impact of such partnerships could be raised to another level by focussing research on issues of classroom, school, local and national significance. The alignment of research and development in these schools, between pupil learning goals, the training of new teachers, the professional development of existing teachers, developing school improvement networks, and the integration of local and national and educational imperatives provides a full expression of the potential of the 'lead school' concept.

In the same way as professional development or training schools take further the role of the lead school in a network, so too could the support agency concept expand from a local to a regional basis. An agency of this type could assume broader responsibilities for continuous professional development, the initial training of teachers, educational research and inter-agency collaboration for community renewal. With such an explicit school improvement agenda, such an organisation would quite appropriately challenge some of the traditional functions of the university schools of education, as well as LEAs. This may well ruffle some feathers initially, and this may be no bad thing! What is certain however, if the school improvement agenda is to be taken seriously, is that radical and responsive ways of challenging and supporting schools at the local level are needed. The role of networking in this endeavour provides the focus for the following section.

The role of networks in supporting school improvement

There has recently been much international interest in the role of networks in supporting school improvement (e.g., OECD, 1999). There are however various interpretations of the network concept. Although networks bring together those with like minded interests, they are more than just opportunities to share 'good practice'. The following definition of networks emerged from an analysis of effective networks identified by the OECD (quotation and discussion in this section based on Hopkins, 2000a: 1):

> Networks are purposeful social entities characterised by a commitment to quality, rigour, and a focus on outcomes. They are also an effective means of supporting innovation in times of change. In education, networks promote the dissemination of good practice, enhance the professional development of teachers, support capacity building in schools, mediate between centralised and decentralised structures, and assist in the process of re-structuring and re-culturing educational organisations and systems.

The qualities exhibited by such networks are however not easily acquired. A number of key conditions need to be in place if networks are to realise their potential as agents of educational innovation. In terms of school improvement, a number of conditions for effective networks can be identified:

- *Consistency of values and focus:* it is important that networks have a common aim and purpose, and that the values underpinning the network are well articulated and 'owned' by those involved. This consistency of values and purpose also relates to the need for the focus of the network to be consistent with the overarching policy framework.
- *Clarity of structure:* effective networks are well organised with clear operating procedures and mechanisms for ensuring that maximum participation is achieved within and between schools. These structures promote involvement that is broad based, preferably with a whole organisation or systemic focus, rather than being narrow, limiting or particular.
- *Knowledge creation, utilisation and transfer:* the key purpose of networks is to create and disseminate knowledge to support educational improvement and innovation. Such knowledge and practice needs to be based on evidence, to focus on the core features of schooling, and to be subject to robust quality assurance procedures.
- *Rewards related to learning:* those who belong to networks need to feel that their involvement is worthwhile. Rewards for networking are best related to supporting professional development and the encouraging of learning. Effective networks invest in people.
- *Dispersed leadership and empowerment:* highly effective networks contain skilful people who collaborate and work well together. The skills required by network members are similar to the skill sets associated

with effective teams and include a focus on dispersed leadership and empowerment.

- *Adequate resources:* networks need to be adequately resourced particularly in terms of time, finance and human capital. It is not necessarily the quantum of resource that is important, more crucially there needs to be flexibility in the way in which it is deployed.

In line with the argument of this chapter, networks in education have a key role to play in supporting innovation and school improvement. Accordingly, networks need to be regarded as support structures for innovative schools, not only in disseminating 'good practice', but also in overcoming the traditional isolation of schools, and to a certain extent even challenging traditional hierarchical system structures. In the past most school systems have operated almost exclusively through individual units; be they teachers, departments, schools or local agencies. Such isolation may have been appropriate during times of stability, but during times of change there is a need to 'tighten the loose coupling', to increase collaboration and to establish more fluid and responsive structures.

It is important to realise however that networks do not just facilitate innovation. By offering the possibility of new ways of working networks can also be an innovation in themselves. This is particularly important in contemporary educational systems, as there is currently a tendency to reduce 'meso-level' support for schools. It may well be that these support structures – the role that local education authorities or school districts, local universities, and other agencies have traditionally played – are also more effective at buttressing the status quo, rather than supporting change and need to be phased out.

Yet paradoxically, in times of innovation and change, the meso-level becomes increasingly important. What is needed however are not outmoded institutions, but more creative and responsive structures for working with and between schools. Networks can provide a means of facilitating innovation and change as well as contributing to large-scale reform. They offer the potential for 're-inventing' the meso-level by promoting different forms of collaboration, linkages, and multi-functional partnerships. These are sometimes referred to as 'cross-over structures' (Fullan, 2000). In this respect the Network enables stakeholders to make connections and to synergise activities around common priorities.

Networks clearly have a role to play during all the phases of a change process. So for example in terms of the typology of change introduced in chapter 3:

- During the 'initiation phase' networks encourage:
  - shared commitment and ownership
  - leadership at a variety of levels
  - external facilitation
  - a clear focus on goals and purposes.

- During the 'implementation phase' networks encourage:
  - understandings about learning and the management of change
  - more flexible and creative use of space, time, communication structures and people
  - social and technical support
  - early success and celebration.
- During the 'institutionalisation phase' networks encourage:
  - widespread use of collaborative ways of working
  - planning for 'scaling up'
  - the redefinition and adaptation of ideas through the use of evidence
  - internally useful data feedback and externally useful evaluation.

To summarise, networks have the potential to support educational innovation and change by:

- providing a focal point for the dissemination of good practice, the generalisability of innovation and the creation of 'action oriented' knowledge about effective educational practices.
- keeping the focus on the core purposes of schooling in particular in creating and sustaining a discourse on teaching and learning
- enhancing the skill of teachers, leaders and other educators in change agent skills and managing the change process
- building capacity for continuous improvement at the local level, and in particular in creating professional learning communities, within and between schools
- ensuring that systems of pressure and support are *integrated* not segmented. For example, professional learning communities incorporate pressure and support in a seamless way
- acting as a link between the centralised and decentralised schism resulting from many contemporary policy initiatives, in particular in contributing to policy coherence horizontally and vertically.

The analysis of the conditions required for effective networking, and the contribution of networks to innovation and change, demonstrate that networks can operate at a number of different levels. In the context of supporting innovation one can discern an evolving typology of Network types. At the basic level networks facilitate the sharing of good practice, at the highest level they can act as agents of system renewal:

- At its most basic level a network could be regarded as simply groups of teachers joining together for a common curriculum purpose and for the sharing of good practice.
- At a more ambitious level networks could involve groups of teachers and schools joining together for the purposes of school improvement with the explicit aim of not just sharing practice but of enhancing teaching and learning throughout a school or groups of schools.

- Over and above this, networks could also not just serve the purpose of knowledge transfer and school improvement, but also involve groups of stakeholders joining together for the implementation of specific policies locally and possibly nationally.
- A further extension of this way of working is found when groups of networks (within and outside education) link together for system improvement in terms of social justice and inclusion.
- Finally, there is the possibility of groups of networks working together not just on a social justice agenda, but also to act explicitly as an agency for system renewal and transformation.

As has been argued at length in this book, the main reason why reforms have not had the desired impact is because government policy on education has not been adequately informed by what is known about how schools improve. This provides a strong argument for governments embracing networks not only as a strategy to assist in the implementation of its reform agenda, but also as an innovation in its own right. Without some form of networking, it is highly unlikely that the aspirations for governmental programmes of educational reform, particularly in decentralised systems, will be realised. If one issue is certain it is that the future of schooling requires a systemic perspective, which implies a high degree of consistency across the policy spectrum and an unrelenting focus on student achievement and learning. Networks, as a natural infrastructure for both innovation and the informing of government policy, provide a means for doing just that.

A policy framework for authentic school improvement

Having critiqued 'performance based' approaches to educational reform, reviewed the implications for policy from the school improvement research, discussed the elements of a local support structure for schools and the role of networks, it is necessary to pull these themes together into a set of guidelines for policy makers. There is no doubt that most governments are committed to the aspirations of school improvement, what they often lack is a considered conceptual framework in which to drive forward and deliver their educational agenda. Successful policy initiatives in the area of school improvement reflect a 'goodness of fit' between the aspirations and implications of the policy being implemented, the values of the school, and the beliefs of teachers. Creating the conditions for such synergy is a key challenge for those at all levels of the educational system (see also Slavin, 1998; Hopkins and Levin, 2000).

Most governments now identify targets for achievement in key learning areas. If these targets are to be realised central policies need to incorporate three further elements.

- The first is making available to schools and local agencies strategies to assist them in realising the goals they have identified, remembering of course that all schools are at different levels of effectiveness. Instead of every school 're-inventing the wheel' governments should be encouraging the development and piloting of curriculum *and* instructional programmes that directly address in implementable ways the targets that they and schools are setting.

- Second, if this could be achieved – a range of policy options related to programmes that *really* work – then schools could begin to select from among a range of options those strategies that address the particular targets they have set, and the learning needs of their students. With such a series of programme options available, schools are then in a position to address more directly the crucial issues of staff development, capacity building and consistency of implementation that are so necessary for ensuring student achievement. The school-level context can facilitate, and to a great extent, determine, successful policy implementation.
- Third, government would then be in a position to target funding to those schools in the greatest need in the far more secure knowledge that what they were going to do would achieve the goals the system as a whole had set itself. In order to challenge schools to be the best they can be, and to support programme development and capacity building, a local infrastructure also needs to be developed. This too needs to be a part of policy formulation. Further there will be the need to focus not just on how innovations impact on individual schools, but on how such innovations can move up the scale and impact across all schools and the system as a whole.

The proposals made in this chapter require a fundamentally new and radical way of thinking about educational reform. In particular, they require a new mindset on the part of policy-makers in attempting to link reform strategies to the achievement of young people in our schools. How might governments move such an agenda forward?

- Even the best of current reform initiatives adopt an *à la carte* perspective to the principles previously outlined. Some may be included, but rarely all of them; the criteria for inclusion often appear to be serendipitous. For example, an initiative may be strong on 'models of teaching' and staff development, but weak on context specificity and capacity building. Most fail to understand the dialectic between classroom and whole-school change, and research and dissemination also usually get short shrift. While the principles outlined may not be the last word on the matter, they do provide an integrated set of research-based criteria against which policies can be formulated and evaluated.
- Reform does require additional resources, but the critical issue is how the resources are deployed. It is vital to link funding to clear plans for improvement that are based on thoughtful use of the best available evidence. It is also important to make sure that all the various forms of additional funding are accessible and coherently focussed, so that schools and districts are not trying to manage multiple funding requests and

multiple programmes that lead them in different directions at the same time. Effective reform may also be impossible without resources for other purposes such as retaining good teachers, maintaining adequate school facilities, or overcoming some of the deep-seated effects of social disadvantage and poverty. However in all cases the essential element is a clear link between resources and outcomes.

- One of the reasons that the relationship between national policy and classroom practice is notoriously fickle is because of a lack of consistency within and between policies. National agencies in particular need to reflect coherence in values and strategy. For example: an inspection agency needs to both challenge and support, and contribute to development by building on school self-evaluation; schemes for the performance appraisal of teachers need to embrace accountability and development, and 'fit' within a whole school context; curriculum agencies need to link curriculum specifications to teaching strategies and schemes for formative assessment; leadership training schemes need to focus on dispersed and instructional leadership; and the agencies responsible for the certification and training of teachers need to find ways of upgrading the profession of teaching. Policy alignment needs therefore to be both horizontal and vertical – reaching across policies and through the various levels of the system. Horizontal co-ordination would suggest that all of these be aligned to support instructional goals and strategies. Vertical co-ordination would mean that classrooms, schools and local authorities receive consistent messages about what is required for success. In this respect, the proliferation of educational agencies and actors in most systems may not be helpful.

- The building of local capacity is as important as a coherent national policy. Key elements of building local capacity are often in existence but not well connected with each other nor linked to a capacity-building agenda. Teachers, school leaders, parents and community leaders need to be supported in learning how to implement and use these and other practices effectively. There also needs to be a closer connection between school improvement work and initial teacher training, so that new teachers come to their work with at least some understanding of key improvement strategies and skills. Building capacity and managing real change requires skills that most administrators now only learn through practice and experience, if they learn them at all. These elements, as well as local research and dissemination could be integrated in ways that are much more powerful than their current separate embodiments. Some new thinking about appropriate organisational forms and delivery modes could have powerful effects in building capacity for change in schools, and in creating the enabling conditions that allow positive change to take place and to become institutionalised.

- Above all, governments should insist that schools be thoughtful in their approach to change and improvement, but not necessarily require that everyone do the same thing in the same way at the same time. The only way to get people to think is to create and support the expectation of thinking. Overall it is unlikely that these proposals would be any more costly than current activities supported by governments. Nor will they be politically problematic. Governments could continue to focus, if they wish, on matters of achievement, standards and accountability, but they would now do so with more confidence that their policies are likely to bring about the conditions they say they desire.

Commentary

Let me finish as I began on a personal note. In this book I have defined 'real school improvement' as an approach to educational change that has a relentless focus on the learning and achievement of students, and on the establishing of a professional learning community within the school. As has been seen this is not an uncontentious position to hold, yet it is a very necessary one. My own personal vision for school improvement also emphasises both its moral purpose and its contribution to educational reform and social justice.

In the introduction I mentioned my hopes for the education and development of my children. What I wish for Jeroen, Jessica and Dylan, is that they not only meet and if possible surpass existing educational standards, but that they also find learning exciting, compelling and intrinsically worthwhile. But not only in an academic sense, as vital as this is. I want more than this for each of them. I wish them to appreciate the richness of their own cultures, to experience the exhilaration of overcoming physical challenges as I have done throughout my life, and to understand the importance of physical activity to health. I wish them to become competent and social beings who have sound, secure and healthy self-concepts to help them face the challenges that await them in their lives.

It is here where the personal and the professional converge. What I want for my children is I believe the same as what most teachers wish for their students. There is a striking quality about fine teachers – they care deeply about their students. Most teachers came into teaching because they wanted to make a difference. A key characteristic of those outstanding teachers in our OECD study was their 'love of children' (Hopkins and Stern, 1996). It may well be that for various reasons, many of which may be to do with the context within which teachers currently work, a degree of cynicism and weariness may dull this initial enthusiasm. But as Michael Fullan commented in *Change Forces* (1993: 10) 'scratch a good teacher and you find a moral purpose'.

It is much easier for individual teachers to express their 'moral purpose' when the institutional climate of the universities and schools in which they train and work espouse and articulate a set of coherent educational values. I do not wish to sound pious, but high quality teachers are committed to the learning of students, so too are outstanding schools. Our research on improving and exemplary schools suggests that they are characterised by a passion for learning; and that they consistently articulate the values on which their curriculum, organisation and teaching methods are based.

In the sense that I mean it here, moral purpose is not 'wishy-washy' idealism, but a ruthless and relentless commitment to the learning of children at both an individual and institutional level. An unending quest for the highest of standards, a low tolerance of failure, and a commitment to student learning is the moral purpose that I see in the outstanding teachers and schools I am privileged to meet and visit.

It is moral purpose that gives the impetus for school improvement: not just in the first place, it also provides the determination to continue on the 'journey'. Without such an authentic or 'real' approach to school improvement, the evidence of practice and research clearly suggests that society will continue to set educational goals that are, on current performance, beyond the capacity of the system to deliver.

References

Abbott, R., Birchenough, M. and Steadman, S. (1988) *GRIDS School Handbooks*, 2nd edn, primary and secondary versions, York: Longman for the SCDC.

Adelman, C. (1993) 'Kurt Lewin and the origins of action research', *Educational Action Research*, 1 (1): 7–24.

Adey, P. and Shayer, M. (1990) 'Accelerating the development of formal thinking in middle and high school students', *Journal of Research in Science Teaching*, 27 (3): 267–85.

Adey, P. and Shayer, M. (1994) *Really Raising Standards*, London: Routledge.

Ainscow, M. and Muncey, J. (1989) *Meeting Individual Needs in the Primary School*, London: Fulton.

Ainscow, M., Hopkins, D., Southworth, G. and West, M. (1994) *Creating The Conditions for School Improvement*, London: David Fulton Publishers.

Ainscow, M., Hargreaves, D. H. and Hopkins, D. (1995) 'Mapping the process of change in schools', *Evaluation and Research in Education*, 9 (2): 75–90.

American Quality Foundation (1992) *The International Quality Study: Best Practices Report*, Cleveland, Ohio: American Quality Foundation and Ernst and Young.

Aoki, T. (1979) 'Toward curriculum enquiry in a new key', Occasional Paper No. 2, Department of Secondary Education, Canada: University of Alberta.

Audi, R. (1995) *Cambridge Dictionary of Philosophy*, Cambridge University Press, Cambridge.

Barber, M. (1996) *The Learning Game: Arguments for an Education Revolution*, London: Victor Gollancz.

Barber, M. (2000) 'The very big picture', *Improving Schools*, 3 (2): 5–13.

Barber, M. and Sebba, J. (1999) 'Reflections on progress towards a world class education system', *Cambridge Journal of Education*, 29 (2): 183–93.

Barth, R. (1990) *Improving Schools from Within*, San Francisco: Jossey-Bass.

Baveja, B. (1988) 'An exploratory study of the use of information-processing models of teaching in secondary school biology science classes', PhD thesis, Delhi, India: Delhi University.

Beare, H., Caldwell, B. J. and Millikan, R. H. (1989) *Creating an Excellent School*, London: Routledge.

Becker, E. (1975) *Escape from Evil*, New York: Free Press.

Bennett, N. (1976) *Teaching Styles and Pupil Progress*, London: Pergamon Press.

Bennett, N. (1988) 'The effective primary school teacher: the search for a theory of pedagogy', *Teaching and Teacher Education*, 4 (1): 19–30.

Bennett, B. and Green, N. (1995) 'Effect of the learning consortium: one district's journey', *School Effectiveness and School Improvement*, 6 (3): 247–64.

Beresford, J. (1998) *Collecting Information for School Improvement*, London: David Fulton Publishers.

Berg, R. and Sleegers, P. (1996) 'The innovative capacity of secondary schools: a qualitative study', *International Journal of Qualitative Studies in Education*, 9 (2): 201–23.

Berman, P. and McLaughlin, M. (1977) 'Federal program supporting educational change: factors affecting implementation and continuation', Santa Monica, CA: Rand Corporation.

Bjornemalm, B. and Ahlstrom, A. (1987) 'School-based review as a basis for a local working plan in Sweden' in R. Bollen and D. Hopkins (1987) *School-based Review: Towards a Praxis*, Leuven, Belgium: ACCO.

Bloom, B. S. (1984) 'The 2 sigma problem: the search for methods of group instruction as effective as one-to-one tutoring', *Educational Researcher*, 13: 4–16.

Bollen, R. and Hopkins, D. (1987) *School Based Review: Towards a Praxis*, Leuven, Belgium: ACCO.

Bowers, D. (1973) 'OD techniques and their results in 23 organisations: the Michigan ICL study', *Journal of Applied Behavioral Science*, 9 (1): 21–43.

Bowles, S. and Gintis, H. (1976) *Schooling in Capitalist America*, New York: Basic Books.

Brophy, J. (1983) 'Classroom organisation and management', *The Elementary School Journal*, 82: 266–85.

Brophy, J. and Good, T. (1986) 'Teacher behavior and student achievement' in M. Wittrock (ed.) *Handbook of Research on Teaching*, 3rd edn, New York: Macmillan.

Brown, S., Duffield, J. and Riddell, S. (1995) 'School effectiveness research: the policy-makers' tool for school improvement', *EEAR Bulletin*, March.

Bruner, J. (1966) *Towards a Theory of Instruction*, Cambridge, MA: Harvard University Press.

Bryk, A. S., Sebring, P., Kerbow, D., Pollow, S. and Easton, J. (1998) *Charting Chicago School Reform*, Boulder, CO: Westview Press.

Caldwell, B. J. and Spinks, J. M. (1988) *The Self-managing School*, Lewes: Falmer Press.

Cambridge University (1994) *Mapping Change in Schools: The Cambridge Manual of Research Techniques*, Cambridge: University of Cambridge Institute of Education.

Carr, W. and Kemmis, S. (1986) *Becoming Critical: Knowing through Action Research*, London: Falmer Press.

Central Advisory Council for Education (England) (1967) *Children and Their Primary Schools*, The Plowden Report, London: HMSO.

Charters, W. and Jones, J. (1973) 'On the risk of appraising non-events in program evaluation', *Educational Leadership*, 2 (11): 5–7.

Cheng, Y. C. (1997) 'The transformational leadership for school effectiveness and development in the new century', paper delivered to International Symposium of Quality Training of Primary and Secondary Principals towards the 21st century, January, Nenjing, China.

Christie, P. (1998) 'Schools as (dis)organisations', *Cambridge Journal of Education*, 28 (3): 281–300.

Clift, P., Nuttall, D. and McCormick, R. (1987) *Studies in School Self-evaluation*, Lewes: Falmer Press.

Cohen, D. (1995) 'What is the system in systemic reform?' *Educational Researcher*, 24 (9): 11–17, 31.

Coleman, J. S., Campbell, E., Hobson, C., McPartland, J., Mood, A., Weinfeld, F. and York, R. (1966) *Equality of Educational Opportunity*, Washington, DC: USPO.

Comer, J. (1992) *For Children's Sake: Comer School Development Program*, discussion leader's guide, New Haven, CT: Yale Child Study Center.

Corcoran, T. and Goertz, M. (1995) 'Instrumental strategies and high performance schools', *Educational Researcher*, 24 (9): 27–31.

Corey, S. M. (1953) *Action Research to Improve School Practices*, New York: Teachers College Press.

Crandall, D. (ed.) (1982) *People, Policies and Practices: Examining the Chain of School Improvement*, volumes 1–10, Andover, MA: The Network.

Crandall, D., Eiseman, J. and Louis, K. S. (1986) 'Strategic planning issues that bear on the success of school improvement efforts', *Educational Administration Quarterly*, 22 (2): 21–53.

Creemers, B. (1994) *The Effective Classroom*, London: Cassell.

Cuttance, P. (1992) 'Evaluating the effectiveness of schools' in D. Reynolds and P. Cuttance (eds) *School Effectiveness*, London: Cassell.

Cuttance, P. (1999) 'School research: the improvement of under-performing and less effective schools', paper prepared for Office of Reviews, Victoria Department of Education, Australia.

Dalin, P. (1973) 'Case studies of educational innovation', IV, *Strategies for Educational Innovation*, Paris: CERI/OECD.

Dalin, P. (1994) *How Schools Improve*, London, New York: Cassell.

Dalin, P. (1998) *School Development, Theories and Strategies*, London, New York: Cassell.

Dalin, P. and Rust, V. (1983) *Can Schools Learn?* London: NFER-Nelson.

Dalin, P., with Rolff, H. G. and Kleekamp, D. (1993) *Changing the School Culture*, London, New York: Cassell.

Deal, T. and Kennedy, A. (1983) 'Culture and school performance', *Educational Leadership*, 40 (5): 14–15.

Depoortere, J., de Soete, M. and Hellyn, J. (1987) in R. Bollen and D. Hopkins (1987) *School Based Review: Towards a Praxis*, Leuven, Belgium: ACCO.

DES (1989) *Planning for School Development: Advice for Governors, Headteachers and Teachers*, London: HMSO.

Downey, L. (1967) *The Secondary Phase of Education*, Boston, MA: Ginn.

Doyle, W. (1987) 'Research on teaching effects as a resource for improving instruction' in M. Wideen and I. Andrews (eds) *Staff Development for School Improvement*, Lewes: Falmer Press.

Duke, D. (1987) *School Leadership and Instructional Improvement*, New York: Random House.

Edmonds, R. (1979) 'Effective schools for the urban poor', *Educational Leadership*, 37 (1): 15–27.

Elliott, J. (1996) 'School effectiveness research and its critics: alternative regions of schooling', *Cambridge Journal of Education*, 26 (2): 199–224.

Elmore, R. F. (ed.) (1990) *Restructuring Schools*, Oakland, CA: Jossey-Bass.

Elmore, R. F. (1995) 'Teaching, learning, and school organisation: principles of practice and the regularities of schooling', *Educational Administration Quarterly*, 31 (3): 355–74.

Elmore, R. F. and Burney, D. (1998) *School Variation and Systemic Instructional Component in Community School District 2, New York City*, University of Pennsylvania, Consortium for Policy Research in Education.

Evans, M. and Hopkins, D. (1988) 'School climate and the psychological state of the individual teacher as factors affecting the use of educational ideas following an in-service course', *British Educational Research Journal*, 14 (3): 211–30.

Evans, R. (1996) *The Human Side of School Change*, San Francisco: Jossey-Bass.

Evertson, C. M. and Harris, A. H. (1992) 'What we know about managing class-rooms', *Educational Leadership*, April: 74–8.

Fisher, J. and Koch, J. (1996) *Presidential Leadership: Making a Difference*, Phoenix, AZ: American Council on Education/Oryx Press series on higher education.

Freeden, M. (1999) 'The ideology of New Labour', *Political Quarterly*, 70 (1): 42–51.

Fullan, M. G. (1982) *The Meaning of Educational Change*, New York: Teachers College Press.

Fullan, M. G. (1985) 'Change processes and strategies at the local level', *The Elementary School Journal*, 85 (3): 391–421.

Fullan, M. G. (1991) *The New Meaning of Educational Change*, London: Cassell.

Fullan, M. G. (1992) *Successful School Improvement*, Buckingham: Open University Press.

Fullan, M. G. (1993) *Change Forces: Probing the Depths of Educational Reform*, London: The Falmer Press.

Fullan, M. G. (1995) 'The school as a learning organisation: distant dreams', *Theory into Practice*, 34 (4) 230–5.

Fullan, M. G. (1999) *Change Forces: The Sequel*, London: Falmer Press.

Fullan, M. G. (2000) 'The return of large-scale reform', *Journal of Educational Change*, 2 (1): 5–28.

Fullan, M. G. and Miles, M. B. (1992) 'Getting reform right: what works and what doesn't', *Phi Delta Kappan*, 73 (10): 745–52.

Fullan, M. G., Miles, M. B. and Taylor, G. (1980) 'Organization development in schools: the state of the art', *Review of Educational Research*, 50 (1): 121–84.

Fullan, M. G., Bennett, B. and Rolheier-Bennett, C., (1990) 'Linking classroom and school improvement', *Educational Leadership*, 47 (8): 13–19.

Galton, M., Simon, B. and Croll, P. (1980) *Inside the Primary Classroom*, London: Routledge and Kegan Paul.

Galton, M., Hargreaves, L., Comber, C. and Will, D. (1999) *Inside the Primary Classroom: 20 Years On*, London: Routledge.

Gardner, H. (1991) *The Unschooled Mind*, New York: Basic Books.

Gardner, H. (1993) *Frames of Mind: The Theory of Multiple Intelligences*, 2nd edn, London: Fontana Press.

Geijsel, F., Sleegers, P., and Berg, R. (1998) 'The need for transformational leadership in large-scale innovation: the case for The Netherlands', paper presented at the annual meeting of the American Educational Research Association, 13–17 April, San Diego, CA.

Geltner, B. and Shelton, M. (1991) 'Expanded notions of strategic instructional leadership', *The Journal of School Leadership*, 1 (43): 38–50.

Gibson, R. (1986) *Critical Theory in Education*, London: Hodder and Stoughton.

Glaser, R. (1991) 'The maturing of the relationship between the science of learning and cognition, and education profile', *Learning and Instruction*, 1: 129–44.

Glass, G. V. (1982) 'Meta-analysis: an approach to the synthesis of research results', *Journal of Research in Science Teaching*, 19 (2): 93–112.

Glickman, C. D. (1993) *Renewing America's Schools: a Guide for School-based Action*, San Francisco: Jossey-Bass.

Good, T. L. (1989) 'The contribution of the researcher on teaching to school improvement', keynote address to the International Congress for School Effectiveness and School Improvement, Rotterdam, January 1989.

Good, T. L. and Brophy, J. E. (1994) *Looking in Classrooms*, 2nd edn, New York: Harper and Row.

Gray, J. (1981) 'A competitive edge: examination results and the probable limits of secondary school effectiveness', *Educational Review*, 33 (1): 25–35.

Gray, J. (1990) 'The quality of schooling: frameworks for judgement', *British Journal of Educational Studies*, 38: 203–23.

Gray, J. and Wilcox, B. (1995) *Good School, Bad School: Evaluating Performance and Encouraging Improvement*, Buckingham: Open University Press.

Gray, J., Jesson, D. and Sime, N. (1990) 'Estimating differences in the examination performances of secondary schools in six counties', *Oxford Review of Education*, 16 (2): 13–58.

Gray, J., Reynolds, D. and Fitz-Gibbon, C. T. (eds) (1996) *Merging Traditions*, London: Cassell.

Gray, J., Hopkins, D., Reynolds, D., Wilcox, B., Farrell, S. and Jesson, D. (1999) *Improving Schools: Performance and Potential*, Buckingham: Open University Press.

Gronn, P. (1999) 'Systems of distributed leadership in organisations', paper presented at the Annual Meeting of American Education Research Association's Conference, Montreal, Canada, 22 April 1999.

Guba, E. and Clark, D. (1965) 'The configurational perspective', *Educational Researcher*, 4 (4): 6–9.

Habermas, J. (1972) *Knowledge of Human Interests*, London: Heinemann Educational Books.

Hallinger, P. (1992) 'The evolving role of American principals: from managerial to instructional to transformational leaders', *Journal of Educational Administration*, 30 (3): 35–48.

Hallinger, P. and Murphy, J. (1985) 'Assessing the instructional management behavior of principals', *Elementary School Journal*, 86 (2): 217–47.

Halpin, A. W. and Troyna, B. (1995) 'The politics of policy borrowing', *Comparative Education*, 31: 303–10.

Handy, C. (1990) *The Age of Unreason*, Boston, MA: Harvard Business School.

Harber, C. and Davies, L. (1997) *School Management and Effectiveness in Developing Countries*, London: Cassell.

Hargreaves, A. (1991) 'Restructuring restructuring: post modernity and the prospects for educational change', *Journal of Education Policy*, 9 (1): 47–65.

Hargreaves, A., Lieberman, A., Fullan, M. and Hopkins, D. (eds) (1998) *The International Handbook of Educational Change*, 4 volumes.

Hargreaves, D. H. (1984) *Improving Secondary Schools*, London: ILEA.

Hargreaves, D. H., Hopkins, D., Leask, M., Connolly, J. and Robinson, P. (1989) *Planning for School Development*, London: Department of Education and Science.

Hargreaves, D. H. and Hopkins, D. (1991) *The Empowered School*, London: Cassell.

Harris, A., Jamieson, I. and Russ, J. (1995) 'A study of effective departments in secondary schools', *School Organisation*, 15 (3): 283–99.

Her Majesty's Inspectorate (1977) *Ten Good Schools*, London: Department for Education and Science.

Hipp, K. (1996) 'Documenting the effects of transformational leadership behaviour on teacher efficiency', paper presented at the Annual Meeting of the American Educational Research Association, 8–12 April, New York.

Hopkins, D. (1982) 'The Problem of Change in Canadian Teacher Education', *Canadian Journal of Higher Education*, 12 (3): 12–31.

Hopkins, D. (1984) 'Change and the organisational character of teacher education', *Studies in Higher Education*, 9 (1): 37–45.

Hopkins, D. (ed.) (1986) *In-service Training and Educational Development*, London: Croom Helm.

Hopkins, D. (1987a) *Knowledge Information Skills and the Curriculum*, London: British Library.

Hopkins, D. (ed.) (1987b) *Improving the Quality of Schooling*, Lewes: Falmer Press.

Hopkins, D. (ed.) (1988) *Doing School Based Review*, Leuven: ACCO.

Hopkins, D. (1990) 'The international school improvement project (ISIP) and effective schooling: towards a synthesis', *School Organisation*, 10 (3): 129–94.

Hopkins, D. (1994) 'Institutional self-evaluation and renewal' in T. Husen and N. Postlethwaite (eds) *The International Encyclopaedia of Education*, New York: Pergamon Press.

Hopkins, D. (1996) 'Towards a theory for school improvement' in J. Gray, D. Reynolds and C. Fitz-Gibbon (eds) *Merging Traditions: The Future of Research on School Effectiveness and School Improvement*, London: Cassell.

Hopkins, D. (1997) *Powerful Learning, Powerful Teaching and Powerful Schools*, Occasional Paper Series, Centre for Teacher and School Development, University of Nottingham.

Hopkins, D. (2000a) 'Schooling for tomorrow: innovation and networks', rapporteur's report on the Portuguese seminar, Lisbon, 14–15 September 2000, Paris: CERI/OECD.

Hopkins, D. (2000b) 'Powerful learning, powerful teaching and powerful schools', *Journal of Educational Change*, 1 (2): 135–54.

Hopkins, D. (2001) *Improving the Quality of Education for All: The Theory and Practice of School Improvement*, London: David Fulton.

Hopkins, D. and Levin, B. (2000) 'Government policy and school development', *School Leadership and Management*, 20 (1): 15–30.

Hopkins, D. and MacGilchrist, B. (1998) 'Development planning for pupil achievement', *School Leadership and Management*, 18 (3): 409–24.

Hopkins, D. and Reynolds, D. (2001) 'The past, present and future of school improvement: towards the third age', *British Journal of Educational Research* (in press).

Hopkins, D. and Stern, D. (1996) 'Quality teachers, quality schools', *Teaching and Teacher Education*, 12 (5): 1–170.

Hopkins, D. and West, M. (1994) 'Teacher development and school improvement' in D. Walling (ed.) *Teachers as Learners: Perspectives on the Professional Development of Teachers*, Bloomington, IN: Phi Delta Kappan.

Hopkins, D., Ainscow, M. and West, M. (1994) *School Improvement in an Era of Change*, London: Cassell.

Hopkins, D., West, M. and Ainscow, M. (1996) *Improving the Quality of Education for All*, London: David Fulton.

Hopkins, D., West, M., Ainscow, M., Harris, A. and Beresford, J. (1997a) *Creating the Conditions for Classroom Improvement*, London: David Fulton Publishers.

Hopkins, D., Harris, A. and Jackson, D. (1997b) 'Understanding the school's capacity for development: growth states and strategies', *School Leadership and Management*, 17 (3): 401–11.

Hopkins, D., Beresford, J. and West, M. (1998) 'Creating conditions for classroom and teacher development', *Teachers and Teaching: Theory and Practice*, 4 (1): 115–41.

Hopkins, D., Harris, A., Youngman, M. and Wordsworth, J. (1999) 'Evaluation of the initial effects and implementation of Success For All in England', *Journal of Research in Reading*, 22 (3): 257–70.

Hopkins, D., and Harris, A., with Singleton, C. and Watts, R. (2000) *Creating the Conditions for Teaching and Learning*, London: David Fulton Publishers.

Huberman, M. (1992a) 'Successful school improvement: reflections and observations', critical introduction in M. Fullan, *Successful School Improvement*, Buckingham: Open University Press.

Huberman, M. (1992b) *Teacher Development and Instructional Mastery* in A. Hargreaves and M. Fullan (eds) *Understanding Teacher Development*, London: Cassell.

Huberman, M. and Miles, M. B. (1984) *Innovation Up Close*, New York: Plenum.

Jackson, D. (2000) 'The school improvement journey: perspectives on leadership', *School Leadership and Management*, 20 (1): 61–78.

Jensen, A. (1969) 'How much can we boost IQ and scholastic achievement?', *Educational Review*, 34: 1–123.

Johnson, D. W. and Johnson, R. T. (1994) *Joining Together: Group Theory and Group Skills*, Allyn and Bacon.

Joyce, B. R. (1991) 'The doors to school improvement', *Educational Leadership*, 48 (8): 59–62.

Joyce, B. R. (1992) 'Cooperative learning and staff development: teaching the method with the method', *Cooperative Learning*, 12 (2): 10–13.

Joyce, B. R. (1997) *Creating a Staff Development System*, Tallahassee, FL: Florida State Department of Education.

Joyce, B. R. and Calhoun, E. F. (eds) (1996) *Learning Experiences in School Renewal*, Eugene, OR: ERIC Clearing House on Educational Management, University of Oregon.

Joyce, B. R. and Calhoun, E. F. (1998) *Learning to Teach Inductively*, Needham, MA: Allyn and Bacon.

Joyce, B. R. and Showers, B. (1980) 'Improving in-service training: the messages of research', *Educational Leadership*, 37 (5): 379–85.

Joyce, B. R. and Showers, B. (1991) *Information-processing: Models of Teaching*, Aptos, CA: Booksend Laboratories.

Joyce, B. R. and Showers, B. (1995) *Student Achievement through Staff Development*, 2nd edn, White Plains, NY: Longman.

Joyce, B. R. and Weil, M. (1996) *Models of Teaching*, 5th edn, Englewood Cliffs, NJ: Prentice-Hall.

Joyce, B. R., Showers, B. and Rolheiser-Bennett, C. (1987) 'Staff development and student learning: a synthesis of research on models of teaching', *Educational Leadership*, 47 (2): 11–23.

Joyce, B. R., Wolf, J. and Calhoun, E. F. (1993) *The Self Renewing School*, Alexandria, VA: ASCD.

Joyce, B. R., Calhoun, E. F. and Hopkins, D. (1997) *Models for Teaching: Tools for Learning*, Buckingham: Open University Press.

Joyce, B. R., Calhoun, E. F. and Hopkins, D. (1999) *The New Structure of School Improvement*, Buckingham: Open University Press.

Kemmis, S. (1982) 'Action research in retrospect and prospect in Deakin University', *The Action Research Review*, Victoria: Deakin University Press.

Kemmis, S. (1983) 'Action research' in T. Husen and T. Postlethwaite (eds) *International Encyclopaedia of Education: Research and Studies*, Oxford: Pergamon.

Kolb, D. (1984) *Experiential Learning*, Englewood Cliffs, NJ: Prentice-Hall.

Kounin, J. S. (1970) *Discipline and Group Management in Classrooms*, Holt, Richards and Wishart: New York.

Leithwood, K. (1993) 'Contributions of transformational leadership to school restructuring', paper read at annual meeting of the University Council for Educational Administration, 29–31 October 1993 at Houston, TX.

Leithwood, K. (1997) 'Distributed leadership in secondary schools', paper presented at AERA annual meeting, March, Chicago.

Leithwood, K., Leonard, L. and Sharratt, L. (1998) 'Conditions fostering organizational learning in schools', *Educational Administration Quarterly*, 34 (2): 243–76.

Leithwood, K., Jantzi, D. and Steinbach, R. (1999) *Changing Leadership for Changing Times*, Buckingham, Philadelphia: Open University Press.

Levin, B. (1995) 'Education and poverty', *Canadian Journal of Education*, 20 (2): 211–14.

Levin, B. (1998) 'An epidemic of education policy: (what) can we learn from each other?' *Comparative Education*, 34 (2): 131–41.

Lewin, K. (1943) 'Forces behind food habits and methods of change', *Bulletin of the National Research Council*, 108: 35–65.

Lewin, K. (1947) 'Group decisions and social change' in T. M. Newcomb and E. L. Hartley (eds) *Readings in Social Psychology*, New York: Henry Holt.

Lewin, K., Lippett, R. and White, R. K. (1939) 'Patterns of aggressive behavior in experimentally created "social climates"', *The Journal of Social Psychology*, 10: 171–99.

Lieberman, A. (1995) 'Practices that support leader development', *Phi Delta Kappan*, 76 (8): 591–6.

Louis, K. S. (1994) 'Beyond "managed change": re-thinking how schools improve', *School Effectiveness and School Improvement*, 5 (1): 2–24.

Louis, K. S. and Leithwood, K. (1998) *Schools as Learning Organisations*, Lisse, Netherlands: Swets and Zeitlinger.

Louis, K. S. and Miles, M. B. (1990) *Improving the Urban High School: What Works and Why*, New York: Teachers College Press.

MacGilchrist, B., Mortimore, P., Savage, J. and Beresford, C. (1995) *Planning Matters*, London: Paul Chapman Publishing.

MacGilchrist, B., Myers, K. and Reed, J. (1997) *The Intelligent School*, London: Paul Chapman.

MacMurray, J. (1961) *Persons in Relation*, London: Faber.

McLaughlin, M. W. (1990) 'The Rand change agent study revisited: macro perspectives, micro realities', *Educational Researcher*, 19 (9): 11–16.

Mannion, P. T. (1998) 'Trusting transformational principals: an empirical surprise', paper read at annual meeting of the American Educational Research Association, April 1998, at San Diego, CA.

Miles, M. B. (1967) 'Some properties of schools as social systems' in G. Watson (ed.) *Change in Schools Systems*, Washington DC: National Training Laboratories.

Miles M. B. (1975) 'Planned change and organizational health' in J. V. Baldrige and T. Deal (eds) *Managing Change in Educational Organizations*, Berkeley, CA: McCutchen.

Miles, M. B. (1986) 'Research findings on the stages of school improvement', mimeo, Center for Policy Research, New York.

Miles, M. B., Ekholm, M. and Vandenberghe (1987) *Lasting School Improvement: Exploring the Process of Institutionalisation*, Leuven, Belgium: ACCO.

Miles, M. B., Saxl, E. R. and Lieberman, A. (1988) 'What skills do educational change agents need? An empirical view', *Curriculum Enquiry*, 18 (2): 157–93.

Mortimore, P. (1991) 'School effectiveness research: which way at the cross-roads?' *School Effectiveness and School Improvement*, 2 (3): 213–29.

Mortimore, P. (1993) 'School effectiveness and the management of effective learning and teaching', *School Effectiveness and School Improvement*, 4 (4): 290–310.

Mortimore, P. (1998) *The Road to Improvement: Reflections on School Effectiveness*, Lisse, Netherlands: Swets and Zeitlinger.

Mortimore, P. (ed.) (1999) *Understanding Pedagogy and Its Impact on Learning*, London: Paul Chapman Publishers.

Mortimore, P. and Whitty, G. (1997) *Can School Improvement Overcome the Effects of Disadvantage?* London: Institute of Education.

Mortimore, P., Sammons, P., Stoll, L., Lewis, D. and Ecob, R. (1988) *School Matters: The Junior Years*, Wells: Open Books (reprinted in 1995 by Paul Chapman).

Murphy, J. (1991) *Restructuring Schools: Capturing and Assessing the Phenomena*, New York: Teachers College Press.

Murphy, J. (1992a) 'School effectiveness and school restructuring: contributions to educational improvement', *School Effectiveness and School Improvement*, 3 (2): 90–109.

Murphy, J. (1992b) 'Effective schools: legacy and future directions' in D. Reynolds and P. Cuttance (eds) *School Effectiveness*, London: Cassell.

Newmann, F., King, B. and Young, S. P. (2000) 'Professional development that addresses school capacity: lessons from urban elementary schools', paper presented to annual meeting of the American Educational Research Association, 3 April, New Orleans.

Nisbet, J. (ed.) (1973) *Creativity of the School*, Paris: OECD.

Nuttall, D., Goldstein, H., Prosser, R. and Rashash, J. (1989) 'Differential school effectiveness', *International Journal of Education Research*, 13 (10): 769–76.

OECD (1999) *Innovating Schools*, Paris: OECD/CERI.

Patterson, J., Purkey, S. C. and Parker, J. (1986) *Productive School Systems for a Non-rational World*, Alexandria, VA: ASCD.

Peters, R. S. (1974) *Psychology and Ethical Development*, London: George Allen and Unwin.

Purkey, S. C. and Smith, M. S. (1983) 'Effective schools: a review', *The Elementary School Journal*, 4: 427–52.

Rapoport, R. (1970) 'Three dilemmas in action research', *Human Relations*, 23: 1–11.

Reynolds, D. (1985) *Studying School Effectiveness*, Lewes: Falmer Press.

Reynolds, D. (1991) 'Changing ineffective schools' in M. Ainscow (ed.) *Effective Schools for All*, London: Fulton.

Reynolds, D. (1992) 'School effectiveness and school improvement' in D. Reynolds and P. Cuttance (eds) *School Effectiveness*, London: Cassell.

Reynolds, D. (1993) 'Changing school improvement strategies for the 1990s', paper presented at ICSEI annual meeting, Sweden.

Reynolds, D., Sullivan, M. and Murgatroyd, S. (1987) *The Comprehensive Experiment*, London: Falmer Press.

Reynolds, D., Hopkins, D. and Stoll, L. (1993) 'Linking school effectiveness knowledge and school improvement practice: towards a synergy', *School Effectiveness and School Improvement*, 4 (1): 37–58.

Reynolds, D., Bollen, R., Creemers, B., Hopkins, D., Stoll, L. and Lagerweij, N. (1996) *Making Good Schools*, London: Routledge.

Rinehart, J. and Lindle, J. C. (1997) 'Pursuing a connection: does Kentucky's education reform reveal a relationship between student achievement and school level governance?', paper presented to the AERA annual conference, Chicago, March.

Rogers, C. (1983) *Freedom to Learn*, 2nd edn, Columbus, Ohio: Merrill.

Rosenholtz, S. (1989) *Teacher's Workplace: The Social Organization of Schools*, New York: Longman.

Rubin, L. (1985) *Artistry and Teaching*, New York: Random House.

Rudduck, J. (1984) 'Introducing innovation to pupils' in D. Hopkins and M. Wideen (eds) *Alternative Perspectives on School Improvement*, London: Falmer Press.

Rudduck, J., Chaplain, R. and Wallace, G. (eds) (1996) *School Improvement: What Can Pupils Tell Us?*, London: David Fulton Publishers.

Rutter, M., Maughan, B., Mortimore, P., Ouston, J. and Smith, A. (1979) *Fifteen Thousand Hours*, London: Open Books.

Sammons, P., Hillman, J. and Mortimore, P. (1995) *Key Characteristics of Effective Schools: A Review of School Effectiveness Research*, London: OFSTED.

Sarason, S. (1982) *The Culture of the School and the Problem of Change*, 2nd edn, Boston: Allyn and Bacon.

Scheerens, J. (1992) *School Effectiveness*, London: Cassell.

Schein, E. (1985) *Organization Culture and Leadership: A Dynamic View*, San Francisco: Jossey-Bass.

Schmuck, R. A. (1984) 'Characteristics of the autonomous school' in D. Hopkins and M. Wideen (eds) *Alternative Perspectives on School Improvement*, London: Falmer.

Schmuck, R. A. and Miles, M. (eds) (1971) *Organizational Development in Schools*, Palo Alto, CA: National Press Books.

Schmuck, R. A. and Runkel, P. (1985) *The Handbook of Organizational Development in Schools*, 3rd edn, Palo Alto, CA: Mayfield.

Sebring, P., Bryk, A., Roderick, M., Camburn, E., Luppescu, S., Thum, Y. M., Smith, B. and Kahne, J. (1996) *Charting Reform in Chicago: The Students Speak*, Chicago: Consortium on Chicago School Research.

Sharan, S. and Shachar, H. (1988) *Language and Learning in the Cooperative Classroom*, New York: Springer-Verlag.

Sheppard, B. (1996) 'Exploring the transformational nature of instructional leadership', *Alberta Journal of Educational Research*, XLII (4): 325–44.

Sizer, T. R. (1989) 'Diverse practice, shared ideals: the essential school' in H. Walberg and J. Lane (eds) *Organizing for Learning: Towards the Twenty First Century*, Reston, VA: NASSP.

Slavin, R. E. (1989) 'PET and the pendulum: faddism in education and how to stop it', *Phi Delta Kappan*, June: 752–8.

Slavin, R. E. (1993) 'Cooperative learning in OECD countries: research, practice and prevalence', Centre for Educational Research and Innovation, Organization for Economic Cooperation and Development.

Slavin, R. E. (1996) *Education for All*, Lisse, The Netherlands: Swets and Zeitlinger.

Slavin, R. E. (1998) 'Sands, bricks and seeds: change strategies and readiness for reform' in A. Hargreaves, A. Lieberman, M. Fullan and D. Hopkins (eds) *International Handbook of Educational Change*, 4, Dordrecht: Kluwer: Academic Press.

Slavin, R. E. and Fashola, O. (1998) *Show Me the Evidence! Proven and Promising Programs for America's Schools*, Thousand Oaks, CA: Corwin Press.

Slavin, R. E. and Madden, N. A. (1999) *Success For All: Research and Reform in Elementary Education*, Mahwah, NJ: Lawrence Erlbaum Associates.

Slavin, R. E., Karweit, N. and Wasik, B. (1994) *Preventing Early School Failure: Research, Policy and Practice*, Boston, MA: Allyn and Bacon.

Slavin, R. E., Madden, N. A., Dolan, L. J. and Wasik, B. A. (1996) *Every Child, Every School: Success for All*, Thousand Oaks, CA: Corwin Press.

Smith, D. and Tomlinson, S. (1989) *The School Effect: A Study of Multi-Racial Comprehensives*, London: Policy Studies Institute.

Stenhouse, L. (1975) *An Introduction to Curriculum Research and Development*, London: Heinemann Educational Books.

Stenhouse, L. (ed.) (1980) *Curriculum Research and Development in Action*, London: Heinemann Educational Books.

Stigler, J. and Hiebert, J. (1999) *The Teaching Gap*, New York: Free Press.

Stoll, L. (1991) 'School effectiveness in action: supporting growth in schools and classrooms' in M. Ainscow (ed.) *Effective Schools for All*, London: Fulton.

Stoll, L. and Fink, D. (1992) 'Effecting school change: the Halton approach', *School Effectiveness and School Improvement*, 3 (1): 19–41.

Stoll, L. and Fink, D. (1996) *Changing Our Schools: Linking School Effectiveness and School Improvement*, Buckingham: Open University Press.

Stringfield, S. and Teddlie, C. (1988) 'A time to summarise: the Louisiana School effectiveness study', *Educational Leadership*, 46 (2): 43–9.

Stringfield, S. and Teddlie, C. (1991) 'Observers as predictors of schools' effectiveness status', *The Elementary School Journal*, 91 (4): 357–76.

Stringfield, S., Ross, S. and Smith, L. (1996) *Bold Plans for School Restructuring*, New York: Lawrence Erlbaum.

Stringfield, S., Millsap, M. and Herman, R. (1998) 'Using "promising programs" to improve educational processes and student outcome' in A. Hargreaves, A. Lieberman, M. Fullan and D. Hopkins (eds) *International Handbook of Educational Change*, 4, Dordrecht: Kluwer: Academic Press.

Strodl, P. and Johnson, B. (1994) *Multicultural Leadership for Restructured Constituencies*, US, Alabama.

Teddlie, C. and Reynolds, D. (2000) *The International Handbook of School Effectiveness Research*, London: Falmer Press.

Teddlie, C. and Stringfield, S. (1993) *Schools Do Make A Difference: Lessons Learned from a Ten-year Study of School Effects*, New York: Teachers College Press.

Thrupp, M. (1999) *Schools Making a Difference: Let's Be Realistic*, Buckingham: Open University Press.

Turan, C. and Sny, C. (1996) 'An exploration of transformational leadership and its role in strategic planning: a conceptual framework', paper presented at annual meeting of the International Society for Educational Planning, September, New Orleans.

Tyack, D. and Cuban, L. (1995) *Tinkering Towards Utopia: A Century of Public School Reform*, Cambridge, MA: Harvard University Press.

van Velzen, W., Miles, M., Ekholm, M., Hameyer, U. and Robin, D. (1985) *Making School Improvement Work: A Conceptual Guide to Practice*, Leuven, Belgium: ACCO.

Verspoor, A. (1989) 'Pathways to change: improving the quality of education in developing countries', World Bank Discussion Paper 53, Washington DC.

Voogt, J. C. (1988) 'Systematic analysis for school improvement (SAS)' in D. Hopkins (ed.) *Doing School Based Review*, Leuven: ACCO.

Walberg, H. (1990) 'Productive teaching and instruction: assessing the knowledge base', *Phi Delta Kappan*, 71 (6): 470–8.

Wallace, R. C., Lemahieu, P. G. and Bickel, W. E. (1990) 'The Pittsburgh experience' in B. Joyce (ed.) *Changing School Culture through Staff Development*, the 1990 ASCD year book, Alexandria, VA: ASCD.

Wang, M., Haertel, G. and Walberg, H. (1993) 'Toward a knowledge base for school learning', *Review of Educational Research*, 63 (3): 249–94.

Weick, K. E. (1976) 'Educational organizations as loosely coupled systems', *Administrative Science Quarterly*, 21: 1–19.

Weick, K. E. (1985) 'Sources of order in under-organised systems: themes in recent organizational theory' in Y. S. Lincoln (ed.) *Organizational Theory and Enquiry*, Beverly Hills, CA: Sage.

West, M. (2000) 'Supporting school improvement: observations on the inside, reflections from the outside', *School Leadership and Management*, 20 (1): 43–60.

West, M. and Hopkins, D. (2001) 'School effectiveness and school improvement: towards a reconceptualisation' in A. Harris and N. Bennet (eds) *Alternative Perspectives on School Effectiveness and School Improvement*, London: Cassell.

West, M., Ainscow, M. and Hopkins, D. (1997) 'Tracking the moving school: challenging assumptions, increasing understanding of how school improvement is brought about', paper presented at ECER annual conference, Frankfurt.

West, M., Jackson, D., Harris, M. and Hopkins, D. (2000) 'Leadership through learning, learning through leadership' in K. A. Riley and K. S. Louis (eds) *Leadership for Change and Several Reforms in International Perspectives*, London: RoutledgeFalmer.

Wilson, B. L. and Corcoran, T. B. (1988) *Successful Secondary Schools: Visions of Excellence in American Public Education*, Lewes: Falmer Press.

Wittrock, M. (ed.) (1986) *Handbook of Research on Teaching*, 3rd edn, New York: Macmillan.

Wohlsetter, P., Smyer, R. and Moheman, S. (1994) 'New boundaries for school-bound management: the higher involvement model', *Educational Evaluation and Policy Analysis*, 16, Fall: 268–86.

Wood, D. (1998) *How Children Think and Learn*, Oxford: Basil Blackwell.

Young, R. (1989) *A Critical Theory of Education*, New York, London: Harvester Wheatsheaf.

Index

Printed in the United Kingdom
by Lightning Source UK Ltd.
117601UKS00002B/123